Java

Today's Programming Language

Volume II

Joslyn A. Smith

ISBN: 978-0-9978172-2-5

Preface

This book is a second in a two-part programming series that uses the Object Oriented paradigm as its platform for programming. This volume provides an in depth, and extensive coverage in programming techniques to a variety of problems. The material in this volume is more detailed than that of the Volume I, and it supports larger and more robust programs. Not only does it lend itself to these two attributes, but you will also learn about re-usability of entities.

Concepts Covered

- Program Design Principles – Cohesion & Coupling. This book begins with these two principles that are used to design and develop mid to large size programming. Once understood, you will see how easy it is to decompose the solution to a program into separate entities (classes), and how to co-ordinate these entities onto one whole – the solution.

- Inheritance & Polymorphism – As you will learn, these two concepts are central to Object Oriented Programming. You will not only learn about these concepts, but you will use them throughout the remainder of the text. You will also learn that these concepts lend themselves to reusability of codes; and, that they also are used to design and develop mid to large size programs.

- Exception and Exception Handling – Sometimes we have brilliant ideas when writing codes, especially when it comes to handling certain programming errors. You will see that although the conditional structures – if/else and switch – work, there may be better ways of detecting possible errors, and how to avoid them from terminating the programming abnormally. That is avoiding the program from crashing. This where Exception and the handling of exception become invaluable.

- Files - while it is useful to be able to read from a file using the class Scanner, this not always the best method. For one thing, you must know the name of the file and where it resides on an external storage device such as a hard drive. The file in question could be buried deep within directories, and having to memorize its path is not practical. In this context you will learn how to write a customize file dialog class, where you can select files by pointing and clicking.

- Reading and writing files, sometimes referred to as streams – input streams and output streams. In most cases when someone mentions reading and writing files, they think of text files only. In this section you will not only learn to read and write text files, but also image files. In this context, you will learn about the two types of file stream formats – byte oriented streams and character oriented streams. Also, most times the file structure that is studied at this level is serial access files. In this section you will learn about random access files – how to create them, write to them, and read from them.

- Elementary Data Structure – you would have studied arrays and probably ArrayList; and of course at least one sorting algorithm and one searching algorithm. Beyond these you will learn about Java collection of interfaces and classes which help in storing, sorting, searching, and general processing of the data efficiently.

- Graphical User Interface – The programs that you have written, except for those that used the JOptionPane class, were text based programs. In this section you will learn a different side to Java, where you will write programs that allow the user to interact with gadgets such as buttons and menu items. In these kinds of applications, the mouse will be used in most cases to gather data, and the output will generally be displayed in dialog box, rather than at the command prompt.

Pre-requisite

- Knowledge of how to construct a class in terms of – naming the class, specifying the fields, the constructors, and methods. Although not necessary, but highly recommended, you should know the difference between instance variables and class variables; instance methods and class methods; and also accessor methods versus mutator methods.
- Understand data types. You should know what primitive data types are and what reference types are. It would also help if you know the different classifications of primitive types.
- Knowledge of the five arithmetic operators (+, -, *, /, %), and the possible operations that can be performed on the primitive types. You should be able to evaluate arithmetic expressions.
- Knowledge of the six relational operators (<, <= >, >=, ==, !=), and how they are used to perform relational expressions. You should be able to evaluate relational expressions.
- Knowledge of the three logical operators (&&, ||, !), and how they are used to form logical expressions. You should able to evaluate logical expressions.
- Knowledge of program control in terms of the selection statements:
    - The **if, if/else** statements, and
    - The **switch** statement.
- Knowledge of program control in terms of the iterative statements:
    - The **while** statement
    - The **do/while** statement, and
    - The **for** statement.
- Knowledge of at least one dimensional arrays and two dimensional arrays
- Knowledge of at least one searching algorithm, and sorting algorithm.

Overview

Chapter 1 - Object Oriented Software Design
In this chapter you will learn the principles of OOD using cohesion and coupling. You will learn about class relationship diagrams; how they are used to model solutions.

Chapter 2 - Inheritance and Polymorphism
In this chapter you will learn the concept of inheritance and polymorphism which are fundamental to Object Oriented Programming (OOP).

Chapter 3 - Exception and Exception Handling
In this chapter you will learn about exception, how it can cause a program to terminate abnormally, and how you can write codes to prevent this from happening.

Chapter 4 - Files and Streams
In this chapter you learn to read and write text files as well as image files. You learn about serial access files as well as random access files.

Chapter 5 - Recursion

In this chapter you will learn about a type of programming technique that causes, not only a statement or a block of statements to be executed repeatedly, but also an entire method calling itself repeatedly.

Chapter 6 - An Introduction to Data Structure

In this chapter you will learn about data structure - particular ways of organizing and storing data for efficient retrieved and manipulation in terms of processing time and hardware resources. In this chapter you learn about the Java Collections Framework that contains classes for this purpose.

Chapter 7 - Specialized Lists – Stack ▪ Queue ▪ LinkedList ▪ HashMap

In this chapter you will learn about four specialized data structures - Stack, Queue, LinkedList, and HashMap.

Chapter 8 - Introduction to Graphical User Interface (GUI)

GUI - a type of program that allows the user to interact with the computer via graphical symbols such as buttons and menus. In this chapter you will learn how to write such programs.

Chapter 9 - Events and Event Handling

The programs we have written so far, called widow base programs, were designed to run sequentially, as coded; hence the next statement to be executed is predictable. With GUI programs, they allow the user to interact with the computer; hence the next statement to be executed is not predictable. In this chapter we will learn how to develop such programs.

Chapter 10 - Graphics

All of the programs that we have written so far are text base programs. In this chapter you learn how to free hand draw onto component, or make static figures onto components.

Contents

Chapter 1 - Object Oriented Software Design...**1**

Objective... 1

Introduction 1

UML Class Relationship Diagram 2

    Dependency Diagram 2

    Association Diagram 4

    Cohesion 7

    Coupling... 20

De-referencing an Object 30

Chapter Summary... 31

Programming Exercises... 32

Chapter 2 Inheritance and Polymorphism **37**

Introduction 37

Generalization Diagrams... 38

Rules Governing Constructors 42

Rules Governing Data Members and Methods... 42

Self-Check... 45

Abstract Class... 47

Self-Check... 52

Polymorphism... 55

    Overloading 55

    Overriding.. 57

    Inclusion... 57

    Casting 58

    Pitfalls Casting Objects 61

    Parametric Polymorphism.. 63

Dynamic Method Lookup 64

The class Object 64

The Keyword final 67

Visibility Modifier 68

Self-Check 69

Interface 71

    Implementing an Interface 71

    Multiple Inheritance by Interface 73

Adapter Class 75

Self-Check 78

Chapter Summary 79

Programming Exercises 80

Chapter 3 Exception and Exception Handling 89

Objectives 89

Introduction 89

Exception Handling 90

Response to an Exception 90

Procedure for Handling Exception 90

Understanding Runtime Errors 91

Exception Classes 93

The Super Class Throwable 93

Exception and Its Associated Packages 94

Checked and Unchecked Exceptions 96

    How to Handle Checked Exception 97

    How to Handle Unchecked Exception 99

Handling Multiple Exceptions 100

    Handling Multiple Unrelated Exceptions 100

    Handling Multiple Related Exceptions 102

    Alternate Handling of Multiple Exceptions 103

Manually Throwing an Exception 105

Using finally Block 108

    How The finally Block Works 108

    try-catch Without Transfer of Control 108

    The try-catch With Transfer of Control 111

    Pitfall: finally Block – with Transfer of Control 113

The *try-with-resources* Statement 117

User Defined Exception Classes 117

Using the throws Clause 122

Nesting try-catch - blocks 124

Rethrowing Exception 125

Chapter Summary 128

Programming Exercises 129

Chapter 4 Input ■ Output using Files and Streams 131

Objectives 131

Introduction 131

Standard Input and Output 132

    err 132

    out 132

    in 132

The class File Class 134

Methods for Testing File Objects 135

    Methods for Accessing File Objects 135

Customized File Class using JFileChooser 139

Java Input ■ Output System 143

Byte Oriented Input Streams 144

    InputStream 144

    FileInputStream 145

    FilterInputStream 145

    DataInputStream 145

BufferedInputStream 146

Byte Oriented Output Streams 150

OutputStream 150

FileOutputStream 151

FilterOutputStream 153

DataOutputStream 153

BufferedOutputStream 157

PrintStream 157

Character Oriented Input Streams 161

The class Reader 162

InputStreamReader 162

Charset 163

FileReader 163

BufferedReader 164

LineNumberReader 165

Character Oriented Output Streams 167

The class Writer 167

OutputStreamWriter 168

FileWriter 169

BufferedWriter 170

PrintWriter 172

The Class StreamTokenizer 177

Random Access File Stream 183

Chapter Summary 188

Programming Exercises 189

Chapter 5 Recursion **197**

Objectives 197

Introduction 197

Recursion 198

Contents

This expression looks intimidating at first, but we already know what n! is. **201**

    Self-Check...204

    Searching a Sorted List...206

    Searching a Non-Sorted List..208

    Recursion vs Iteration – Which Approach Is Better...............211

        Execution Time..211

        Memory Usage 215

        Programming Level of Difficulty.....................................217

    Self-Check...218

    Chapter Summary..218

    Programming Exercises...219

Chapter 6 An Introduction to Data Structure.............................223

    Objectives..223

    Introduction...223

    Collection Framework..224

        When To Use Set, List, Queue, or Map.........................225

        The Interface - Collection 226

        The Interface - Set...227

        The Class HashSet...227

        The Class TreeSet..228

        Single Operations...230

        Bulk Operations...230

        Sorting Bulk Operation..232

        The interface - List 234

        Classes That Implement List..234

        When To Use ArrayList over Vector 235

        Classes That Implements Map.......................................240

    Chapter Summary..247

Contents

Chapter 7 Specialized Lists – Stack ▪ Queue ▪LinkedList▪ **249**

Objectives 249

   Stack 249

   Queue 262

   LinkedList 268

   Structure of a LinkedList 268

   Representing LinkedList in Java 271

   Creating a LinkedList in Java 272

Chapter Summary 282

Programming Exercises 282

Chapter 8 Graphical User Interface Programming **287**

Objectives 287

Introduction 287

   Components and Containers 288

Creating Frames 288

   Changing Properties of a Frame 290

   AWT versus Swing 296

   The ContentPane 297

   Setting up Menus 299

   Setting the Menu bar 299

   Adding Menu Choices to the Menubar 301

   Adding Menu Items to the Menu Choices 303

   Buttons 308

   Layout Managers 309

   FlowLayout Manager 309

   GridLayout Manager 312

   BorderLayout Manager 314

   GridBagLayout Manager 317

JPanel 332

Chapter Summary 336

Programming Exercises 337

Chapter 9 Event and Event Handling **341**

Objectives 341

Introduction 341

Event and Event Listener Listener 342

Listener Interfaces and Adapter classes 350

HyperlinkListener Interface 358

KeyListener Interface and KeyAdapter class 359

Chapter Summary 360

Programming Exercises 361

Chapter 10 Graphics **367**

Objectives 367

Introduction 367

JLabel 368

Creating Picture Scenes 368

Rendering Text 374

The class Font 374

The class Graphics 376

The Method paint 379

Geometric Shapes and Figures 380

Making Free Hand Drawing 385

Chapter Summary 390

Programming Exercises 391

Index **393**

Chapter 1 - Object Oriented Software Design

Objective

After reading this chapter you will:

- Understand the concept of Object Oriented Design
- Be able to apply Object Oriented Design principles to designing software systems.
- Understand UML class relationships – dependency and association – in order to decompose problem definitions into component.
- Understand the concepts cohesion and coupling – in order to assemble the components (classes) into complete programs.

Introduction

Object-oriented design (OOD) is the philosophy of developing an object-oriented model of a software system, by defining the classes and their interactions with one another. The major benefits of OOD are easy maintainable systems, easy understandable systems, easy expandable systems, and reusable components of a system.

In this chapter you will learn the principles of OOD including class diagrams. You will learn about the different kinds of relationships that can be formed among classes, how to use these relationships to model the solution to an entire system. OOD demands that the programmer defines principles to decompose problem definitions into separate entities; it also demands that the programmer determines the relationship among the entities, which eventually leads to the solution of the problem. The principle that we will use to achieve the former is called cohesion; and the principle to achieve the latter is called coupling.

The chapter closes with a survey of misinterpretations and pitfalls that could occur during the design and implementation phases. Before studying the pitfalls, however, we will develop an entire system using the concept of Object Oriented Design along with the Uniform Modeling Language.

UML Class Relationship Diagram

The Unified Modeling Language (**UML**) as we know from volume I is a standardized specification language that uses a set of diagrams to model objects, with the ultimate aim of solving problems. UML features several types of diagrams for different purposes - component diagrams, composite structure diagram, deployment diagram, object diagram, package diagram, and class diagram. We will continue to use class diagram, this time using it to solve more complex problems than we had encountered in volume I. As we have mentioned then, one of the applications of the **UML** is to design class diagrams.

The term UML class diagram really means UML Class Relationship diagram. There are four types of class relationship diagrams that can be formulated using UML notation. They are UML Dependency diagram, UML Association diagram, UML Generalization diagram, and UML Realization diagram. We will discuss class dependency and association diagrams in this chapter. Generalization and realization diagrams will be discussed in chapter 2 when we discuss inheritance.

Dependency Diagram

The UML dependency relationship is the least formal of the four relationship diagrams, as we will see shortly. The default of any relationship is bi-directional. However, when applied to designing class diagrams it is limited to unidirectional relationship. The UML dependency diagram uses a broken line to show the relationship between two classes. In addition, an open arrow head is used to show the directional relationship between classes. **Figure 1.1** shows two classes **A** and **B** that have unidirectional dependency. The relationship between these two classes means that class **A** depends on class **B**, for information that is contained in an instance of B.

Figure 1.1 UML Class diagram; class A depends on class B

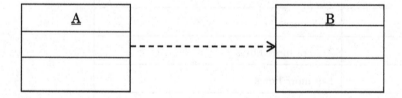

In **Figure 1.1**, the unidirectional dependency diagram means that class **A** uses class **B**. In this situation, the relationship is restricted to the following meaning.
   (a) Class **A** receives an instance of class **B** as a parameter to at least one of its methods, or
   (b) Class **A** creates an instance of class **B**, local to one of its methods.

In this kind of relationship, class **B** cannot be an attribute of class **A**. Hence class **A** cannot contain an instance of **B**.

Listing 1.1 shows the interpretation of the UML unidirectional dependency relationship. Notice that method1 in class **A**, accepts reference parameter **b**. Also, method2 in class **A** creates a reference of **B** local to method2 in **A**.

Listing 1.1 UML dependency relationship between class A and class B

```
1.   public class A
2.   {
3.        public void method1(B b)
4.        {
5.        }
6.        public void method2()
7.        {
8.              B b = new B();
9.        }
10.  }
```

```
1.   public class B
2.   {
3.        public void method()
4.        {
5.        }
6.        public void method2()
7.        {
8.        }
9.   }
```

It is not enough to know that one class depends on another, but equally important is to know the frequency on which one class depends the other. The following table is a frequency chart showing the possible frequency occurrences.

Frequency	Meaning
0.. 1	Zero or one time
1	Only once
0 .. *	Zero or more times
1 .. *	1 or more times
n	Only n times, $n > 1$
0 .. n	Zero or more times, where $n > 1$
1 .. n	1 or more times, where $n > 1$

Figure 1.2 shows another feature of a UML class dependency diagram. Not only does the class A depends on the class B, but it depends on it from one to any number of times, as indicated by the symbols above the arrow.

Figure 1.2 UML Class diagram; class A may depend on class B multiple times

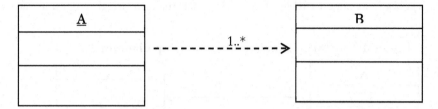

Self-Check

1. Given that A and B are two classes, and that class B depends on class A. Draw a unidirectional dependency relationship diagram between both classes.

2. Given that A and B are two classes. What must be true, in order to establish a unidirectional dependency between class B and class A.

3. Given that Q represents a class. Which of the following classes establish a dependency relationship of class P on class Q?

(a) class P
```
{
    Q q;
    P()
    {
        q = new Q();
    }
}
```

(b) class P
```
{
    P()
    {
        Q q = new Q();
    }
}
```

(c) class P
```
{
    P()
    {

    }
    void add( Q q);
    {

    }
}
```

(d) class P
```
{
    P()
    {

    }
}
```

(e) class P
```
{
    P()
    {
        Q q = new Q();
    }
}
```

Association Diagram

A class association diagram defines a relationship that is much stronger than dependency relationship. **Figure 1.3** shows the UML association relationship class diagram between class **A** and class **B**. The solid line with an open ended arrow establishes a unidirectional association relationship between these classes. The strength of an association relationship class diagram means that class **A** will contain at least one instance variable of class **B**, which makes class **B** structurally a part of class **A**.

Figure 1.3 A UML Association relationship diagram

Example 1.1 Let us consider the classes **Person** and **Name** as shown in **Figure 1.4**. The class **Person** is a composition of two fields, the first which is of type **Name**, the second of type **String**. This relationship establishes the fact that the class Name forms part of the physical structure of the class Person.

Figure 1.4 Association diagram of class Person with respect to class Name.

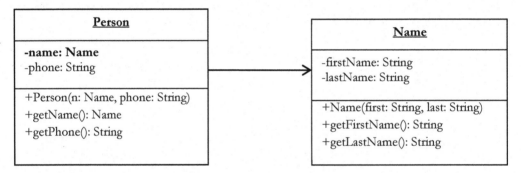

If we were to remove the field **name** from the class Person, then the class Person, having just the field, **phone**, would not have conveyed a meaning that we are talking about a person. Hence by including the field, **name** to Person, at least intuitively adds the meaning person. **Figure 1.5** shows the class Person without the field **name**. But one would say that we could list the fields of the class Name as attributes of the class Person. While this would work, it would weaken the effect of modularity, as you will see in the next section.

Figure 1.5 class Person without the field name

Person
-phone: String
+Person(phone: String) +getPhone(): String

Self-Check

1. What condition(s) must exist for the class A to have an association relationship on class B?

2. If class A has an association relationship with class B, draw the association diagram between both classes.

3. Differentiate between the concept of association relationship and dependency relationship, as they pertain to programming.

4. Given that Q represents a class. Which of the following classes establish an association relationship of class P on class Q?

(a) class P
```
{
    Q q;
    P()
    {
        q = new Q();
    }
}
```

(b) class P
```
{
    P()
    {
        Q q = new Q();
    }
}
```

(c) class P
```
{
    P()
    {
    }
    void add( Q q);
    {

    }
}
```

(d) class P
```
{
    P()
    {

    }
}
```

(e) class P
```
{
    P()
    {
        Q q = new Q();
    }
}
```

5. There are two classes, Circle and Shape. Define both classes where the class Shape defines an association relationship on the class Circle.

6. There are two classes, Circle and Shape. Define both classes where the class Shape defines an dependency relationship on the class Circle.

7. Define two classes, Sentence and Words, where the class Sentence has an association relationship with an array of potential Word objects.

8. Using Question 5, draw a unidirectional association relationship between both classes.

Cohesion

In object oriented programming design, the solution to a problem may be so complex that it may involve several classes. The entire set of classes in the design is sometimes referred to as the software system; and each class in the system is referred to as a component of the system. The design and implementation of large-scale software systems draw attention to the need for well-defined design methodologies and modeling techniques that can reduce the complexity of the solution, and at the same time increase the probability of a correct solution. While there may not be a one-shop, quick-fix solution to good software design, there are some well proven methodologies that have been used as guidelines towards good software designs. Two of methodologies are cohesion and coupling. In this section we will discuss cohesion, and the next section we will discuss coupling.

With respect to object oriented design, the concept of cohesion focuses on the logical construction of each component within the system; where each component is required to concentrate on a single objective. In turn, each module, or method within the component should be responsible to carry out one precise task.

The quality of a software system is generally measured by the strength, or the cohesiveness of each of the components. The strength of a cohesive system is measured from low cohesive to high cohesive. A low cohesive system is a system that focuses on multiple tasks. The more tasks it has to perform, is the weaker the cohesiveness of the system. A highly cohesive system on the other hand focuses on only one task. A lowly cohesive system is considered to be a poorly designed system; whereas, a highly cohesive system is considered to be of a good design.

In designing, a highly cohesive method has several advantages than a very low cohesive one. A highly cohesive method is simpler to understand, simpler to re-use, easier to maintain, easier to code, and is easier to debug. If methods are highly cohesive, then the class itself will be highly cohesive. Hence the class is easy to understand, because it is designated to relay a single complete thought. Above all, a change in one component may not necessitate a change in any of the other components. In an environment where there is low cohesion, errors are harder to detect and correct. In an effort to correct an error, you may inadvertently create new ones.

As we said earlier, the concept of cohesion can be readily applied to object oriented software design, in that the design requires the programmer to decompose problem definitions into highly cohesive components. Rarely are all systems purely cohesive. Some components may have to establish relationship such as dependency relation, or association relation among other components.

Example 1.2 Consider the following narrative:

Design a Java program that carries out banking operations on customers' account. The concept of banking is characterized by customers and their account balances. The program should be able to:

- Store the customers' account information in a database.
- Make deposits.
- Make withdrawals.
- Search for an account, given the account number.

- Delete an account from the active accounts in the database, and store any deleted account into a separate database

Solution I

A programmer who does not know about the concept of cohesion would more likely write a single class, along with a test class, to solve problems of this kind. This class would encapsulate all of the characteristics described in the problem. That is, the class would be responsible for:

- The collection of data and dissemination of information for names.
- The collection data and dissemination of information for addresses.
- The collection of data and dissemination of information for customer.
- Create bank accounts, update bank account, and dissemination of information about bank accounts.
- Create database, store bank accounts in database, search database for accounts, and remove accounts from database.

A system of this kind would be considered loosely cohesive; one that would be difficult to debug if there is a logic error; and almost impossible to maintain if any segment requires change to it.

Solution II

A second approach would be to combine the concept of name, address, customer, and bank account as one component; thus keeping the database component separate. But just like the first solution, the bank account component would have too much responsibility. Let us consider a third possibility.

Solution III

When we analyze the problem, we see that in order to have a highly cohesive system, there are at least six components, excluding the test class. These components are as follow:

- A **bank account** component that is characterized by customer and an initial balance.
- With respect to customer, a **customer** is an entity that is characterized by name, address, and account number.
- When it comes to address, an **address** is characterized by street, city, state, and zip code.
- A name can also be characterized as a component which has at least a first name and a last name.
- The concept database, which is a repository for banking transactions, can also be considered another component.
- Lastly, we may need a component that can be used to read data and display information.

Figure 1.6 shows the system consisting of these six components, not including the test class. At the moment there is no defined relationship between any of them. It is only a decomposition of the various components within the system.

Figure 1.6 A software system of six components

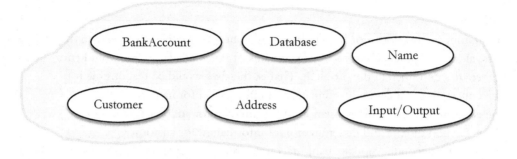

In general, when designing an object oriented software system, the first thing that you want to do is to determine what the possible components are, and what the responsibility of each will be. In the current example, the entity Name will define names only; the entity Address will be restricted to facilitating address only. As it stands, there is no relationship between a name and an address object. Should there be an error within any of the two, then we would directly focus on the one that has the problem. There would be no need to interfere with any of the other entites. These two components are now said to be highly cohesive.

In terms of customer on the other hand, in real life a customer has a name and an address. Against this background, the entity Customer will have both attributes - Name and Address. That is, both entities must be physically a part of the Customer entity. This consideration therefore establishes an association relationship between the component Customer, and the components Name and Address. This situation is represented by **Figure 1.7**.

Figure 1.7 Association relationship between Customer, and the pair Name **and** Address

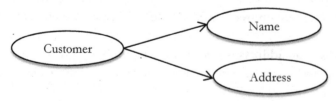

With regards to the ease of detecting and correcting errors, if we know for sure that the entities Name and Address are clear of any logic errors, but the component Customer has some form of logic error, then the problem must lie with the current component. Either that it has introduced new variables that are causing the problem; or, the established components are being used improperly.

With regards to the component Bank account, a bank account obviously has customer as one of its attributes. In this situation the component BankAccount has to establish an association relationship between itself and the component, Customer, as shown in **Figure 1.8**.

Figure 1.8 Association relationship between BankAccount and Customer

In terms of maintenance or debugging purposes, if we know for sure that the component Customer is flawless, and a problem surfaces in the BankAccount entity, then without any question we would narrow our effort to the local definition of the component, in terms of its newly defined variables and methods.

With regards to the entity Database, it receives bank account objects, via one of its methods, and store them. This establishes a dependency relation of Database upon BankAccount. See **Figure 1.9**.

Figure 1.9 Dependency relationship of Database upon BankAccount

Any component such as BankAccount appearing as field in the Database would be secondary to the operation of storing and retrieving data. In other words, whether or not such fields are included, they would not greatly influence the definition of the entity Database. This runs parallel to the discussion in **Example 1.1**, where we discussed dependency relationship.

The next step in the design process is to construct the class notation diagram for each of these components. We will use the names in **Figure 1.6**, for the name in each of the class notation diagram that is to be drawn. Against this background, it does not matter the order in which the diagrams are drawn; what matters is the relationship one entity will have on another one. In this regard, let us design the UML diagram for the class Customer.

The narrative tells us what attributes constitute a customer object. That is, with respect to customer, a customer is characterized by name, address, and account number. When we analyze this statement, it is obvious that the fields for the component Customer are: component type Name, component type Address, and a component of type String, for the account number. This leads us to conclude that the fields Name and Address will form an association relationship with the class Customer. See **Figure 1.10**. Although not specified in the problem, it is possible that a customer may want to change the account number of any number of reasons. Against this background we include a mutator method that does exactly that.

Figure 1.10 Fields Name and Address define association relationship with Customer

Customer
-name : **Name** -addr : **Address** -acc_no: String
+Customer(n: Name, a: Address, acc: String) +getName(): Name +getAddress(): Address +getAccountNumber(): String +changeAccountNumber(acc: String): void

As you will notice, this component is solely responsible for addressing customers' information; it does not address the concerns of any of the other components. From all indications, each of the methods, by nature of their names and return type, will focus one task; thus making the component itself highly cohesive.

As you have noticed in Figure 1.10, no mention was made about the physical structure of the classes Name and Address; yet it is possible to use them to code the class Customer, as shown in **Listing 1.2**. When it comes time to compile this class however, you would be required to supply the necessary code for these classes, in order for the class Customer to compile.

Listing 1.2 Class Customer

```
1.    public class Customer
2.    {
3.        private Name name;
4.        private String acc_no;
5.        private Address address;
6.
7.        public Customer (Name n, String ac, Address addr)
8.        {
9.            name = n;
10.           acc_no = ac;
11.           this.address = addr;
12.       }
13.       public Name getName()
14.       {
15.           return name;
16.       }
17.       public Address getAddress()
18.       {
19.           return address;
20.       }
21.       public String getAccountNumber()
```

```
22.        {
23.              return acc_no;
24.        }
25.        void changeAccountNumbsr(String acc)
26.        {
27.              acc_no = acc;
28.        }
29. }
```

Next, we will design the class BankAccount. This component we know is characterized by Customer objects, and an initial balance, as stated in the opening sentence of the problem description. This means that there is an association relation between itself and the class Customer.

It is customary that when an account is opened, an initial deposit is also made. This tells us that the constructor will not only accept Customer object, but also an initial deposit which will be used to offset the balance in the account upon creating the account. This implies that it is necessary to have a field that will act as an accumulator for the balance.

The problem also specifies that one should be able to make deposits and withdrawal any number of times. These activities necessitate a mutator method for each action – deposit, and withdraw. In addition, we will also need accessor methods for each of the fields. **Figure 1.11** shows the class diagram representing the entity BankAccount.

Figure 1.11 The entity BankAccount

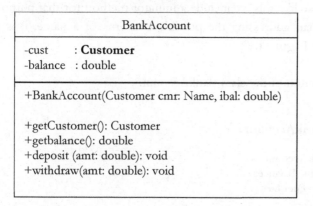

Whereas the method withdraw seems straightforward; i.e., a withdrawal is a subtraction, the account could end up with a negative balance. To avoid this from happening, one approach is to test whether or not the amount to be withdrawn exceeds the actual balance in the account; and if this is the case, we may want to let the program alert the customer. If we take this approach, then we will see that the method called **withdraw** will have three responsibilities – testing the data, alerting customer by providing a message, and withdrawing, by subtracting values. In this context, this method is lowly cohesive, since it has three responsibilities. This in turn weakens the cohesiveness of the class itself. To strengthen the cohesiveness of this method would be to let it carry out the subtraction for withdrawal only; then we would design a separate method to do the testing. In addition, let the class that is implementing this aspect of this component determine the alert message. In this context, this version has a higher degree of cohesiveness than the previous one. In particular, see the method called isSufficient. **Figure 1.12** shows a modified version of the component BankAccount.

Figure 1.12 The entity BankAccount

BankAccount
-cust   : **Customer**   -balance : double
+BankAccount(Customer cmr: Name, ibal: double)   +getCustomer(): Customer   +getbalance(): double   +deposit (amt: double): void   +withdraw(amt: double): void   +isSufficient(amt: double): boolean

In the design of this system, the entities Name and Address are quite simple, when compared to the other components. The entity Name is comprised of three fields of type String – first name, last name and middle name (if any). Usually an entire name is not changed; but may be a last name may change due to marriage. In a case like this we include a mutator method for that purpose. Since this component has nothing else than addressing the possible concerns of a name, it is considered a highly cohesive component. See **Figure 1.13**.

Listing 1.3 shows the definition of the class BankAccount.

Listing 1.3 Class BankAccount

```
1.    public class BankAccount {
2.         private double balance;
3.         private Customer cust;
4.
5.         public BankAccount (Customer c, double amt)
6.         {
7.             cust = c;
8.             balance = amt;
9.         }
10.        public Customer getCustomer()
11.        {
12.            return cust;
13.        }
14.        public void deposit(double amt)
```

```
15.        {
16.            balance += amt;
17.        }
18.        public void withdraw(double amt)
19.        {
20.            balance -= amt;
21.        }
22.        public double getAmount()
23.        {
24.            return balance;
25.        }
26.        public boolean isSufficient(double amt)
27.        {
28.            return balance >= amt;
29.        }
30. }
```

Figure 1.13 shows the UML class notation diagram representing the name object of an individual. Notice that we have included a mutator method that can be used to change ones last name, if there is ever the need to do so.

Figure 1.13 The entity Name

Name
-firstname: String -lastname: String -middlename: String
+Name(first: String, last: String, middle: String,) +getFirstname():String +getLastname():String +getMiddleName():String +change:LastName(n: String): void

Listing 1.4 shows the definition of the class Name.

Listing 1.4 Definition of the class Name

```
1.    class Name
2.    {
3.        String first;
4.        String last;
5.
6.        Name(String f, String l)
7.        {
8.            first = f;
9.            last = l;
10.       }
```

```
11.
12.      String getFirst()
13.      {
14.          return first;
15.      }
16.
17.      String getLast()
18.      {
19.          return last;
20.      }
21. }
```

Like the component Name, the component Address is highly cohesive. It is comprised of five fields of type String – street, city, zip, and state, country. See **Figure 1.14**.

Figure 1.14 The entity Address

Address
-street: String -city: String -state: String -zip: String -country: String
+Address(street: String, city: String, state: String, zip: String) +getStreet() : String +getCity()   : String +getState( ) : String +getZip()   : String +getCountry(): String

Listing 1.5 shows the definition of the class Address. Notice that everything in this class has to do with the concept of address. The only missing elements are methods to modify the fields.

Listing 1.5 The definition of the class Address

```
1.   class Address
2.   {
3.        String street, city, state,  zip;
4.
5.        Address(String str, String city, String st, String zip)
6.        {
7.            street = str;
8.            this.city = city;
9.            state = st;
10.           this.zip = zip;
```

```
11.      }
12.         String getStreet() {
13.             return street;
14.         }
15.         String getCity() {
16.             return city;
17.         }
18.         String getState() {
19.             return state;
20.         }
21.         String getZip() {
22.             return zip;
23.         }
24. }
```

Analyzing the entity Database we see that it is more complex than all of the other components. But as complex as this may seem however, its singly purpose as far as the banking activities are concern is a focus on database operations only:

- Add bank accounts to a growing list[1] of bank accounts.
- Search the list for a given accounts.
- Obtain copy of a bank account if it is in the database.
- Find the location of a bank account, if that account is in the database, to a lesser extent.
- Remove an account from the list of accounts.

On the surface, **Figure 1.15** seems to be an accurate response to the five requirements above. The method, **add**, accepts a bank account object and adds it to the list; the method **delete**, removes the account from the list; the method **search**, searches the list and returns its index; and the method **getAccount**, simply returns an account from the list.

Figure 1.15 The entity Database

Database
-list   : ArrayList -account   : BankAccount
+ Database () +add(account: BankAccount): void +delete(accountNumber: String): BankAccount +search (accountNumber: String): int +getAccount(accountNumber: String): BankAccount

---

[1] For an expandable list, the class ArrayList is more appropriate than an array which is non-expandable.

On closer examination of this solution, there are several assumptions that are being made. The method called **add** undoubtedly has only one function; that is, it appends an account to the growing list of accounts.

The method called **delete** has the potential of doing more than one tasks. The acceptance of the account number as parameter, suggests that it uses the account number to conduct a search for the bank account. Not only does it searches the list, but it also removes the account object from the list if it is there, and it also returns a copy of it. This method exhibits low cohesiveness. A better approach would be for the method to receive the index, and use it to remove and return the object that it removes.

The method called search should be a mutator method, designed to make note of three pertinent pieces of information that are consistent with a search - whether or not an item is in the list; if the item is in the list, where in the list it is; and thirdly, which account it is, if it is in the list. With this modification there should now be three accessor methods, one for each of the three pieces of information produced by the search method. This modification strengthens the degree of cohesiveness of both the method; hence the class on the whole is strengthened.

Lastly, the method getAccount, by accepting as parameter the account number, has the potential of executing multiple tasks – searching, determining if the account is in the list, and returning a copy of that object. This method should depend on the outcome of the search method, and should only be called if an account is found to be in the list. That is, the method search should be made to accept an account number as parameter, and conduct the search as discussed in the previous paragraph. **Figure 1.16** shows a more cohesive class than the one shown in Figure 1.15.

Figure 1.16 The entity Database

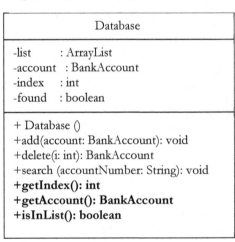

Listing 1.6 shows the class definition of the UML diagram representing the entity, Database.

Listing 1. 6

```
1.    import java.util.ArrayList;
2.
3.    class Database
4.    {
5.        ArrayList<BankAccount> list;
6.        BankAccount ba;
7.        int index;
8.        boolean found;
9.        Database()
10.       {
11.           list = new ArrayList<BankAccount>();
12.       }
13.       void search(String key)
14.       {
15.           found = false;
16.           int i = 0;
17.
18.           while(!found && i < list.size()) {
19.               BankAccount b = list.get(i);
20.               if(b.getCustomer().getAccountNumber().equalsIgnoreCase(key))
21.               {
22.                   ba = b;
23.                   found = true;
24.                   index =i;
25.               }
26.               else
27.                   i++;
28.           }
29.       }
30.       void add(BankAccount b) {
31.           list.add(b);
32.       }
33.       BankAccount delete(int i) {
34.           return list.remove(i);
35.       }
36.       int getIndex(){
37.           return index;
38.       }
39.       boolean inList(){
40.           return found;
41.       }
42.       BankAccount getAccount() {
43.           return ba;
44.       }
45.       int size()  {
46.         return list.size();
47.       }
48.       boolean isEmpty() {
```

```
49.          return list.isEmpty();
50.      }
51.      ArrayList getList(){
52.          return list;
53.      }
54.  }
```

As we have stated, the quality of a software system is generally measured by the cohesiveness of each of the components. If the components when connected do not have cycles of dependencies, but form a perfect tree, then the system is in general a highly cohesive. The result of the above analysis, with the exception of the component called Input/Output, results in a tree, as shown in **Figure 1.17**. A highly cohesive system generally gives rise to a lowly coupled system.

Figure 1.17 The graph of a cohesive system generally forms a perfect tree

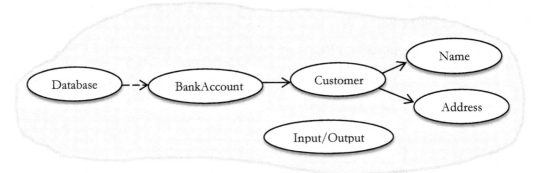

Self-Check

1. Which of the following statements is true concerning a class? Select one.
    (a) In a class, fields can ONLY be user-defined types.
    (b) In a class, fields can ONLY be primitive data types or existing Java classes.
    (c) In a class, fields can be primitive data types, existing Java types, or user-defined types.
    (d) In a class, fields can ONLY be primitive data types such as int, float, etc.

2. Write a class called Person. A person has a name and a social number. Assume that a class Name exists with first name and last name. Design the class Person such that it accepts a Name object and a social security number. Provide accessor methods to return the Name object and also the social security number.

    Write a class called Registration that accepts two values - a Person object, and an array called courses [ ] - representing strings of course titles. No student is allowed to register for more than five (5) at any one time. Write a method that determines if a student has registered for too many courses. You are responsible for providing the requisite variables, and any other methods deemed necessary.

Coupling

Whereas cohesion describes the relationship of elements within a single component of a system, coupling on the other hand describes the interdependent relationships among the components. In order for the system to work harmoniously, the components must be connected in such a way that they work harmoniously with one another as well. The nature of the connections is important, as it will determine the stability of the system. For instance, if there is a change in one component of the system, will thisnchange require change in any other component; and if so, to what extent.

In objected oriented design, if every component has a reference to every other component in a system, then this interdependent relationship is said to be tightly coupled. In a tightly coupled system, we often find cyclic relationship among components. **Figure 1.18** shows a highly coupled system. In the figure, the components BankAccount, Customer and Address form a cycle.

Figure 1.18 A highly coupled system

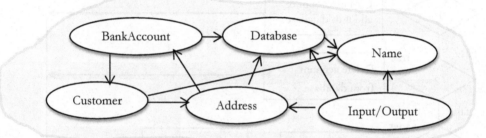

Tightly coupled systems generally present major programming challenges. A tightly coupled system increases the possibility of too much information flow through it, which in term has the potential of creating redundancies along the way. In a tightly coupled system, a change in one component could have ripple effect of changes in other components. As a result, modification to a tightly coupled system can prove difficult, if not impossible to maintain.

Instead of creating a system that is highly coupled, it is better to create a loosely coupled one, by designing a separate component that supervises the cohesive portion of the system. In general, a loosely coupled system is more desirable than a tightly coupled one. **Figure 1.19** shows a loosely coupled system of components that is supervised by a tester component.

Figure 1.19 A loosely coupled system

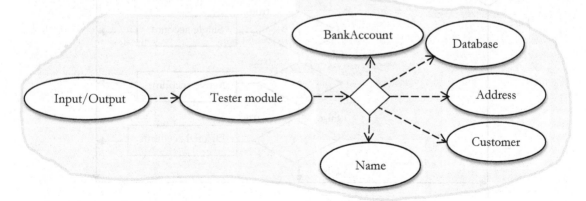

This system represents one of dependency relationship, rather than an association relationship. Notice that there is no cyclic relationship among any of the components. In addition, the system is governed by a decision control node that accepts input generated from the Input/Ouput component, and selects the component that is to be accessed. As the arrows show, no one component is directly in control of another component. In its implementation, the tester component will provide options for selecting which component gets accessed. This solution is best illustrated by a flowchart. See **Figure 1.20**.

Figure 1.20 Test component coordinates the other components

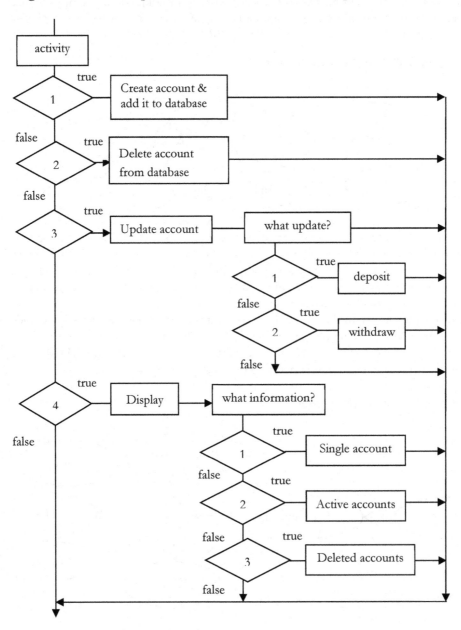

Figure 1.20 illustrates four major activities – create a new account and add it to the database, delete an existing account from the database, update an existing account, and display information.

Prior to the creation of the various components object for a BankAccount we first create a database object for keeping a list of the current customers, and one for the list of closed account. Perhaps we could create these objects as follows:

> Database db = new Database( );
> Database close = new Database( );

The creation of a BankAccount object and adding it to the database is best described by the flowchart shown in **Figure 1.21.** In this situation the user inputs the data needed to create the respective object, in the order shown in the flowchart.

Figure 1.21 Creating a BankAccount object

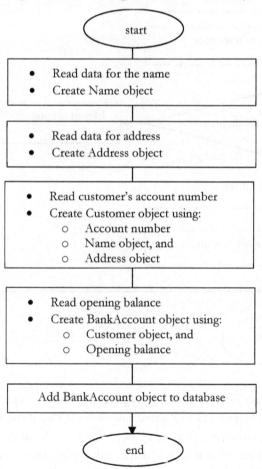

The deletion of an account, and the storing of it, first require determining whether or not the account exists. To determine if the account exists you will need the account number in order to conduct the search. Once it is determined that the account exists, then it is just a matter of obtaining the location where it it resides, and removing it, and storing in the list of deleted accounts. If the accoount does not exists, inform the user that it does not exists. This algorithm is illustrated in **Figure 1.22**.

Figure 1.22 Deleting an account and storing it in a list of deleted accounts

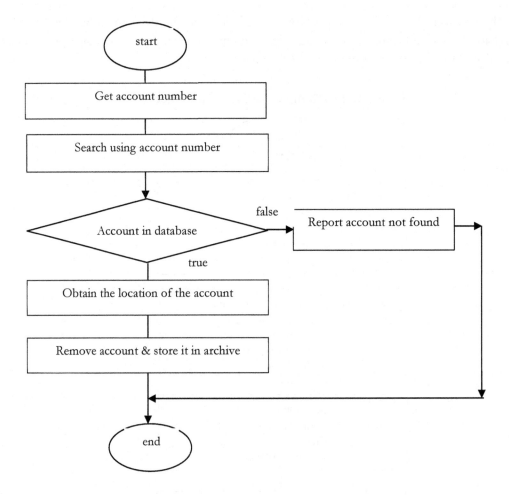

The third option, the updating of an account, runs parallel to removing an account, in that the account in question must first be located. The difference however is that if the account is located it is not removed, instead we must ascertain from the user whether the update is a deposit, or a withdrawal. Deposit is quite simple; this is just a matter of getting the amount representing the deposit and adding it to the existing balance, to form a new balance. Withdrawal other the other hand requires determining if there is sufficient funds in the account to effect the withdrawal. Finally, if the account does not exist in the database, the user should be alerted. See **Figure 1.23** for an illustration.

Figure 1.23 Updating an account

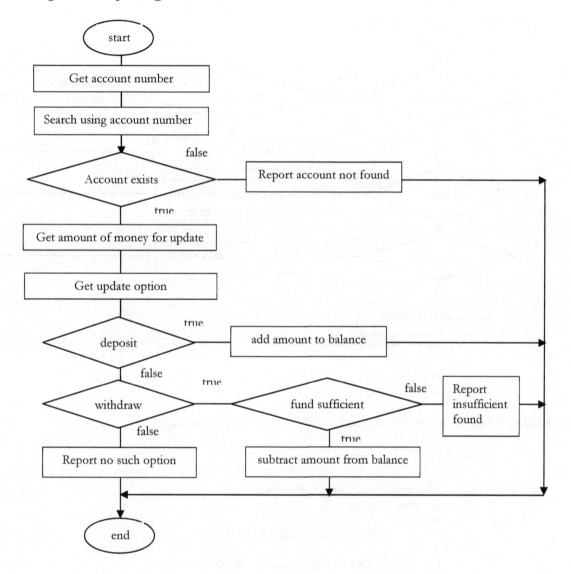

The displaying of information is summarized in **Figure 1.24**, where the information to be displayed is either about a single customer, a list of the current customers, or a list of the closed accounts.

Figure 1.24 Displaying account information

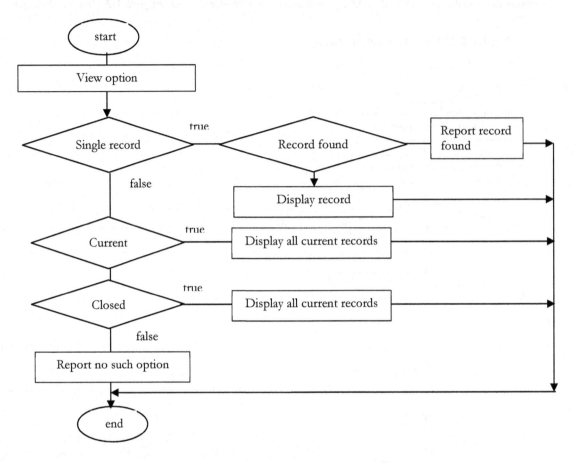

Listing 1.7 shows the class GetData that will be used to input the data.

Listing 1.7

```
1.   import javax.swing.JOptionPane;
2.   class GetData
3.   {
4.       public static double getDouble(String s)
5.       {
6.           return Double.parseDouble(getWord(s));
7.       }
8.       public static int getInt(String s)
9.       {
10.          return Integer.parseInt(getWord(s));
11.      }
12.      public static String getWord(String s)
13.      {
```

```
14.              return JOptionPane.showInputDialog(s);
15.          }
16.  }
```

Listing 1.8 shows the test class called TestBankAccount which creates the database objects for storing the current customers, and the closed accounts. See **Lines 15** and **16** respectively. The outer while loop which spans **Lines 22** thru **159** keeps the application running until the boolean variable established on **Line 20** is set to **true**. The menu, defined on **Line 24**, allows the user to select the option of creating a new account, updating an existing account, closing an account, viewing account information, or terminating the application. The outer switch statement beginning on Line 26 allows the user to make the selection. The first case **Lines 28** thru **51** creates a new account and adds it to the database of active accounts. The second option case 2, **Lines 52** thru **80** allows the user to update an account, if possible. Option 3 which spans **Lines 81** thru **93** shows how an account is removed from the active list and get stored into the list of closed accounts, where possible. Option 4 which spans **Lines 94** thru **151** determines which account or set of accounts is displayed. Finally, option 5 which spans **Lines 153** thru **156** terminates the application.

Listing 1.8 The test class TestBank.java

```
1.      package BankAccount;
2.
3.      import java.text.DateFormat;
4.      import java.util.Date;
5.      import java.text.NumberFormat;
6.      import javax.swing.JOptionPane;
7.      import javax.swing.JTextArea;
8.      import javax.swing.JScrollPane;
9.      import java.util.ArrayList;
10.
11.     public class TestBankAccount
12.     {
13.         public static void main(String args[])
14.         {
15.             Database db = new Database();  // Creating database for active accounts
16.             Database close = new Database();  // Creating database for inactive accounts
17.             DateFormat df = DateFormat.getDateInstance(DateFormat.LONG);
18.             Date now = new Date();
19.             NumberFormat nf = NumberFormat.getCurrencyInstance();
20.             boolean done = false;
21.
22.             while (!done)
23.             {
24.                 int menu = GetData.getInt("\tUnited Bank of Java\n" + "\t" + df.format(now) + "\n"
25.                     + "\nPlease Choose From the Following:" + "\n1. Create New Account\n2. Update
26.                     Existing Account Account "+ "\n3. Close an Account\n4. View Account
                        Information\n5.
27.                     Exit");
```

```
28.              switch(menu)
29.              {
30.                  case 1: //Creating a BankAccount object and storing it in the database
31.                      // Creating Name object
32.                      String f = GetData.getString("Enter First Name") ;
33.                      String l = GetData.getString("Enter Last Name") ;
34.                      Name n = new Name(f,l);
35.
36.                      // Creating Address object
37.                      String str = GetData.getString("Enter Street Name") ;
38.                      String city = GetData.getString("Enter City") ;
39.                      String st = GetData.getString("Enter State") ;
40.                      String zip = GetData.getString("Enter Zip") ;
41.
42.                      // Creating Customer object
43.                      Address addr = new Address(str,city,st,zip);
44.                      String accNo = GetData.getString("Enter Account Number") ;
45.                      Customer c = new Customer(n,accNo,addr);
46.
47.                      // Creating BankAccount object
48.                      double amount = GetData.getDouble("Enter First Deposit") ;
49.                      BankAccount ba = new BankAccount(c, amount);
50.
51.                      // Add BankAccount object to the database
52.                      db.add(ba);
53.              break;
54.          case 2: //Update Account
55.              accNo = GetData.getString("Enter Account Number of Account you'd like to update") ;
56.              db.search(accNo);
57.              if (!db.inList())
58.                  JOptionPane.showMessageDialog(null, "Account not found.");
59.              else
60.              {
61.                  int option = GetData.getInt("Would you like to (1) Deposit, (2) Withdraw");
62.                  switch(option)
63.                  {
64.                      case 1:
65.                          double amt = GetData.getDouble("Enter amount you'd like to deposit");
66.                          BankAccount b = db.getAccount();
67.                          b.deposit(amt);
68.                      break;
69.                      case 2:
70.                          double amnt = GetData.getDouble("Enter amount you'd like to withdraw") ;
71.                          BankAccount bnk = db.getAccount();
72.                          if (!bnk.isSufficient(amnt))
73.                              JOptionPane.showMessageDialog(null,  "Insufficient  funds,  withdrawal
                               cannot be done.");
74.                          else
75.                              bnk.withdraw(amnt);
76.                      break;
```

```
77.                     default:
78.                         JOptionPane.showMessageDialog(null, "Invalid selection. To return to main
                            menu, please deposit or withdraw $0");
79.                         break;
80.                     }
81.                 }
82.         break;
83.         case 3: //Close Account
84.             accNo = GetData.getString("Cose account - Please enter Account No.)");
85.             db.search(accNo);
86.             if (!db.inList())
87.                 JOptionPane.showMessageDialog(null, "Account not found.");
88.             else
89.                 {
90.                     BankAccount b = db.getAccount();
91.                     int index = db.getIndex();
92.                     db.add( db.delete(index) );
93.                     JOptionPane.showMessageDialog(null, "The Account " + accNo + " has been closed.");
94.                 }
95.         break;
96.         case 4: //View Account
97.             int view = GetData.getInt("What information would you like to view?\n1. Single
                account\n2. All active accounts\n3. All inactive accounts\n");
98.
99.             switch(view)
100.             {
101.                 case 1: // View a single account
102.                     accNo = GetData.getString("View – account. Please enter Account No.");
103.                     db.search(accNo);
104.                     if(!db.inList())
105.                         JOptionPane.showMessageDialog(null, "Account not found.");
106.                     else
107.                         {
108.                             BankAccount bb = db.getAccount();
109.                             String s = "Customer\t" + bb.getCustomer().getName().getFirst() + "\t" +
                                bb.getAmount() ;
110.                             JOptionPane.showMessageDialog(null,    s,    "Bank    Account    " +
                                bb.getCustomer().getAccountNumber(),
                                JOptionPane.INFORMATION_MESSAGE);
111.                         }
112.                     break;
113.                 case 2: // View all active accounts
114.                     ArrayList list = db.getList();
115.                     if(list.isEmpty())
116.                         JOptionPane.showMessageDialog(null, "List is empty");
117.                     else
118.                         {
119.                             int i = 0, length = db.size();
120.                             String s = "";
121.                             while(i < length)
```

```
122.                        {
123.                            BankAccount b = (BankAccount)list.get(i);
124.                            s = s + "Customer Name: " + b.getCustomer().getName().getFirst() + " "
                                + b.getCustomer().getName().getLast() + "\nAccount number: " +
                                b.getCustomer().getAccountNumber() + "\n"
125.                            + b.getCustomer().getAddress().getStreet() + ", " +
                                b.getCustomer().getAddress().getCity() + ", " +
                                b.getCustomer().getAddress().getState() + ", "
126.                            + b.getCustomer().getAddress().getZip() + "\n" +
                                nf.format(b.getAmount()) + "\n";
127.                            i++;
128.                        }
129.                        display(s, "Active Accounts", JOptionPane.INFORMATION_MESSAGE);
130.                    }
131.                break;
132.                    case 3: // View all closed accounts
133.                        ArrayList closed = db.getList();
134.
135.                        if(closed.isEmpty())
136.                            JOptionPane.showMessageDialog(null, "List is empty");
137.                        else
138.                        {
139.                            int i = 0, length = db.getSize();
140.                            String s = "";
141.                            while(i < length)
142.                            {
143.                                BankAccount b = (BankAccount)closed.get(i);
144.                                s = s + "Name " + b.getCustomer().getName().getFirst() + " " +
                                    b.getCustomer().getName().getLast() + "\tAccount number: " +
                                    b.getCustomer().getAccountNumber() + "\n";
145.                                i++;
146.                            }
147.                            display(s, "Closed Accounts",
                                JOptionPane.INFORMATION_MESSAGE);
148.                        }
149.                    break;
150.                        default:
151.                        JOptionPane.showMessageDialog(null, "Invalid option.");
152.                        break;
153.                }// End view
154.            break;
155.            case 5: //Exit
156.                    done = true;
157.            break;
158.            default:
159.                    JOptionPane.showMessageDialog(null, "Account not found.");
160.            break;
161.        }
162.     }
163. }
```

```
164.        static void display(String s, String heading, int MESSAGE_TYPE)
165.        {
166.            JTextArea text = new JTextArea(s, 20, 30);
167.            JScrollPane pane = new JScrollPane(text);
168.            JOptionPane.showMessageDialog(null, pane, heading, MESSAGE_TYPE);
169.        }
170.    }
```

De-referencing an Object

Just as it is important to construct a cohesive set of classes, we must also be able to deference any component of the system. For instance, one of the requirements of the output was to produce the following information:

Fist, lastname

Account #

Street, City, State, zip, and $ amount.

The code that is actually responsible for this output is generated from the lines in the following display.

```
123.    BankAccount b = (BankAccount)list.get(i);
124.    s = s + "Customer Name: " + b.getCustomer().getName().getFirst() + "    " +
        b.getCustomer().getName().getLast()      + "\nAccount      number:      " +
        b.getCustomer().getAccountNumber() + "\n"
125.    + b.getCustomer().getAddress().getStreet() + ", " + b.getCustomer().getAddress().getCity() +
        ", " + b.getCustomer().getAddress().getState() + ", "
126.    + b.getCustomer().getAddress().getZip() + "\n" + nf.format(b.getAmount()) + "\n";
```

Line 123 retrieves a bankAccount object **b**. The class BankAccount as you know has field Customer, hence the method, getCustomer(), which returns a Customer object. But the class Customer has fields, Name and Address; hence methods, getName() and getAddress() respectively. In the case of getName of type Name, the class Name has fields, firstName and lastName. In this context chaining the classes via their respectively reference to display one's first name we structure the code as follows:

> b.getCustomer().getName().getFirst()

This construct is exactly the opposite of forming the cohesivity among the classes – BankAccount, Customer, and Name. The pattern holds true for the class Address.

Self-Check

1.   What is meant by the term coupling? How is it difference from cohesion?

2.   Write a class called Dealer that has fields of type Vehicle and Customer. The field for Vehicle is a class that has fields make, model, and VIN. The field Customer has fields Name and account number. The field called Name is also an existing class with fields - last name and first name.

      (a) Define the class Dealer so that a Dealer object can be created either by a customer object alone, or by a customer object and a vehicle object.

      (b) Provide accessor methods for each type of fields in the class Dealer.

      (c) Provide a mutator method that changes the vehicle object. (A test class is not necessary).

      (d) Suppose the class Name has a method getLastName(), that returns the last name of a customer. If the reference variable **deal** is an instance of Dealer, write appropriate Java code that will extract and return the last name of a customer.

Chapter Summary

- Object-oriented design (OOD) is the philosophy of developing an object-oriented model of a software system, by defining the classes and their interactions with one another.

- The major benefits of OOD are easy maintainable systems, easy understandable systems, easy expandable systems, and reusable components of a system.

- The Unified Modeling Language (**UML**) uses a set of diagrams to model objects. This language features several types of diagrams, among which is the class diagram.

- Class diagrams are of four types, two of which are dependency diagram and association diagram.

- With respect to object oriented design, two of the more popular concepts for programming are cohesion and coupling.

- Cohesion focuses on the logical structure of the entity. That is, keep all related fields within the same unit.

- Coupling on the other hand focuses on coordinating the behavior of the entities.

- A highly cohesive system is more desirable than a loosely cohesive one.

- A loosely coupled stem is more desirable than a highly coupled one.

- Sometimes it can be beneficial in using flowchart of pseudocode to express the algorithm of a process.

- Apart from constructing a cohesive system of classes, we must also be proficient in de-referencing an object of the system.

Programming Exercises

1. The establishment called ABC Enterprise requires a Java program to keep a database of the inventory of the products that it sells. Each product is identified by its manufacturer, its name, the quantity, and unit price. Note: a manufacturer is characterized by its company's name and address
   In addition to storing the information, the program should be able to make updates to the quantity and/or the price as time goes on. That is, when a sale is made, the quantity of that product must be reduced; similarly, when a product is re-ordered, the quantity of that product must be increased. Also, when there is a change in the price of a product, the price must be changed. The change must be interpreted as a replacement of the value. New products may be added to the inventory at any time; also, a product may be removed from the inventory at any time. Maintain a separate list the products that have been deleted from the database of active products.

   Your program must be able to produce three kinds of reports, namely:
   Locate a single product and display its name, price and quantity alone.
   The inventory report should be structured as follows:

Product	Purchase Date	Quantity	Price	Manufacturer	State
Telephone	01/20/2013	10	254.99	Motorola	FL
Computer	01/06/2013	15	756.99	CBS	NY
:	:	:	:	:	:
:	:	:	:	:	:

   The list of deleted products should be structured as follows:

Product	Date	Manufacturer
Paper reams	01/20/2013	Morgan Jewelry
:	:	:

   In your design, convince yourself that you need a minimum of four classes, not including the test class – Product, Manufacturer, Address, and Database. You may use the class called GetData.java, **Listing 1.6**, for inputting the data. Use a scrollable pane to display your output.

2. Imagine that you were required to write a Java program which will store, manipulate, and print student registration information.

    As part of the solution, identify the following classes:

    (a) Student
    (b) Admissions.

    The class Student has the following fields – Name, Address, Id number, and Date, where:

    (a) Name is a user defined class comprising of at minimum first name and last name.
    (b) Address is a user defined class comprising of fields - street, city, state, and zip code.
    (c) Date is a predefined class in the java.util package
    (d) Id number a string variable that uniquely identifies a student.

    The class Admissions stores and manipulates the student information (student record). Because the list of students grows dynamically, it is best to use a dynamic data structure such as the ArrayList to store the information. This class should do the following, among other possible activities:

    (a) Add student to the list
    (b) Remove student from the list. This would first involve locating the record in order to remove it. In order to determine which record to remove you must supply the Id number as the search argument.

    You are to provide a test class that coordinates the activities of the classes outlined above, by:

    *   Creating student objects and adding them to the database of the Admissions object
    *   Removing a student from the database
    *   Change a student's last name
    *   Displaying list of currently registered students
    *   Displaying list of all students that were dropped from the course

    The output must be formatted as follows, and must be placed in a scrollable pane.

    CURRENTLY ENROLLED
    Id number: 123456
    Name: Williams, John
    Address: 2525 Hartsfield Road
             Tallahassee, FL 33319
    Date: September 5, 2010

                 :

                 :

    STUDENT WHO WERE DROPPED
    Id number: 56789-0
    Name: Roberts, Kay-Anne

Date: September 5, 2010

                    :

                    :

3. Write a Java program which will store, manipulate, and print student registration information. As part of the solution, identify the following classes:
    (c) Student
    (d) Admissions.

The class Student must have the following fields – Name, Address, Id number, Courses, and Date, where:
(e) Name is a user defined class comprising of at minimum first name and last name.
(f) Address is a user defined class comprising of fields - street, city, state, and zip code.
(g) Date is a predefined class in the java.util package
(h) The field Courses is a set of no more than five (5) string values representing the courses being registered for. Course names supplied are assumed to be valid and contains no blank space, for instance COP3804 is valid but not COP 3804.
(i) Id number a string variable that uniquely identifies a student.
The class Student must be capable of adding courses and dropping courses

The class Admissions stores and manipulates the student information (student record). Because the list of students grows dynamically, it is best to use a dynamic data structure such as the ArrayList to store the information. This class should do the following, among other possible activities:
(c) Add student to the list
(d) Remove student from the list, which would first involve locating the record in order to remove it. In order to determine which record to remove you must supply the Id number as the search argument.

You are to provide a test class that coordinates the activities of the classes outlined above, by:
• Creating student objects and adding them to the database of the Admissions object
• Manipulating student record by:
    o Adding a course(s)
    o Dropping a course(s)
• Removing a student from the database
• Displaying list of currently registered students
• Displaying list of all students that were dropped from the course

The output must be formatted as follows:

CURRENTLY ENROLLED
Id number: 123456
Name: Williams, John
Address: 2525 Hartsfield Road
             Tallahassee, FL 33319

Date: September 5, 2009
Courses: COP3804, MATH2050, ENG3300
             :
             :

STUDENT WHO WERE DROPPED
Id number: 567890
Name: Roberts, Kay-Anne
Date: September 5, 2009
             :
             :

Note: Use the class GetData provided to enter the data from the keyboard.

4. Parking Ticket Simulator

    You are required to write a Java program to simulate police action re parked cars at parking meters.

    In modeling the solution, convince yourself that the program could have at least the following classes:

    - A class that models a parked car. This class is characterized by a car object, and the number of minutes that the car has been parked. A car object is characterized by its make, model, color, and license number.
    - A class that models a parking meter. This class is characterized by the number of minutes of parking time that has been purchased.
    - A class that models a parking ticket. This class is characterized by, among other things, parked car objects and police officer objects. In addition it reports:
        o   The make, model, color, license number of the illegally parked car.
        o   The amount of fine. The amount of fine is determined as follows: $25.00 for the first hour, or part of an hour that the car is parked illegally, plus $10.00 for every additional hour or part of an hour that the car is parked illegally.
        o   The name and badge of the officer issuing the ticket.
        o   The date upon which the ticket was issued
    - A class that models a police officer who is inspecting the parked car. This class is characterized by the following:
        o   The officer's name and badge number. The name is an object characterized by at least first and last name.
        o   The parked car object and the parking meter object to determine of the whether or not the car's time has expired
    - A class that features storing, searching, and retrieving officer's copy of parking tickets.

Design a menu as shown below.

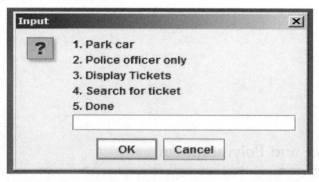

Display your output in a scrollable pane similar to the display shown below.

Chapter 2 Inheritance and Polymorphism

Objectives

After reading this chapter you will:

- Understand the concept of inheritance
- Be able to differentiate between subclass and superclass
- Know what an abstract class is.
- Be able to define concrete class from abstract class
- Understand the concept of polymorphism
- Know the four forms of polymorphism
- Know what visibility modifiers are, and their effect on classes.
- Be able to write programs that are easily extendable and modifiable by applying inheritance.

Introduction

The concept inheritance is a fundamental principle of Object Oriented Programming (OOP). This concept allows you to define a new class from an existing one. That is, this new class is an extension of the existing one. The existing class is referred to as the direct superclass of the new class, and derived class is referred to as the direct subclass of the existing class. A direct superclass does not have any intervening class between itself and its direct subclass; conversely, a direct subclass does not have any class between itself and its direct superclass. Hence, in OOP, whenever the term subclass is used, it means direct subclass; and whenever the term superclass is used, it means direct superclass.

Generalization Diagrams

When applied to large scale programming, generalization diagrams are used to model inheritance. This kind of relationship indicates that the subclass is a specialized model (child) of a general (parent) model. This relationship is also known as an "is a" relationship since the child class **is a** type of the parent class. In the general sense the parent model can have multiple children, and any child model element can have one or more parents, typically a single parent has multiple children. Java however does not permit a child to have multiple parents. UML generalization diagrams use a solid line, solid head one directional arrow to model generalization diagrams.

Let **A** and **B** be two classes as shown in **Figure 2.1**, the directional arrow with closed head as shown, means that class **B** inherits the features of class **A**. Hence, class B is the subclass class A; and vice versa, class A is the superclass of class B.

Figure 2.1 Class B is a subclass of class A; vice versa, class A is the superclass of B

Java allows one and only one direct superclass for any direct subclass. A superclass on the other hand can have any number of subclasses. In addition, a subclass can serve as a superclass for any number of subclasses, relatively to itself. **Figure 2.2** shows that class **A** has two subclasses, **B** and **C**; and subclass **C** is the superclass for class **D**, making **D** an indirect subclass of **A**.

Figure 2.2 Classes B and C are subclasses of class A; class D is a subclass of C

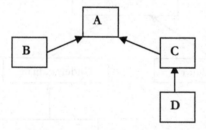

Conceptually two or more classes can be combined to form a new one. Although this is true with programming languages such as C++, Java does not support it. **Figure 2.3** shows that class **R** is derived from class **P** and class **Q**. As we have said, Java does not support this form of inheritance.

Figure 2.3 Class R inherits classes P and Q; this not supported by Java

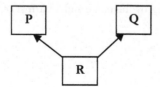

In terms of code, Java uses the keyword **extends** to denote inheritance. Using Figure 2.1, where **A** represents the superclass of **B**, the general format for defining inheritance is as follows:

```
<modifier> class B extends A
{
        // new instance fields for class B
        // new constructors for class B
        // new member methods for class B
}
```

A subclass may add its own fields, constructors and methods, as indicated in the format.

Example 2.1 Consider the following situation, where:
   A person is represented by the name and the age.
   A student is represented by the name, age, and major.
   A graduate student is represented by the name, age, major, and thesis option.
   An instructor is represented by a name, age, and a salary.

These entities can be represented in a hierarchy of classes, as shown in **Figure 2.4**, where Instructor and Undegraduate are both direct subclasses of the class Person; and Graduate is a direct subclass of Undergraduate.

Figure 2.4 Hierarchy of classes

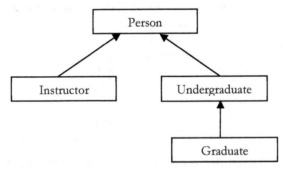

In developing this hierarchy of classes, the class Person serves as the superclass for all the subclasses. Its definition is shown in **Listing 2.1**.

Listing 2.1 Super class Person

```
1.    // A person is represented by the name and a birth year
2.    public class Person
3.    {
4.          private String name;
5.          private int birthYear;
```

```
6.
7.          public Person(String n, int byear)
8.          {
9.              name = n;
10.             birthYear = byear;
11.         }
12.         public String toString()
13.         {
14.             return "Person: " + name + ", birth year: " + birthYear;
15.         }
16. }
```

As shown, the class **Person** is defined the usual way that we are accustomed to writing classes. It has two parameters, a constructor, and a single accessor method that returns a string containing the name and age of the individual.

With respect to instructor, the attributes are name, age, and salary. This implies that an instructor is a person who gets a salary. In terms of generalization, an instructor a specialized form of person; one who gets a salary. As such the class instructor inherits the definition of the class Person, as shown in **Listing 2.2.**

Listing 2.2 Subclass Instructor inherits the class Person

```
1.   //An instructor is represented by a name, age, and a salary
2.   public class Instructor extends Person
3.   {
4.       private double salary;
5.       public Instructor(String n, int age, double s)
6.       {
7.           super(n, age);
8.           salary = s;
9.       }
10.      public String toString()
11.      {
2.           return "Instructor[super=" + super.toString() + " salary = " + salary + "]";
13.      }
14. }
```

The class **Instructor** is defined a little different from the regular way to which we have been accustomed. **Line 2** shows the heading for the class Instructor; in particular, notice the phrase **Instructor extends Person**. By definition, Person is the superclass, and Instructor is the subclass. **Line 4** shows a member variable – **salary**. This variable is unique to Instructor and is not a member of the class Person.

Lines 5 thru **9** show the constructor definition for the class **Instructor**. **Line 5** has parameters **name**, **age**, and **salary**. Since the superclass **Person** contains the codes for initializing **name** and **age**, we can use that constructor to carry out the initialization of these two variables. **Line 7** shows how this is achieved. The code **super(n, age)** calls the constructor of the superclass by passing to it the value in the variables, n and age. The variable **salary** is initialized locally.

The class has a single method - **public String toString()**. **Line 12** returns the **name**, **age**, and **salary** of the **Instructor**. Notice that the variables **name** and **age** are private members of the class **Person**, therefore they cannot be accessed directly from within the class Instructor. In order to access these variables you will have to access the public method in the superclass. In the current situation the statement **super.toString()** returns these values through the toString() method. In particular, the qualifier **super** is used to refer to the toString() method in the superclass.

The class **Undergraduate** is defined in a similar way to the class Instructor. See **Listing 2.3**. Notice that whereas the class Instructor has added field **salary**, Undergraduate has added field called **major**.

Listing 2.3 Subclass Undergraduate and extension of the class Person

```
1.    // A student is represented by the name, age, and major
2.    public class Undergraduate extends Person
3.    {
4.          private String major;
5.
6.          public Undergraduate(String n, int age, String m)
7.          {
8.               super(n, age);
9.               major = m;
10.        }
11.
2.         public String toString()
13.        {
14.              return "Undergraduate[super= " + super.toString() + "\nmajor=" + major + "]";
15.        }
16. }
```

Finally, the class **Graduate** inherits the class **Undergraduate**, which indirectly inherits the class **Person**. See **Listing 2.4**. Although the class **Graduate** indirectly inherits the class **Person**, we do not **extends** twice. That is, **class Graduate extends Undergraduate extends Person** is syntactically incorrect. The word **extends** can only be used once.

Listing 2.4 Subclass Graduate inherits class Undergraduate

```
1.    // A graduate student is represented by the name, age, major, and thesis option
2.    public class Graduate extends Undergraduate
3.    {
4.          private String thesis;
5.
6.          public Graduate(String n, int age, String m, String thesis)
```

```
7.        {
8.              super(n, age, m);
9.              this.thesis = thesis;
10.       }
11.
2.        public String toString()
13.       {
14.             return "Graduate[super = " + super.toString() + "\nThesis = " + thesis + "]";
15.       }
16. }
```

In Listing 2.4, Line 8 calls the constructor of its superclass to carry out the initialization of its inherited fields name, age and major. The effect of this call is referred to as the chaining of constructors, since the super class of Graduate will call its super class, thus forming a chain.

Rules Governing Constructors

Constructors, although they are considered part of the definition of the subclass, they cannot be called directly by a subclass. However, they can be called indirectly by using the Java keyword **super** as a call to the superclass. Its format is as follows:

> **super**(<argument>);

When used, the statement must be the first executable statement in the constructor of the subclass. Refer to **Listings 2.2, 2.3** and **2.4**; **Lines 7, 8**, and **8** respectively.

Rules Governing Data Members and Methods

- Private members of the superclass cannot be accessed directly by its subclasses. Instead, you must provide non-private accessor methods to return their values.
- Private methods in a superclass cannot be accessed directly by its subclasses. Instead, you must provide non-private methods in the superclass.

- You can use the Java modifier **super** to reference the non-private method in the superclass. The format of using it is as follows:

> **super.nameOfMethod**(<argument>);

- Non-private variables in the superclass can be referenced directly by their names in the subclass, if the names are not in the subclass. If they are in both classes, you must use the modifiers **super** and **this**, to differentiate between them. Usually, we use accessor methods to return their values.

- A subclass class can override the definition of its inherited method. That is, a subclass can redefine a method it inherits from a superclass. The new method will undoubtedly have the same signature as the superclass, but usually they have different code in the body. At runtime the object type determines which method is invoked

Listing 2.5 shows a possible driver class. As seen in the listing, **Lines 8** thru **12** creates different kinds of Person objects, and adds them to a growing list of objects.

Listing 2.5 The test class that creates and stores objects

```
1.   import java.util.ArrayList;
2.
3.   // Create and store Person, Undergraduate, Graduate, and Instructor objects
4.   public class Driver{
5.       public static void main(String[] args)
6.       {
7.           ArrayList <Person>list = new ArrayList<Person>();
8.           list.add(new Person("Perry", 1959));
9.           list.add(new UnderGraduate("Sylvia", 1979, "Computer Science"));
10.          list.add(new Graduate("James", 2003, "Computer Science", "GUI"));
11.          list.add(new Instructor("Edgar", 1969, 65000));
12.          print(list);
13.      }
14.      static void display(ArrayList list)  {
15.          int length = list.size(),
16.          person = 0,
17.          ugrad  = 0,
18.          grad   = 0,
19.            ins   = 0;
20.
21.          for (int i = 0; i < length; i++)
22.          {
23.              Object o = list.get(i);
24.
25.              if ( o instanceof  Person)
26.                  person++;
27.              else if (o instanceof Graduate)
28.                  grad++;
29.              else if (o instanceof UnderGraduate)
30.                  ugrad++;
31.              else if (o instanceof Instructor)
32.                  ins++;
33.          }
34.          System.out.println("\n# of instructors:  \t " + ins + "\n# of undergraduates: "
                 + ugrad + "\n# of graduates:  \t " + grad + "\n# of Persons: \t\t " + person);
35.      }
36. }
```

The output shown in **Figure 2.5,** does not make any distinction between the different types of objects. Hence it shows that all of the objects are Person objects.

Figure 2.5 Output generated for each class in the hierarchy

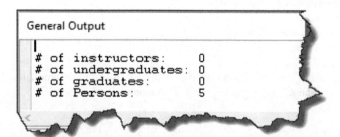

```
General Output

# of instructors:      0
# of undergraduates:   0
# of graduates:        0
# of Persons:          5
```

It is showing that all of the objects are of type Person. Indeed they are, but one would want to know the specific type of Person object. To achieve this we need to re-arrange the order of testing for the objects. That is, instead of first testing for Person the superclass, as shown on **Line 25** of Listing 2.5, reverse the order. That is, test from the subclass up to the superclass. See **Listing 2.6, Lines 27 thru 33**.

Listing 2.6

```
1.    import java.util.ArrayList;
2.
3.    public class Driver
4.    {
5.        public static void main(String[] args)
6.        {
7.            ArrayList<Person>list = new ArrayList<Person>();
8.            list.add(new Person("Perry", 35));
9.            list.add(new UnderGraduate("Sylvia", 24, "Computer Science"));
10.           list.add(new Graduate("James", 30, "Computer Science", "Graphical User Interface"));
11.           list.add(new Instructor("Edgar", 45, 65000));
12.           list.add(new Graduate("Barry", 32, "Computer Science", "Compiler Construction"));
13.           print(list);
14.       }
15.       static void display(ArrayList list)
16.       {
17.           int length = list.size(),
18.           person = 0,
19.           ugrad  = 0,
20.           grad   = 0,
21.           ins = 0;
22.
23.           for (int i = 0; i < length; i++)
24.           {
25.               Object o = list.get(i);
```

```
26.
27.                 if ( o instanceof Graduate )
28.                     grad++;
29.                 else if (o instanceof UnderGraduate)
30.                     ugrad++;
31.                 else if (o instanceof Instructor)
32.                     ins++;
33.                 else if (o instanceof Person )
34.                     person++;
35.             }
36.         System.out.println("\n# of instructors:  \t " + ins + "\n# of undergraduates: " + ugrad
           + "\n# of graduates:  \t " + grad + "\n# of Persons: \t\t " + person);
37.     }
38. }
```

Having change the order of testing for the objects, **Figure 2. 6** shows the correct output.

Figure 2. 6

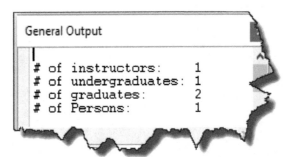

General Output

```
# of instructors:      1
# of undergraduates:   1
# of graduates:        2
# of Persons:          1
```

Self-Check

1. Define the following terms: **inheritance, superclass,** and **subclass**.

2. What are the two ways that the keyword **super** can be applied?

3. Show the output from the following program.

```
class A extends B
{
    A(int x)
    {
        System.out.println("In construct A - x is: " + x);
    }
}
```

```
class B
{
        B()
        {
                System.out.println("In construct B");
        }
}
class Test
{
        public static void main(String[] arg)
        {
                A a = new A(10);
        }
}
```

4. What problem arises when you attempt to compile the following program?

```
class A extends B
{
    A(int x)
    {
        System.out.println("In construct A - x is: " + x);
        super(x);
    }
}

class B
{
    B(int y)
    {
        System.out.println("In construct B - y is: " + y);
    }
}

class Test
{
    public static void main(String[] arg)
    {
        A a = new A(10);
    }
}
```

5. Consider the following description. Every employee and every student is a person. Every instructor and every administrator is an employee. Every associate and every undergraduate is a student; furthermore, every graduate has attribute of an undergraduate, and every post graduate has attributes of a graduate.
    Draw an inheritance diagram showing the relationship among the entities. Mark clearly the name of each entity.

6.   How many times can we have the **extends** clause in the class header when creating subclasses?

7.   Explain the significance of the calls **super("Hello")** and **this("Hello")**, as they pertain to the Java Programming language. Give one example of each to support your answer.

8.   Where must the following Java statement appear in a subclass?

super();

(a) It can be anywhere, as long as it is in the constructor.
(b) It should be the last statement in the constructor.
(c) It should be the first executable statement in the constructor.
(d) It should come before the **this()** statement in the constructor.
(e) It should be the first executable statement in a method.

Abstract Class

An abstract class is a special type of Java class that has zero or more abstract methods. An abstract method is one that is declared, but its body is not implemented; only a prototype of the method is specified. The classes that we have been accustomed to, had all of their methods defined. These classes are called concrete classes. Abstract classes are used to declare common characteristics of subclasses.

An abstract class cannot be instantiated. It can only be used as a superclass for other classes that extend the abstract class. Like concrete class, an abstract class can contain fields, constructors and concrete methods. An abstract class can include methods that contain no implementation. These are called abstract methods. The abstract method declaration must end with a semicolon rather than a block. If a subclass has any abstract methods, whether declared or inherited, then the class must be declared abstract. Abstract methods are used to provide a template for the classes that inherit the abstract methods. The general format for defining an abstract class is shown below.

```
<modifier> abstract class A
{
    <member variables>
    < constructors>
    < concrete methods>
    <modifier> abstract return_type  method_name( <parameter>);
}
```

In the above format, notice in the class declaration the keyword **abstract**. Also, notice the keyword **abstract** appears in the method prototype. In addition, instead of specifying the body of the method, it is terminated with the semi-colon.

As mentioned earlier, abstract classes cannot be instantiated; they must be subclassed, and the subclasses must provide the actual implementations for the abstract methods. Any implementation specified can, of course, be overridden by subclasses. If a subclass does not provide implementation for all of the abstract methods that it inherits, then the subclass is also an abstract class, as such that subclass must be prefaced with the keyword **abstract**.

Example 2.2

Write a Java program to calculate the wages for employees of a company. There are two types of employees – managers and hourly workers. A manager is paid a fixed salary. An hourly worker is not paid a fixed amount. If an hourly paid employee works 40 hours or less the gross pay is calculated as the number of hours worked times the rate of pay. If an hourly paid employee works more than 40 hours for the week, the gross pay is calculated as forty hours times the rate of pay, plus an overtime payment calculated at $1\frac{1}{2}$ the pay rate times the number of excess hours. The hourly rate is fixed at $25.00.

The program must calculate the gross pay and the net pay for each employee. The deduction for a manager is 1/5th gross pay. The deduction for anyone who works regular forty hours or less is 1/6th the gross pay, and the deduction for anyone who works over forty hours is 1/6th the gross pay regular pay, plus 1/8th of the overtime amount.

Solution

You should convince yourself that technically there are three categories of employees – manager, regular hourly worker who works forty hours or less, and overtime worker who works more than forty hours per week. In each case, the worker gets a gross pay; similarly each worker has some form of deduction, and each gets a net pay after the deduction has been taken out of the gross. Against this background we can see that all three share these commonalities. The method of carrying out these calculations is different however. With this in mind we can define:

   (a) A class for the manager

   (b) A class for the regular worker, and

   (c) A class for the overtime worker.

These three classes will return the gross pay, the deduction, and the net pay per individual. In addition, they will carry out calculations to determine these values. The method of carrying out these calculations will differ however. Against this background we could define an abstract class to handle all of the commonalities – getting the gross pay, getting the deduction, and getting the net pay. In addition, we can specify the abstract method to indicate that all three classes will carry out some calculations. Let us call these classes **Wages**, **Manager**, **RegularPay**, and **OvertimePay**; the class **Wages** being the abstract class. **Figure 2.7** shows a hierarchy of these classes.

Figure 2.6 Class hierarchy representing the different types of workers

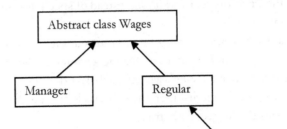

As you read, assume that the following constants exist - **MANAGER_TAX, REGULAR_TAX, RATE, OVERTIME_RATE, OVERTIME_TAX**, and **FORTY**.

Listing 2.7 shows the abstract class Wages.

Listing 2.7 The abstract class Wages

```
1.    abstract class Wages
2.    {
3.        double amount, gross, deduction, netPay;
4.
5.        Wages(double a)
6.        {
7.            amount = a;
8.        }
9.        double getGross()
10.        {
11.            return gross;
12.        }
13.        double getDeduction()
14.        {
15.            return deduction;
16.        }
17.        double getNet()
18.        {
19.            return netPay;
20.        }
21.
22.        abstract void calculate();
    }
```

Line 1 shows the declaration of the abstract class. It is prefaced with the keyword **abstract**. **Line 25** shows the declaration of the abstract method **calculate()**. All other features of the class are similar to the concrete classes to which we have been accustomed. All three classes that inherit this abstract class will report some gross pay, calculate some deductions, and get some net pay - hence the need for the three concrete methods. Each of the three classes however, will no doubt carry out these calculations differently; hence the need for the abstract method.

The class **Manager**, shown in **Listing 2.8** is a concrete class because it defines the abstract method **calculate**. See **Lines 9** thru **13**. This method calculates the three values – **gross, deduction,** and **netPay** - based on the value that was passed to the superclass. Hence the three accessor methods in the superclass can return these values for a **Manager** object.

The gross pay for the manager class is any amount that the constructor gets as argument. The method **calculate()** – as shown in **Line 10** thru **13** - simply assigns to the variable **gross** the value in the variable **amount**; the deduction is carried out per the rule as shown on **Line 11**; and lastly, the deduction is subtracted from the gross pay to give the net pay – standard calculations.

Listing 2.8 concrete subclass Manager derived from Wages

```
1.    class Manager extends Wages
2.    {
3.            static final double MANAGER_TAX = 1.0/5;
4.
5.            Manager(double amount)
6.            {
7.                super(amount);
8.            }
9.        void calculate()
10.        {
11.                gross = amount;
12.                deduction = gross * MANAGER_TAX;
13.                netPay = gross - deduction;
14.        }
15. }
```

The class **RegularPay** is a concrete class, as shown in **Listing 2.9**. It also defines the abstract method inherited from the abstract class **Wages**.

Listing 2.9 Concrete subclass RegularPay derived from abstract class Wages

```
1.    class RegularPay extends Wages
2.    {
3.            static final double RATE              = 25,
4.                            REGULAR _TAX = 1.0/6;
5.
```

```
6.        RegularPay(double amount)
7.        {
8.            super(amount);
9.        }
10.       void calculate()
11.       {
12.           gross = amount * RATE;
13.           deduction = gross * REGULAR_TAX;
14.           netPay = gross - deduction;
15.       }
16.   }
```

This class is similar to the **Manager** class, except that the **amount** variable represents the number of hours worked for a person who works forty hours or less. The **calculate()** method, though similar to the one in **Manager** class, calculates the gross pay differently than the manager class's definition. Nevertheless, all three field variables are assigned their respective values.

The class **OvertimePay**, a concrete class is somewhat different from the other two, in that it inherits all calculations from the **RegularPay** class, and adds to each quantity the extra amounts. See **Listing 2.10**.

Listing 2.10 concrete class OvertimePay, inherited from RegularPay

```
1.    class OvertimePay extends RegularPay
2.    {
3.        double overtimeHours;
4.
5.        OvertimePay(double amount)
6.        {
7.            super(FORTY);
8.            overtimeHours = amount - FORTY;
9.        }
10.       void calculate()
11.       {
12.           super.calculate();
13.           gross = super.getGross() + overtimePay();
14.           deduction = super.getDeduction() + overtimePay() * OVERTIME_TAX;
15.           netPay = gross - deduction;
16.       }
17.       double overtimePay()
18.       {
19.           return overtimeHours * OVERTIME_RATE * RATE;
20.       }
21.   }
```

In this listing the amount parameter in the constructor represents the number of hours worked. Because this number exceeds forty, we must send forty to the **RegularyPay** class to carry out the calculations based on regular pay. The excess hours is now assigned to the variable **overtimeHours**. This value is used to carry out the overtime gross pay as shown in method **overtimePay()**.

The method **calculate()** is different from the previous two, in the sense that this method calls the superclass's **calculate()** method to carry out the calculations for the forty hours regular pay. See **Line 13**. The gross pay is now based on the amount calculated from the superclass plus the extra from the **overtimePay()** method. See **Line 14**. The deduction is calculated in likewise manner. See **Line 15**.

Self-Check

1. What is meant by the term abstract class? Give one example of an abstract class.

2. Apart from abstract methods, what else can an abstract contain? Given one example of an abstract class that can or cannot include any other elements of a concrete class.

3. Given that A is an abstract class, and B is a subclass of A. If class B inherits class A, but class B does not define all the abstract methods that it inherits, what would happen if you attempt to compile the code?

4. Which of the following is a legal definition of an abstract class?

(I)	(II)	(III)

```
class Animal
{
    abstract void grow();
}
```

```
abstract Animal
{
    abstract void grow();
}
```

```
class abstract Animal
{
    abstract void grow();
}
```

(IV)   (V)

```
abstract class Animal
{
    abstract void grow();
}
```

```
abstract class Animal
{
    abstract void grow()
    {
        System.out.println("Grow animal !");
    }
}
```

5. True or false? Abstract classes that has constructor(s) can be instantiated.

6. What will happen if you compile and execute the following program?

```
1.   class A                        1.   class B extends A
2.   {                              2.   {
3.       int x;                     3.       public static void main(String[] arg)
4.       A(int i)                   4.       {
5.       {                          5.           B b = new B(2);
6.           x = i * 2;             6.       }
7.           System.out.println("x is " + x);   7.
8.       }                          8.       B(int i)
9.   }                              9.       {
                                    10.          super(i);
                                    11.          System.out.println("i is " + i);
                                    12.      }
                                    13.  }
```

7. A bank maintains the accounts for its customers. The bank allows customers to make deposits, withdrawals, and to get their balance at any time. Each customer is identified by a field for an account number and a field called Customer. (We assume that this class Customer has already been defined).

From the set of responses below select the ONE that best describes an abstract class for this situation.

(I)

```
public abstract class Banking
{
    String accNumber;
    Customer customer;
    Banking(Customer cust, String accno)
    {
        customer = cust;
        accNumber = accno;
    }
    void deposit(double amount);
    double withdraw(double amount);
    double getBalance();
}
```

(II)

```
abstract interface Banking
{
    String accNumber;
    Customer customer;
    Banking(Customer cust, String accno)
    {
        customer = cust;
        accNumber = accno;
    }
    void deposit(double amount);
    double withdraw(double amount);
    static double money = getBalance();
}
```

(III)

```
public final abstract class Banking
{
        String accNumber;
        Customer customer;
        Banking(Customer cust, String accno)
        {
            customer = cust;
            accNumber = accno;
        }
        void deposit(double amount);
        double withdraw(double amount);
        static double money = getBalance();
}
```

(IV)

```
public abstract class Banking
{
        String accNumber;
        Customer customer;
        Banking(Customer cust, String accno)
        {
            customer = cust;
            accNumber = accno;
        }
        void deposit(double amount);
        double withdraw(double amount);
        static double money = getBalance();
        Banking b = new Banking(customer)
}
```

8. Consider the following Java code.

```
abstract class A
{
    A() {  }
}

class B extends A
{
    B() {  }
}
```

Assume that there is a test class; select those statements that will compile.
   (a) B b = new B();
   (b) A a = new A();
   (c) A a = new B();
   (d) B b = new A();
   (e) B b = new (B);

9. Design an abstract class called Shape. This class contains a single constructor that accepts a single numeric value that is used to calculate various values, one of which is area. Include an abstract method called findArea that can be defined to find the area of any shape. Also provide a concrete method to return the area.

   Design two concrete classes, Circle and Square, that inherit the class Shape. Each of these classes finds the respective area; i.e. area of circle and area of square.

10. Consider the following program. What output is generated from it?

```
class A                                        class B extends A
{                                              {
    A(String x)                                    B(int p, int q)
    {                                              {
      System.out.print(x);                             super(p);
    }                                                  System.out.println("and q is " + q);
    A(int p)                                       }
    {                                          }
        this("Hi there ");
        System.out.println("p is " + p);
    }
}

class AB
{
    public static void main(String[] arg)
    {
        A a = new A(10);
        B b  = new B(100, 200);
    }
}
```

Polymorphism

The term polymorphism, when applied to Object Oriented Programming, means that a reference variable can be used to create objects from a linear descendant of classes. It can also be used to call methods from the different objects. Of course we could use different variable declarations for each object, but our intention is to understand the concept of polymorphism as it relates to Object Oriented programming. In terms of Java, polymorphism exhibits itself in five ways – overloading, inclusion, overriding, casting, and parametric.

Overloading

Overloading polymorphism occurs when a class has multiple constructors, or when a method has multiple definitions in the same class. **Listing 2.11** shows the class Manufacturing containing two overloaded constructors and three overloaded methods.

Listing 2.11 Class with overloaded constructors and overloaded methods

```
1.   public class Manufacturing
2.   {
3.       private String name;
4.       private double price;
5.
6.       public Manufacturing(String name)
```

```
7.        {
8.               this.name = name;
9.        }
10.       public Manufacturing(String name, double price)
11.       {
12.              this(name);
13.              this.price = price;
14.       }
15.       public void change(String name)
16.       {
17.              this.name = name;
18.       }
19.       public void change(double price)
20.       {
21.              this.price = price;
22.       }
23.       public void change(String name, double price)
24.       {
25.              change(name);
26.              change(price);
27.       }
28. }
```

Given the above class definition, and given the following declaration:

> Manufacturing **m;**

This reference variable **m** can be used to create objects from either of the two constructors. The difference will be resolved during runtime when the compiler examines their parameters of the constructors.

> m = new Manufacturing("Table", 250.50);
>
> m = new Manufacturing("Chair");

Similarly, the same reference variable can be used to call any of the overloaded methods. The compiler will know which of the three methods to call during runtime, by examining their parameters, as shown in the following statements:

> m.change(350);
>
> m.change("Sofa", 150.25);
>
> m.change("Table");

Overriding

Overriding polymorphism occurs when a subclass redefines the definition of a method that it inherits from a superclass. This type of polymorphism is used when different subclasses have different behaviors based on some intrinsic characteristic of the subclass. As an example, the **calculate()** method in subclass **OvertimePay** overrides the **calculate()** method that it inherits from its superclass **RegularPay**, as shown below.

```
class RegularPay extends Wages          class OvertimePay extends RegularPay

void calculate()                        void calculate()
{                                       {
   gross = amount * RATE;                  super.calculate();
   deduction = gross * REGULAR_TAX;        gross = super.getGross() + overtimePay();
   netPay = gross - deduction;             deduction = super.getDeduction() +
}                                          overtimePay() * OVERTIME_TAX;
                                           netPay = gross - deduction;

                                        }
```

Inclusion

Inclusion polymorphism occurs if a subclass class inherits a concrete method from its superclass, whether directly or indirectly, and the subclass does not override the method. In our current example there are three concrete methods that were inherited from the superclass **Wages**. These are **getGross()**, **getDeduction()**, and **getNet()**. All of the subclasses made use of these methods without overriding any of them. In this case they can be called form within the subclass, without qualifying them with the keyword **super**, as shown below.

```
class OvertimePay extends RegularPay
   void calculate()
   {
        super.calculate();
        gross = getGross() + overtimePay();
        deduction = getDeduction() + overtimePay() * OVERTIME_TAX;
        netPay = gross - deduction;

   }
```

Casting

Casting, sometimes called coercion polymorphism, occurs when a type is coerced into being another type. There are two types of conversions – implicit conversion, and explicit conversion. Implicit conversions are performed automatically when the type on the right of the assignment operator can be safely promoted to the type on the left. Consider the following segment of code.

```
byte b = 20;
int i = b;
```

In this piece of code the amount of storage required for the byte value of 20 is one byte. The amount require for the **int** is 32 bits. This is sufficient memory to store the 20. This is a case of implicit conversion, no casting is required. The same cannot be said if the types were to be switched around. Consider the following segment of codes.

```
int i = 20;
byte b = i;
```

In this piece of code 32 bits are required to store the value 20, which is perfect. However only 8 bits are allocated to store data in **b**, which is not sufficient. As a result the code does not compile. To fix this situation, we must explicitly cast the **int** value to a byte as shown below.

```
int i = 20;
byte b = (byte)i;
```

Just like primitive types, casting can be performed between classes. There times when it is necessary to explicitly convert from one type to another. We can cast from a subclass to a superclass; as well as we can cast from a superclass to a subclass. Casting from a subclass to a superclass is reliable because the subclass contains all the information about their superclass. Casting from subclass to a superclass can be done implicitly; but casting from a superclass to a subclass must be done explicitly. Consider **Listing 2.12**.

Listing 2.12

```
1.   import java.util.ArrayList;
2.
3.   class TestWages
4.   {
5.       public static void main(String[] arg)
6.       {
7.           String s = "Employee\t  Gross\tDeduction\tNetPay";
8.           ArrayList list = new ArrayList();
9.
```

```
10.             Wages w = new RegularPay(40);
11.             list.add(w);
12.
13.             w = new OvertimePay(50);
14.             list.add(w);
15.
16.             w = new Manager(4000);
17.             list.add(w);
18.
19.             display(s, list);
20.        }
21.        static void display(String s, ArrayList list)
22.        {
23.             System.out.println(s + "\t" );
24.             for (int i = 0; i < list.size(); i++)
25.             {
26.                 Wages o = list.get(i);
27.
28.                 o.calculate();
29.
30.                 f( o instanceof OvertimePay)
31.                     System.out.print("Overtime:\t " + o);
32.                 else if(o instanceof RegularPay)
33.                     System.out.print("Regular:\t " + o);
34.                 else if(o instanceof Manager)
35.                     System.out.print("Manager:\t " + o);
36.             }
37.        }
38. }
```

In analyzing the code we see that **Line 8** creates an ArrayList, and that three employees were created and added to the list – a RegularPay, an OvertimePay, and a Manager employees, **Lines 10** thru **17**. When attempting to compile the program, it failed on **Line 26**. See **Figure 2.8**.

Figure 2. 8 – Compilation fails

```
TestWages.java:26: error: incompatible types: Object cannot be converted to Wages
            Wages o = list.get(i);
                              ^
1 error
```

The problem arises with what the ArrayList method **get** which returns a generic Object[1].

---

[1] Later we will learn that the class Object is the superclass of all classes.

This return type must be converted into type Wages. (Wages is an indirect subclass of th_ _ Object). The correction to Line **26** is to explicitly cast the type Object, to type Wages. That is:

> Wages o = (Wages)list.get(i);

Figure 2.9 shows the correct output when the program is executed.

Figure 2.9 Output from the program

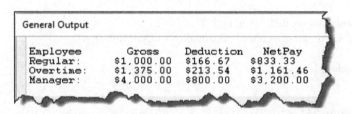

```
General Output

Employee     Gross      Deduction   NetPay
Regular:     $1,000.00  $166.67     $833.33
Overtime:    $1,375.00  $213.54     $1,161.46
Manager:     $4,000.00  $800.00     $3,200.00
```

In general, converting a subclass to a super class requires no explicit casting since the superclass has a wider scope than the subclass. For instance, consider the following two sets of code from our example on Wages:

list.add(new RegularPay(40)); RegularPay m = (RegularPay)list.get(i); **Wages w = m;**	list.add(new OvertimePay(40)) OvertimePay m = (OvertimePay)list.get(i); **Wages w = m;**

These are cases of implicit casting. Notice that Wages is the superclass of both RegularPay and OvertimePay.

Casting from a superclass to a subclass must be done explicitly. Consider the following two cases.

List.add(new RegularPay(40)); Wages w = list.get(i); RegularPay **m = w;**	list.add(new RegularPay (40)); Wages w = list.get(i); **RegularPay m = (RegularPay)w;**

In either case implicit casting took place. The scope of the left identifier, Wages, is wider than, or equal to, the type returned from the list. The third line of the code on the left does not compile since its scope is narrower. This is a case where explicit casting is required, as shown in the code on the right.

Listing 2.13 shows the complete definition of the abstract class, Wages.

Listing 2.13

```
1.    import java.text.NumberFormat;
2.
3.    abstract class Wages{
4.    static final double MANAGER_TAX   = 1.0/5,
5.                       REGULAR_TAX  = 1.0/6,
6.                       RATE = 25,
7.                       OVERTIME_RATE = 1.5,
8.                       OVERTIME_TAX = 1.0/8,
9.                       FORTY        = 40;
10.        double amount, gross, deduction, netPay;
11.        static NumberFormat cf = NumberFormat.getCurrencyInstance();
12.
13.        Wages(double a) {
14.           amount = a;
15.        }
16.        double getGross() {
17.           return gross;
18.        }
19.        double getNet() {
20.           return netPay;
21.        }
22.        double getDeduction() {
23.            return deduction;
24.        }
25.        abstract void calculate();
26.        public String toString() {
27.           return cf.format(gross) + " "+ cf.format(deduction) +" " + cf.format(netPay) + "\n";
28.        }
29. }
```

Pitfalls Casting Objects

There are restrictions to casting objects. The following section outlines castings that are prohibited. We begin by looking at siblings; see **Figure 2.10**.

Figure 2.10 Sibling classes

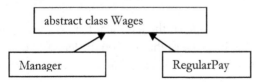

As shown in **Figure 2.10**, the classes Manager and RegularPay are siblings; as such they cannot not be casted from one type to the other. For instance, the following two statements look syntactically correct.

RegularPay reg = new RegularPay(30);
Manager mgr = (Manager)reg;

Although both statements compile, upon execution the second fails to execute, as shown in **Figure 2.11**

Figure 2.11 Execution error. Siblings cannot be cast from one type to another.

```
Exception in thread "main" java.lang.ClassCastException: RegularPay cannot be cast to Manager
    at TestWages.output(TestWages.java:40)
    at TestWages.main(TestWages.java:26)
```

Another situation is, attempting to cast a superclass object into that of a subclass type. Using our example, consider the following statements:

list.add(new RegularPay(40));
    :

Wages w = list.get(i);
RegularPay m = (RegularPay)w;
OvertimePay op= (OvertimePay)m;

These statements seem syntactically valid. They compile. However, the last poses execution problem, as shown in **Figure 2.12**. The problem arises because the original object (1st line), was of type RegularPay, hence casting cannot be applied.

Figure2.12 Super class object cannot be cast to a subclass type.

```
Exception in thread "main" java.lang.ClassCastException: RegularPay cannot be cast to OvertimePay
    at TestWages.main(TestWages.java:14)
```

In this case the casting is inappropriate. Since all **OvertimePay** are **RegularPay,** a reference to the method **overtimePay()** would not have been known by the class RegularPay.

Finally, it is only concrete classes that can be casted, since we cannot create objects of an abstract class. Using our current example, the following statement will not compile.

Manager mgr = (Manager)w;

Where the reference **w** is of type **Wages**. As a matter of fact, the compilation process may not get this far, since you could not possibly create object of the abstract class, **Wages**.

Parametric Polymorphism

Parametric polymorphism sometimes referred to as generics is a technique used to inform the compiler of the type a class, an interface, or a method is to expect. This has the effect of giving the compilation process the task of detecting certain types of errors, rather than having the execution process detecting the errors. Two of the benefits of using generics is for stronger type checking at compilation time; secondly, the elimination of type casing. Recall the problem we encountered in **Listing 2.12** with the statement:

Wages o = list.get(i);

The only fix at the time was to cast the return value. That is,

Wages o = **(Wages)**list.get(i);

This goes for the descendants of Wages also. With parametric polymorphism you use the diamond operator to specify the type of object under consideration, and thereby avoiding type casting. **Line 8** of **Listing 2.14** shows how this is done. In addition, the formal parameter of the method output specifies the type of object that are stored in the ArrayList. Against this background it is not necessary to cast the return value shown on **Line 20**.

Listing 2.14 Avoid Casting

```
1.    import java.util.ArrayList;
2.
3.    class TestWages
4.    {
5.        public static void main(String[] arg)
6.        {
7.            String s = "Employee   Gross\tDeduction\tNetPay\n";
8.            ArrayList<Wages> list = new ArrayList<Wages>();
9.
10.           list.add(new OvertimePay(50));
11.           list.add(new Manager(4000));
12.           list.add(new RegularPay(40));
13.
14.           System.out.println(output(s, list));
```

```
15.        }
16.        static String output(String s, ArrayList<Wages> list)
17.        {
18.            for (int i = 0; i < list.size(); i++)
19.            {
20.                Wages w = list.get(i);
21.                w.calculate();
22.
23.                if (w instanceof OvertimePay)
24.                    s += "Overtime: " + w.toString();
25.                else if( w instanceof RegularPay)
26.                    s += "Regular : " + w.toString();
27.                else if (w instanceof Manager)
28.                    s += "Manager : " + w.toString();
29.                else
30.                    s += "Unknown person - no payment is due\n";
31.            }
32.            return s;
33.        }
34. }
```

Not only is it not necessary to cast the object, it is not necessary to explicitly identify the object in order to call the respective calculate method. The Java Virtual Machine (JVM) determines that automatically. **Line 21** shows the method, **calculate** being called. No effort was made to distinguish which one of the calculate method to call – RegularPay, OvertimePay, or Manager. The compiler was able to detect and differentiate which one to call.

Dynamic Method Lookup

We have seen that polymorphism can occur in five forms – overloading, inclusion, overriding, casting, and parametric. Against this background, we may ask, at what point will Java knows which method it must call? It will not know until when the program is executing. That is, during compilation, the compiler cannot attach a reference to any particular instance method. However, during runtime, the JVM determines the appropriate method to call, based on the type of the current object, as we saw in **Listing 2.14 Line 21.**

The class Object

The class Object is the highest in the hierarchy of classes defined in the collection of Java predefined classes. Every class, including user defined classes, inherits this class, whether directly or indirectly. That is, every class that is defined without an explicit **extends** clause, extends the class Object; as such every class is permitted to redefine the methods that it inherits. The two most frequently methods that are overridden are the **toString()** method and the **equals()** method.

The toString() method, if not redefined, returns a representation of the object to which it refers. By default it specifies the name of the class from which the object is created followed by the address at which the reference to the object is stored. For example, consider the following two statements:

Wages w = new Manager(5000);
System.out.println(w.toString());

When these statements were executed the **toString()** method yielded the output as shown in **Figure 2.13**

Figure 2.13 Default output value returned by the toString() method

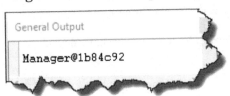

General Output

Manager@1b84c92

This output shows the name of the class from which the object was created (**Manager**), and the address where the reference to the object was stored.

Let us remodel the abstract class **Wages** and redefinition the **toString** method that it automatically inherited from the class **Object**. In redefining the method let us format the three values and return then as a string of information. See **Listing 2.15**.

Listing 2.15 Redefining the toString() method

```
1.   import java.text.NumberFormat;
2.
3.   abstract class Wages
4.   {
5.       static final double MANAGER_TAX       = 1.0/5,
6.                           REGULAR_TAX       = 1.0/6,
7.                           RATE              = 25,
8.                           OVERTIME_RATE     = 1.5,
9.                           OVERTIME_TAX      = 1.0/8;
10.                          FORTY             = 40;
11.      double amount, gross, deduction, netPay;
12.      static NumberFormat cf = NumberFormat.getCurrencyInstance();
13.
14.      Wages(double a)
15.      {
16.          amount = a;
17.      }
18.      abstract void calculate();
19.      public String toString()
20.      {
```

```
21.        return cf.format(gross) +  "     "+  cf.format(deduction)  +"    "  +
               cf.format(netPay) + "\n";
22.    }
23. }
```

Lines 19 thru 22 shows the new definition of the **toString()** method. Notice that we have abandoned the accessor methods since the **toString()** method can deliver the same information. Note though, if you think that you may want individual values then retain them.

We have also modified the method **output()** in the test class to accommodate the change in the **Wages** class. See **Listing 2.16**.

Listing 2.16 Each reference calls its own toString() method

```
1.    import java.text.NumberFormat;
2.
3.    class TestWages
4.    {
5.        public static void main(String[] arg)
6.        {
7.            NumberFormat cf = NumberFormat.getCurrencyInstance();
8.            String s = "Employee\tGross\tTax\t\t\tNet\n";
9.            Wages w;
10.
11.           w = new Manager(5000);
12.           s = output(s, w, cf);
13.
14.           w = new OvertimePay(50);
15.           s = output(s, w, cf);
16.
17.           w = new RegularPay(40);
18.           s = output(s, w, cf);
19.
20.           System.out.println(s);
21.       }
22.       static String output(String s, Wages w, NumberFormat cf)
23.       {
24.           w.calculate();
25.
26.           if (w instanceof OvertimePay)
27.               s += "Overtime: " + w.toString();
28.           else if( w instanceof RegularPay)
29.               s += "Regular : " + w.toString();
30.           else if (w instanceof Manager)
31.               s += "Manager : "  + w;
32.           else
33.               s += "Unknown person - no payment is due\n";
34.           return s;
```

```
35.        }
36. }
```

Lines **27** and **29** show the **toString()** method being called explicitly for each type of object. Line 31 shows it being called implicitly. The result we get is the same as the previous version.

The Keyword final

We have seen the modifier **final** used in conjunction with identifiers to define constants. We can also use it to prevent a class from being inherited. If it does not make sense for a class to be inherited, then you can use the modifier final to prevent the inheritance to occur. For example, in our example, there is no practicality in extending the class OvertimePay. In this regard you can bar this class from being inherited, by using the keyword **final**. **Line 1** of **Listing 2.17** shows how this is done.

Listing 2.17 Use of the modifier final to prevent inheritance

```
1.    final class OvertimePay extends RegularPay
2.    {
3.         double overtimeHours;
4.
5.         OvertimePay(double amount)
6.         {
7.             super(FORTY);
8.             overtimeHours = amount - FORTY;
9.         }
10.        void calculate()
11.        {
12.            super.calculate();
13.            gross = super.getGross() + overtimePay();
14.            deduction = super.getDeduction() + overtimePay() * OVERTIME_TAX;
15.            netPay = gross - deduction;
16.        }
17.        double overtimePay()
18.        {
19.            return overtimeHours * OVERTIME_RATE * RATE;
20.        }
21. }
```

A third use of the modifier final is to prevent a method from being redefined. For this to work the method must a concrete method. It cannot be an abstract method. The format is shown below.

```
final return_type methodName( <parameter>)
{
    // method definition
}
```

Visibility Modifier

Java has four ways of controlling access to fields, methods, and classes. These modifiers, taken in increasing order of protection or visibility are: private, no modifier (called default package level), protected, and public. You have already encountered **private** modifier and **public** modifier. The modifier **private** is usually used to hide members of a class. This means that these members can only be accessed from inside the class where they are declared, and cannot be accessed directly from outside the class. When no modifier is used, you can get direct access to classes and members of classes that are within the same package, but not from outside the package. This is also known as default package. A class with **protected** modifier allows the members of a class to be accessed by the subclasses, or by classes within the same package.

A subclass can override a **protected** method in its superclass, and it can change its visibility from **protected** to **public**. However, a subclass cannot change a public modifier to a **protected** modifier. In other words, a subclass cannot weaken the accessibility of a method defined in its superclass. It is for this reason why when you redefine the **toString()** method you must write the method signature in full. That is, you must write as:

```
public String toString()
{
    return ...
}
```

The method cannot be prefaced with either the modifier **private** or **protected**; neither can it be left at package level since these have narrower scope than **public**.

You use the **public** modifier to allow access to a class, and class members from anywhere; hence the word public.

Figure 2.14 summarizes the accessibility of the members in a class.

Figure 2.14 Summary of access visibility

Access Modifier	From within the same class	From the same package	From a subclass	From a different package
public	√	√	√	√
protected	√	√	√	
Default packag	√	√		
private	√			

To put these concepts into context of programming, **Figure 2.15** shows an example of access visibility between two packages named p1 and p2; and among five classes named C1, C2, C3, C4 and C5.

Figure 2.15

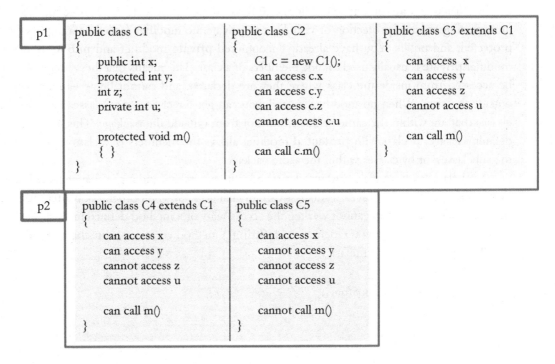

In class C2 of package p1, the reference variable c of class C1 can access all, but the private field, u, of class C1. The field u is private, therefore it cannot be accessed by members outside of its class. Likewise class C3 can access all, but C1 by inheritance, except the field u of class C1, because field u is private. Referring to package p2, the class C4 which inherits class C1 from package p1cannot access the private field u, nor can it access the field z, since z is at package level protection. Finally, looking at class C5 in package p2, and class C1 of package p1, the reference variable c of class C1 can only be used to access the field x, of class C1, since this field is public.

Self-Check

1. As it pertains to object oriented programming, differentiate between the techniques, method overloading and method overriding. Give **ONE** example of each.

2. As it pertains to polymorphism select from the following the word which best describes each phrase (casting, overriding, and inclusion).

_____ Polymorphism occurs when a subclass redefines the body of the method implementation of the super class.

_____ Polymorphism occurs when an object type is cast or coerced into being another object type.

_____ Polymorphism occurs if a subclass class inherits its methods from its super class, whether direct or indirect super class, and does not carry out any modification to any of the methods it inherits.

3. Name the five ways that polymorphism exhibits itself, and briefly describe each form.

4. What is wrong with the following Java code?

```
final class First
{
        private int a;
        int b;

        First()
        {
            a = 10;
            b = 20;
        }
}
```

```
class Second extends First
{
        public void method()
        {
            System.out.println(a + b);
        }
}
```

Select the correct answer(s).
(a) Because the variable **a** is private, no class other than First can access it.
(b) The class Second cannot extend First because the class First is a terminal class.
(c) You cannot call println() method without passing a String parameter to it.
(d) The word final is not a keyword to describe a class; it is only used for constants.
(e) Nothing is wrong with the code. It will compile and execute fine.

5. Which of the following statement(s) is(are) false about classes?
(a) A final class cannot have a superclass.
(b) A final class can be extended.
(c) A final class can have instances.
(d) A final class can only be inherited by an abstract class.

6. True/False. As it pertains to inheritance, some classes are instances of the class Object.

7. The following program has syntax errors. Find these errors and correct them.

```
final class First
{
        private int a, int b;

        public void display()
        {
            a = 10;
            b = 20;
            System.out.println(a + b);
        }

}
```

```
class Second extends First
{
        void method()
        {
            System.out.println(a + b);
        }
}
```

Interface

Another core feature of Java is the concept of interface. This concept presents a level of abstraction to the object oriented paradigm. An interface is a special form of abstract class, in that it contains abstract methods, and may have constants as well. A class that inherits an interface promises to provide the definition for all of the abstract methods that it inherits; otherwise such class must be explicitly be defined as an abstract class. The general format for defining an interface is as follows:

```
public interface A
{
        <constants>
        <abstract method>
}
```

As noted, the keyword **interface** is used to denote the entity – not the word **extends**. Typically, an interface lists those methods that are common among objects. However, each object will provide its own way of implementing the methods.

In an interface all constants are by default class constants, and are public. Hence, you may define a constant without having to use the keywords – public, static, and final. Likewise, all methods are public and abstract; hence, you need not specify these attributes in the declaration.

Implementing an Interface

When an interface is to be inherited, the keyword **extends** is not used; instead the keyword **implements** is. The general format for implementing an interface is as follows:

```
public class B implements A {
        <fields>
        <Constructor>
        < Methods unique to B >
        <Definition of inherited methods>
}
```

The keyword **implements** means that the class opens a contract between itself and the interface, whereby the class promises to furnish the definition for all the abstract methods in the interface. Failure to do so will result in syntax error, unless you explicitly specify that the class is abstract.

Consider for instance two shapes – square and circle. We can find the area of a circle, as well as the area of a square. Note the requirement is finding area. But as you know, the method of finding the area of a circle is different from that of finding the area of a square. Similarly, we can find the perimeter of a square, as well as that of a circle – re-call that the perimeter of a circle is called circumference. In this situation we could define an interface with two abstract methods – findArea and findPerimeter. Also, since the perimeter of a square is four times the length of one of its side, we can include a constant with the value 4. **Listing 2.14** shows the definition of the interface called Shape. The definition contains a constant called FOUR with value 4, and two abstract mutator methods – findArea and find Perimeter.

Listing2.18 Interface Shape

```
1.   public interface Shape
2.   {
3.        static final int FOUR = 4;
4.
5.        public abstract void findArea();
6.        public abstract void findPerimeter();
7.   }
```

Listings **2.19** and **2.20** show that the classes Square and Circle inherit the abstract class Shape, and that each supplies its own definition to the abstract methods- findArea and findPerimeter.

Listing 2.19 Class Square.java

```
1.   public class Square implements Shape
2.   {
3.        double length, area, perimeter;
4.
5.        public Square(double length)
6.        {
7.             this.length = length;
8.        }
9.        public  void findArea()
10.       {
11.            area =  length * length;
12.       }
13.       public void findPerimeter()
14.       {
15.            perimeter = Shape.FOUR* length;
16.       }
17.  }
```

Listing 2.20 Class Circle

```
1.   public class Circle implements Shape
2.   {
3.        double radius, area, perimeter;
4.
5.        public Circle(double r)
6.        {
7.             radius = r;
8.        }
9.        public  void findArea()
10.       {
11.            area =  Math.PI * radius * radius;
12.       }
13.       public void findPerimeter()
14.       {
15.            perimeter =  2 * Math.PI *radius;
16.       }
17.  }
```

Multiple Inheritance by Interface

As we have stated, Java does not support multiple inheritance by inheriting multiple classes; however, it supports the concept with interfaces. The general format for implementing multiple inheritance through interface is as follows:

```
public class B implements A, P, Q
{
    <fields>
    <Methods unique to B>
    <Definition of inherited methods>
}
```

Where A, P and Q are interfaces.

Going back to the current example about geometric figures, suppose the class Circle wants to display its result in a dialog box, and the square wants to display its output using the console. In this scenario, both objects want to display information, but by different method. We could translate this idea into defining an interface, and both classes could then inherit this interface and specify its own definition for displaying the information. **Listing 2.21** shows the definition of an interface called **Display**, with a single abstract method called **displayOutput**.

```
Listing 2.21
1.
2.    public interface Display
3.    {
4.         void displayOutput( );
5.    }
```

Listing 2.22 shows that the class Square inherits both interfaces. See **Line 1**. Also it supplies the definition for the method displayOutput. See **Line 17** thru **20**.

```
Listing 2.22

1.    public class Square implements Shape, Display
2.    {
3.         double length, area, perimeter;
4.
5.         public Square(double length)
6.         {
7.              this.length = length;
8.         }
9.         public  void findArea()
10.        {
```

```
11.              area =  length * length;
12.          }
13.          public void findPerimeter()
14.          {
15.              perimeter = Shape.FOUR * length;
16.          }
17.          public void displayOutput()
18.          {
19.              System.out.println("Area of the square: " + area + " sq units\n" + "Perimeter is: "
                 + perimeter + " units");
20.          }
21.  }
```

As does the class Square, the class Circle also inherits both interfaces, and defines the method, displayOutput differently by using the JOptionPane dialog box. See **Lisitng 2.23**, **Lines 20** thru **25**.

Listing 2.23
```
1.
2.    import javax.swing.JOptionPane;
3.
4.    public class Circle implements Shape, Display
5.    {
6.        double radius, area, perimeter;
7.
8.        public Circle(double r)
9.        {
10.            radius = r;
11.        }
12.        public  void findArea()
13.        {
14.            area =  Math.PI * radius * radius;
15.        }
16.        public void findPerimeter()
17.        {
18.            perimeter =  2 * Math.PI * radius;
19.        }
20.        public void displayOutput() {
21.            String s = "Area of the square: " + area + " sq units\n" +"Circumference is: "
22.            + perimeter + " units";
23.            JOptionPane.showMessageDialog(null, s, "Circle",
24.            JOptionPane.INFORMATION_MESSAGE);
25.        }
26.  }
```

Adapter Class

An adapter class is a concrete class that acts as a bridge between an interface and the class(es) that want to implement the interface, by providing an empty implementation of all the methods it inherits from the interface. In turn any class that inherits an adapter class will redefine only those methods that are relevant to it.

In the example discussed above, we found the area and perimeter of circles and squares. What if in addition to finding these measures, we were asked to find the volume of right cylinders and of cubes? From Figure **2.16** we see that cylinder can be defined as a subclass of circle, since the volume of the *cylinder* = *area of its circular base* * *its height*. That is, the class cylinder could require the superclass, Circle, to calculate the area of the circle that forms its base; and the class Cylinder multiply this result by its height. Also, the surface area of the *cylinder* = *perimeter (circumference) of the cylinder* * *its height*. This circumference can be calculated by the superclass Circle, and the result multiplied by its height. Similar analysis can be made of the cube. The *volume* = *area of the square base* * *height*; and its *surface area is 6* * *the area of one of its sides*.

Figure 2.16 Hierarchy of shapes

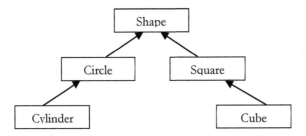

From this analysis we can include an abstract method in the interface for finding volume (findVolume). See **Listing 2.24**. We have also included the constant SIX.

Listing 2.24

```
1.   public interface Shape {
2.        public static final int FOUR = 4;
3.        public static final int SIX = 6;
4.
5.        public  abstract void findArea( );
6.        public abstract void findPerimeter( );
7.        public abstract void findVolume( );
8.   }
```

Looking back at Figure 2.16, we know that neither circle nor square has volume. So if they inherit the interface Shape, then they are forced to define the method volume. In order to avoid defining methods that are unwanted by some classes, we define the intermediate adapter class, from which subclasses can choose only those methods that are relevant to them. **Figure 2.17** shows the modified hierarchy that includes the block representing the adapter class.

Figure 2.7 Hierarchy of shapes

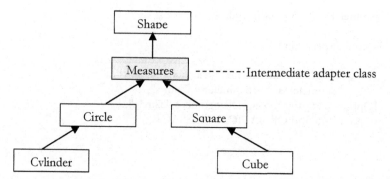

Listing 2.25 shows the definition of the adapter class, Measures. Notice that each method is faked. There is no statement within any of them. A class that inherits this class will re-define the requisite method it chooses.

Listing 2.25 Adapter class

```
1.   public class Measures implements Shape
2.   {
3.        public void findArea(){ }
4.        public void findPerimeter(){ }
5.        public void findVolume(){ }
6.   }
```

As mentioned earlier, classes that are derived from an adapter class have a choice of what methods they choose to over-ride. In **Listing 2.26** we see that the class Circle chooses to re-define the methods findArea, findPerimeter, and displayOutput. It chooses not to mention the method, volume; since a circle does not have volume.

Listing 2.26

```
1.   import javax.swing.JOptionPane;
2.
3.   public class Circle extends Measures implements Display {
4.        double radius, area, perimeter;
5.
6.        public Circle(double r)
7.        {
8.             radius = r;
```

```
9.        }
10.       public void findArea()
11.       {
12.           area = Math.PI * radius * radius;
13.       }
14.       public void findPerimeter()
15.       {
16.           perimeter = 2 * Math.PI * radius;
17.       }
18.       public void displayOutput()
19.       {
20.           String s = "Area of the square: " + area + " sq units\n" +
21.               "Perimeter is: " + perimeter + " units";
22.           JOptionPane.showMessageDialog(null, s, "Circle",
23.           JOptionPane.INFORMATION_MESSAGE);
24.       }
25. }
```

If an interface has accessor methods, then those methods would be required to return a representative value in the adapter class. When a class subclass redefines the method, then it will return the appropriate value at that time.

Whenever inheritance involves class and interfaces, we can only inherit one class at a time, but multiple interfaces can be inherited. This means only one extends clause can be coded, but several interfaces can be listed, each separated by a comma. The **extends** clause must precede the **implements** clause. Line 3 of Listing 2.26 shows the class Circle inheriting a class (Measures) and also an interface (Display).

When it comes to cylinder, we do not think of them as having perimeter. Therefore in defining the class Cylinder, we think of it having surface area and volume. See **Listing 2.27**.

Listing 2.27 Cylinder a subclass of Circle

```
1.   import javax.swing.JOptionPane;
2.
3.   public class Cylinder extends Circle
4.   {
5.      double height, volume, surface;
6.
7.      public Cylinder(double r, double h)
8.      {
9.           super(r);
10.          height = h;
11.      }
12.      public void findArea()
13.      {
14.          super.findArea();
15.          surface = perimeter * height + 2 * area;
16.      }
```

```
17.     public void findVolume()
18.     {
19.          super.findArea();
20.          volume = height * area;
21.     }
22.     public void displayOutput()
23.     {
24.          String s = "Area of the cyliner: " + surface + " sq units\n" +   "Volume is: " +
25.                     volume + " units";
26.                     JOptionPane.showMessageDialog(null, s, "Circle",
27.                     JOptionPane.INFORMATION_MESSAGE);
28.     }
29. }
```

Self-Check

1. Which of the following statements are **false** about classes?
    (a) An abstract class can be extended.
    (b) An abstract class cannot be inherited.
    (c) An abstract class can have any type of member that a concrete class can have, in addition to any abstract method.
    (d) All abstract classes must have at least one abstract method.
    (e) An abstract class cannot inherit a concrete class.
    (f) A concrete class does not have to define all of the abstract methods that it inherits from an abstract class.

2. What are the similarities and differences between the following pairs of terms?
    (a) A class and an interface
    (b) An abstract class and an interface
    (c) An abstract class and a concrete class.

3. A bank maintains the accounts for its customers. The bank offers customers two types of accounts - a checking account and a savings account. The checking account charges customers a fixed service charge of $25.00 per month. The savings account yields a fixed interest rate of 3% per year on the monthly balance. The bank allows customers to make deposits, withdrawals, and to get their balance at any time. From the set of responses below select those that best describe an interface for this situation.

I

```java
public interface Banking {
    double CHECKING_RATE = 25;
    final double SAVING_RATE  = 0.03
    void deposit(double amount);
    double withdraw(double amount);
    double getBalance();
}
```

II

```java
public interface Banking {
    static double CHECKING_RATE = 25;
    double SAVING_RATE  = 0.03
    void deposit(double amount);
    abstract double withdraw(double amount);
    double getBalance();
}
```

III

```java
public interface Banking {
    static double CHECKING_RATE = 25;
    static final double SAVING_RATE  = 0.03
    public abstract void deposit(double amount);
    double withdraw(double amount);
    double getBalance();
}
```

IV

```java
public interface Banking {
    double CHECKING_RATE = 25;
    double SAVING_RATE  = 0.03
    void deposit(double amount);
    double withdraw(double amount);
    static double money = double getBalance();
}
```

V

```java
public interface Banking {
    double CHECKING_RATE = 25;
    double SAVING_RATE  = 0.03
    void deposit(double amount);
    double withdraw(double amount);
    static double getBalance() { return 0.0;}
}
```

Chapter Summary

- Inheritance, the creation of a new class from an existing one, is a powerful concept in Object Oriented Programming. An existing class can either be a concrete class or an abstract class.

- A concrete class is one that has all its method defined.

- In an abstract class all of its methods do not necessarily have to be defined.

- The existing class is called the superclass of the new class.

- The newly created class is referred to as the subclass of the exiting class.

- The new class can add members that are unique to it.

- A subclass can redefined any of the methods that it inherits, except if the method is prefaced with the keyword **final**, in which case the subclass cannot override the method.

- If a class is prefaced with the keyword **final**, it cannot be inherited.

- The term polymorphism means that an object can exists in multiple forms. The kinds of polymorphism exhibited in Java re overloading, overriding, inclusion, casting and parametric.

Programming Exercises

1. Write a class called Person. A person has a name and a social number. Assume that a class Name exists with first name and last name. Design the class Person such that it accepts a Name object and a social security number. Provide accessor methods to return the Name object and also the social security number.

    Write a class called Registration that accepts two values - a Person object, and an array called courses[ ] - representing strings of course titles. No student is allowed to register for more than five (5) at any one time. Write a method that determines if a student has registered for too many courses.

    (You are responsible for providing the requisite variables, and any other methods deemed necessary)

2. Write an abstract class called Manufacturer that has two concrete subclasses – Local and International. Among concrete methods, the abstract class has an abstract method called calculate, that calculates the taxes for items that are manufactured locally as well as internationally. Items that are manufactured locally are taxed a fixed rate of 7% per unit, while items that are manufactured internationally are pays a flat rate of $450.00 per shipping container, plus an additional $3.50 handling fee. Write a test class to test your system of classes.

3. Design an abstract class called Shape. This class contains a single constructor that accepts a single numeric value that is used to calculate various values, one of which is area. Include an abstract mutator method called findArea that can be defined to find the area of any shape. Also provide a concrete method in the abstract class to return the area.

    Design two concrete classes, Circle and Square, that inherit the class Shape. Each of these classes use the value obtained by the abstract class to find the respective area; i.e. area of circle and area of square. You are responsible for providing any relevant variable(s).

    Write a test class to implement your set of classes for finding areas.

4. Cryptography, the study of secret writing, has been around for a very long time, from simplistic techniques to sophisticated mathematical techniques. No matter what the form however, there are some underlying things that must be done – encrypt the message and decrypt the encoded message.

   One of the earliest and simplest methods ever used to encrypt and decrypt messages is called the Caesar cipher method, used by Julius Caesar during the Gallic war. According to this method, letters of the alphabet are shifted by three, wrapping around at the end of the alphabet. For example,

Plain Text	a	b	c	d	e	f	g	h	i	j	k	l	m	n	o	p	q	r	s	t	u	v	w	x	y	z
Caesar Shift	d	e	f	g	h	i	j	k	l	m	n	o	p	q	r	s	t	u	v	w	x	y	z	a	b	c

When encrypting a message, you take each letter of the message and replace it with its corresponding letter from the shifted alphabet. To decrypt an encoded message, you simply reverse the operation. That is, you take the letter from the shifted alphabet and replace it with the corresponding letter from the **plaintext** alphabet. Thus the string **the quick brown fox** becomes **wkh txlfn eurzq ira**

Another type of cipher is known as Transposition cipher. In this type of cipher, letters in the original message are re-arranged in some methodical way – for instance, reverse the letters in each string. Thus the string **the quick brown fox** becomes **eht kciuq nworb xof**

Yet there is still another cipher method called Reverser cipher. This method does not only reverse the letters in each word, but as does the Transposition cipher, but it also reverses the result generated from the Transposition cipher. Hence the original message **the quick brown fox** becomes **xof nworb kciuq eht**

Class design

Here are three Cryptography methods – **Caesar, Transposition** and **Reverser**. They all have something in common. They encrypt and decrypt messages. That is, they take a string of words and translate each word using the encoding algorithm appropriate for that cipher. Thus each class cipher will need polymorphic encode() and decode() methods, which take a word and encodes and decodes it according to the rule of the particular cipher.

From a design perspective, the encrypt() method and the decrypt() methods will be the same for every class. They simply break message into words and have each word encode or decode. However, the encode and decode methods will be different for each cipher. **Figure 1** shows a hierarchy of the classes.

Figure 1. Inheritance hierarchy

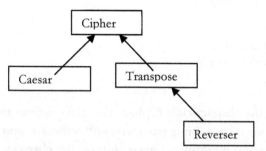

From the above analysis a partial abstract class Cipher is depicted be by **Listing 1**.

```java
import java.util.StringTokenizer;

public abstract class Cipher
{
    private String message; // The message string
    StringBuffer  encrypted_message, decrypted_message;
    public Cipher(String text)
    {
    // Complete the definition
    }
    public final void encrypt()
    {
        /** The message string is tokenized into individual words, and each word is encoded by
            calling the encode method
        */
    encrypted_message = new StringBuffer("");
    StringTokenizer words = new StringTokenizer(message);


        while(words.hasMoreTokens())
        {
            String s = words.nextToken();
            s = encode(s) + " ";
            encrypted_message.append(s);
        }
    }
    public final void decrypt(String message)
    {
/* The encoded message string is tokenized into individual words, and each word is
            encoded  by calling the decode method
        Complete the method and return the decoded word
     */
    }
    String getEncodedMessage() {
        return encrypted_message.toString();
```

```
}
String getDecodedMessage(){
return decrypted_message.toString();
}

public abstract String encode(String s);
public abstract String decode(String s);
}
```

The class Caesar inherits the abstract class Cipher. This class defines the methods code and decode. The method encode takes a String parameter and returns a String result. It takes each character of the parameter and performs a Caesar shift on the character. That is, a shift with possible wrap around can be coded as follows:

```
char ch = word.charAt(i);
ch = (char)('a' + ch - 'a' + 3) % 26);
```

The method decode does the reverse. **Listing 2** shows a partial definition of this class - Caesar

```
// Listing 2.
public class Caeser extends Cipher
{
    public Caeser(String s)
    {
        super(s);
    }
    public String encode(String word)
    {
        StringBuffer result = new StringBuffer();
        for (int i = 0; i < word.length(); i++)
        {
            char ch = word.charAt(i);
            ch = determineCharacter(ch, Constants. ENCODE_SHIFT);
            result.append(ch);
        }
        return result.toString();
    }
    public String decode(String word)
    {
        // Complete the method and return the decoded word
    }
    public char determineCharacter(char ch, int shift)
    {
        if(Character.isLowerCase(ch))
            ch = (char)('a' + (ch - 'a' + shift) % Constants.WRAP_AROUND);
        return ch;
    }
}
```

Similarly, the class Transpose inherits Cipher and defines the methods code and encode. **Listing 3** shows an incomplete definition of the class Transpose.

// Listing 3

```
public class Transpose extends Cipher
{
    Transpose(String s)
    {
        super(s);
    }
    public String encode(String word)
    {
        //Complete the method and return the encoded word
    }
    public String decode(String word)
    {
        // Complete the method and return the decoded word
    }
}
```

The class Reverser inherits the class Transpose. **Listing 4** shows an incomplete definition of this class.

// Listing 4

```
public class Reverser extends Transpose
{
    Reverser(String s)
    {
        super(s);
    }
    String reverseText(String word)
    {
        // Complete the method and returns the reverse transposed version;
    }
}
```

Things to do - rom the above discussion
- Complete the classes Cipher, Caesar, and Transpose, and Reverser. In addition
- Define an interface called Constants that will store the value **26** in the identifier **WRAP_AROUND**; similarly, store **3** in the identifier, **ENCODE_SHIFT**, and **23** in the identifier **DECODE_SHIFT** (needed to decode the encoded message). The code in the method **determineCharacter(char ch, int shift)** accounts for lower case letters only. Extend the code to include both upper and lower case letters.

Use the following test class to implement your other classes.
```
import javax.swing.JOptionPane;

class TestEncryption {
```

```
public static void main(String arg[]) {
    String code, output = "";
    String text = JOptionPane.showInputDialog("Enter message");
    output += "The original message is \n" + text + "\n";

    Cipher c = new Caeser(text);
    c.encrypt();
    code = c.getEncodedMessage();
    output += "\nCeasar Cipher\nThe encrypted message is \n" + code + "\n";
    c.decrypt(code);
    code = c.getDecodedMessage();
    output +="The decrypted message is \n" + code + "\n";

    c = new Transpose(text);
    c.encrypt();
    code = c.getEncodedMessage();
    output += "\nTranspose\nThe encrypted Transpose message is \n" + code + "\n";
    c.decrypt(code);
    code = c.getDecodedMessage();
    output +="The decripted Transpose message is \n" + code + "\n";
    Reverser r = new Reverser(text);
    r.encrypt();
    code = r.reverseText( r.getEncodedMessage() );
    output += "\nReverser\nThe encrypted Reverse message is \n" + code+ "\n";
    code = r.decode(code);
    output+="The decrypted Reverse message is \n" + code;

    System.out.println(output);
    }
}
```

A typical output from the program can be seen in **Fig. 2**.

Figure 2

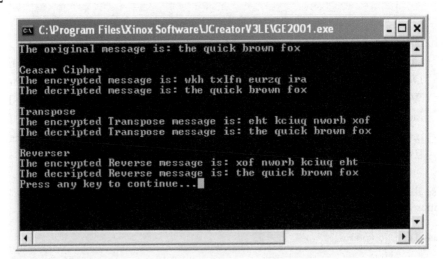

5. Write a Java application program that calculates the perimeter, area and volume of geometric figures, where possible. Because it cannot be assumed that all the triangles involved in this problem are right angled triangles, instead of using the formula ½* base * height, us instead the formula:

   area = $\sqrt{[s(s-a) * (s-b) * (s-c)]}$, where

   s = ½(a + b + c), where
   a, b, and **c,** are the sides of the triangle, and **s,** the perimeter.

   The permissible figures are shown below:

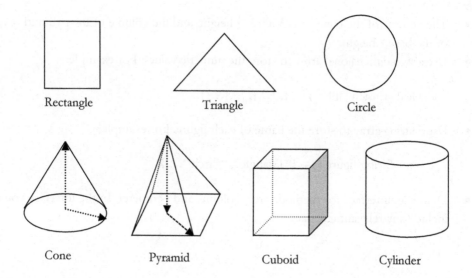

Rectangle	Triangle	Circle

Cone	Pyramid	Cuboid	Cylinder

   In your solution you make use of the classes already defined in the chapter, and continue to define the classes Cone, Pyramid, and Cuboid.

   Use the following data set to test your program: (The data is in italic bold). Also, present the output in a tabular for shown below. Output data must end with two decimal places. Entries that are not applicable must be indicated with a dash.

Figure	Side/radius	Side	Side	Height	Perimeter	Area	Volume
Triangle	3	4	5	-	xx.xx	xx.xx	-
Circle	3	-	-	-	-	xx.xx	xx.xx
Cylinder	10	-	-	20	-	xx.xx	xx.xx
Cuboid	4	4	10	-	-	xx.xx	xx.xx
Rectangle	10	20	-	-	xx.xx	xx.xx	-
Cone	4	-	-	10	-	xx.xx	xx.xx
Pyramid	6	6	-	12	-	xx.xx	xx.xx

Note:
- The volume of the cone is: $1/3\ \pi*r2\ *$ height, and the volume of the pyramid is $1/3\ *$ area of the base * height.
- Use a two dimensional array to store the numeric values: For example:

  double dimension [ ][ ] = {{...}, {...}, ...,{...}};

- Use a string array to store the name of each figure. For example,

  String figure [ ]= {"Triangle", "Circle"...,};

- Define an interface for methods area, volume, and perimeter. In the interface you may also include any relevant constants.

Chapter 3 Exception and Exception Handling

Objectives
After reading this chapter you will:
- Understand the concept of exception
- Know the difference between checked exception and unchecked exception
- Understand the exception hierarchy
- Know the procedure for handling exception
- Know how to define your own exception class

Introduction
An exception is an abnormal event that is likely to happen when a program is executing, the result of which will terminate the program prematurely, if the condition that causes the abnormality is not handled appropriately. For instance, the computer could run out of memory; not usually, but there is a possibility that it can happen; or calling the **parseInt** method with an argument that cannot be parsed into an integer; dividing a non-zero integer by integer zero; or attempting to access an array outside of its boundary.

Exception must be distinguished from other types of programming errors. Programming errors can be categorized into three types – syntax errors, logic errors, and runtime errors. Errors that occur during compilation as we know, are called syntax errors, or compilation errors. These errors result from the lack of compliance with the rules of the programming language. Logic errors on the other hand occur when the program produces unintended results, but the program does not terminate abnormally. Runtime errors occur when the program requires the computer to perform tasks that are impossible for it to carry out. For instance, asking the computer to parse a non-digit string into a number is an impossibility. If these conditions are not handled appropriately, the program will terminates abnormally.

Exception Handling

The concept of exception is a customary way in Java to indicate that an abnormal condition has occurred. When a method encounters an abnormal condition that it cannot handle itself, it may throw an exception. Throwing an exception is like tossing a ball out of a window hoping that there is someone on the outside who will catch it, and deal with it in such a way that no damage is done. Hence, the primary objective of handling an exception is to transfer control from where the error occurred to a section of the program that can take care of the situation such that the program will not terminate abnormally. The section of code that deals with the exception is called an exception handler. When you write your code, you must position exception handlers strategically, so that your program will catch and handle all exceptions that are likely to be thrown.

Response to an Exception

In response to an exception, the programmer has one of three options. One way of addressing the exception is to ignore, and do nothing. But as we stated earlier the program will terminate abnormally. This could not be good for a well-intended program. A second option would be to let the user fix the problem, but usually the user of the program is not a programmer. Therefore such a person would not be able to fix the code; hence we would be back at the first situation described above. The best solution therefore would be for the programmer to design the program in such a way that if an exception occurs, some form of program control mechanism would be in place to pass the exception to an appropriate block of codes within the program where the exception would be taken care of.

Procedure for Handling Exception

In response to an exception, Java uses the ***try-throw-catch-finally*** model to handle an exception. The general format for handling exceptions is a follows:

```
try
{
        <throw new ExceptionObject>
}
catch(ExceptionObject e)
{
        <handle exception>
}
        :
finally {
        <handle exception>
}
```

Where:

- The **try** block encloses the code that may generate an exception. If no exception arises, then the block ends normally.
- An exception as we will see later in this chapter is an object. The **throw** clause is the statement which says what exception object is to be thrown. This clause is optional.
- The **catch** block is that point in the code that handles the exception. If no exception is thrown, this clause is bypassed. A try block may be able to detect multiple kinds of exception object. As such there can be multiple catch blocks associated with a single try block.
- The **finally** block gets executed regardless of whether or not an exception is thrown. This block is optional. If coded, it must be placed after any catch block.

Catch block(s) must immediately follow the try block. If there are two or more catch blocks in a series, each must be unique. That is the parameter of each catch block must be different. If there is a series of catch blocks, they must be arranged in the order of, the most specific exception object to be caught, to the more general object. Also, there can only be one finally block associated with a try block as we stated earlier. Whether or not an exception is thrown, the finally block gets executed, if it is specified. If no handler is found, the application is aborted.

Self-Check

1. As it pertains to programming what is an exception?
2. Differentiate between logic error and exception.
3. Differentiate between syntax error and exception.
4. Define the programming model that Java uses to deal with exception.
5. What will happen if an exception is raised, thrown and not caught?
6. What is the purpose of the *try* block?
7. What is the purpose of the *catch* block?
8. What is peculiar about the finally block?

Understanding Runtime Errors

As mentioned earlier, runtime errors occur when a program attempts to perform tasks that are impossible. **Listing 3.1** shows a program that simply reads string values continuously. As each value is read, it is used as argument to the parseInt method. The program is supposed to terminate when the digit 4 is entered. Is this simple enough?

```
1.  // Listing 3.1 Line 15 causes exception
2.
3.  import javax.swing.JOptionPane;
4.
5.  class Exception
6.  {
```

```
7.        public static void main(String[] arg)
8.        {
9.            boolean done = false;
10.
11.          while (!done)
12.          {
13.              String s = JOptionPane.showInputDialog("Enter an integer");
14.
15.              int i = Integer.parseInt(s);
16.              if (i == 4)
17.                  done = true;
18.          }
19.      }
20.  }
```

During the execution of the program the string "**w**" was entered and stored in the variable **s**, as shown in **Figure 3.1**.

Figure 3.1 The string w **was entered as input**

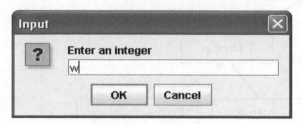

The **parseInt** method expects a string value that can be parsed into an integer. See **Line 15**. Upon encountering the string "**w**" this becomes an impossible task for the method to perform; hence this gives rise to runtime error; the kind described as an exception. As a result the program terminates abnormally. See the error message in **Figure 3.2**.

Figure 3.2 NumberFormatException **occurs - cannot parse letter** w **to an integer**

```
General Output

1  Exception in thread "main" java.lang.NumberFormatException: For input string: "w"
2      at java.lang.NumberFormatException.forInputString(NumberFormatException.java:65)
3      at java.lang.Integer.parseInt(Integer.java:492)
4      at java.lang.Integer.parseInt(Integer.java:527)
5      at MyException.main(MyException.java:13)
6
7
```

In Figure 3.2, notice that five lines of information are displayed in response to the invalid input. The first line, **Line 1**, tells us why the program failed – **NumberFormatException**; the cause of which is the invalid input string, **w**. The method parseInt could not parse the letter into an integer value. **Line 2** shows where the class NumberFormatException.java attempted to resolve the issue on

Line 65 of its code. Prior to that the class Integer attempted to resolve the problem twice – once on Line 527 of its code; and next, line 492 of its code. Finally, **Line 5** of Figure 3.3 shows that the exception was propagated by **Line 13** of method main of our class MyException.java. Since there was no mechanism in place to deal with the exception, the program terminated unsuccessfully.

Exception Classes

In Java, exceptions are objects. Hence, when a program throws an exception, it throws an object containing various pieces of information. The object that it throws is a descendant of a super class called **Throwable**. That is, the class **Throwable** serves as the base class for an entire family of exception classes. This class and most members of its family are found in java.lang. Others are found in packages such as **java.util**, and **java.io**. A small part of this family hierarchy is shown in **Figure 3.3**.

Figure 3.3 Small portion of exception hierarchy of classes

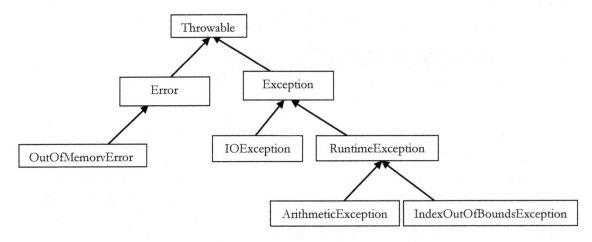

As you have seen in Figure 3.4, the super class of all exceptions is the class Throwable, which has only two direct subclasses, namely: **Error** and **Exception**.

The Super Class Throwable

The class Throwable is the superclass of all exceptions in the Java language. Only objects that are instances of this class, or any of its subclasses are thrown by the JVM, or can be thrown using the Java throw statement. Similarly, only objects of this class, or one of its subclasses can be the argument type in a catch clause.

Of its five overloaded constructors the two most popularly used ones are:

Throwable()   Constructs a new Throwable with no detail message.

Throwable(String message)   Constructs a new Throwable with the specified detail message.

Three of the more frequently used methods of the thirteen methods are:

getMessage()   Returns the detail message of this Throwable object, or null if this Throwable does not have a detail message.

toString()   Returns a short description of this Throwable object.

printStackTrace()   Prints this Throwable and its back trace to the console.

The class **Error** refers to catastrophic events, from which the program is not likely to recover. The programmer cannot design any code within the program to deal with exceptions of this category. The following are subclasses of **Error**:

- **ClassFormatError**. This error is thrown when the Java Virtual Machine attempts to read a class file and determines that the file is malformed, or otherwise cannot be interpreted as a class file.

- **VirtualMachineError**. This error is thrown to indicate that the virtual machine is broken, or has run out of resources necessary for it to continue operating.

- **NoClassDefFoundError** This error is thrown if the Java Virtual Machine or a class loader tries to load in the definition of a class and no definition of the class could be found.

- **OutOfMemoryError**. This error it thrown when the Java Virtual Machine cannot allocate an object because it is out of memory, and no more memory could be made available by the garbage collector.

This book does not further the discussion of Error, or its subclasses, since we cannot embed any code in our program that can catch exceptions of these types.

The subclass **Exception** refers to abnormal conditions that can be caught and be dealt with, in the program. Exceptions of this category can be dealt with by transferring control to a block of codes where the exception is expected to be dealt with. The next section lists these exception classes along with their associated package. In addition to throwing objects whose classes are declared in Java, you can throw objects of your own design. To create your own class of Throwable objects, your class must be a subclass of the Throwable, or any of its descendants.

Exception and Its Associated Packages

You can, and should catch the exceptions that are represented by objects of classes derived from the class Exception. There is a special set of exceptions in this category called **RuntimeException**. These exceptions are generally not thrown by the programmer. The JVM will throw them automatically. However, the programmer should arrange to catch them and to deal with them. The following section outlines the subclasses of Exception and the package in which they are found.

java.util Package
- RuntimeException
  - EmptyStackException
  - NoSuchElementException
    - InputMismatchException

java.io Package
1. IOException
   - EOFException
   - FileNotFoundException
   - InterruptdIOException
   - UTFDataFormatException

java.lang Package
2. ClassNotFoundException
- CloneNotSupportedException
- IllegalAccessException
- InstantiationException
- InterruptException
- NoSuchMethodException
- **RuntimeException**
  - ArithmeticException
  - ArrayStoreException
  - ClassCastException
  - IllegalArgumentException
    - IllegalThreadStateException
    - NumberFormatException
  - IllegalMonitorStateException
  - IndexOutOfBoundsException
    - ArrayIndexOutOfBoundsException
    - StringIndexOutOfBoundsException
  - NegativeArraySizeException
  - NullPointerException
  - SecurityException

java.net
3. IOException
   - MalformedURLException
   - ProtocolException
   - SocketException
   - UnknownHostException
- UnknownServiceException

java.awt Package

4.   AWTException

Checked and Unchecked Exceptions

In Java an exception is raised in one of two events of programming – either during compilation time, or during run-time. As a result Java defines two categories of exceptions - they are referred to as checked exception and unchecked exception. Unchecked exceptions are those exceptions that are not examined at compiled time. This means that code will compile, even though to the human it may be evident that there is a problem with it. In Java, the class RuntimeException, and all of its subclasses are unchecked exceptions. All other exceptions are checked exceptions. This means that the compiler examines them during the compilation of the code. This also means that the programmer must be aware of these kinds of exceptions, and account for them during compilation time. **Listing 3.2** shows an example of unchecked exception.

```
1. // Listing 3.2 Compilation time – exception is not checked
2.
3. class UncheckedException
4. {
5.      public static void main(String [] arg)
6.      {
7.           int x = 20/0;
8.      }
9. }
```

In the Listing, it is evident that **Line 5** will generate ArithmeticException as a result of the division by zero. However, the code compiled successfully – the compiler did not concern itself about this kind of error when compiling the program. The error manifests itself during the execution of the program. This means that the programmer must be aware of the possible type of exception and make provision to deal with them.

Listing 3.3 on the other hand shows an example of checked exception. In this example the code appears to be syntactically correct – it indicates the creation of an object. See **Line 9**.

```
1. // Listing 3.3 Compilation time – exception is checked
2.
3.    import java.io.FileReader;
4.
5.    class CheckedException
6.    {
7.         public static void main(String[] arg)
8.         {
9.              FileReader f = new FileReader("input.txt");
10.         }
11. }
```

As shown in **Figure 3.4**, the code in **Line 9** generated syntax error. The compiler expected the code to say how it would handle the situation if the file in question was not found. At this point nothing more can be done except to fix code.

Figure 3.4 Unreported checked exception

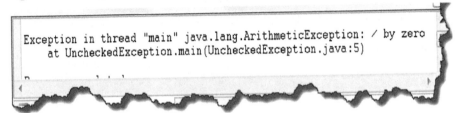

As we have seen, Listing 3.2, UncheckedException, compiled successfully. However, upon attempting to execute the code, **Line 7** failed to execute, as shown in **Figure 3.5**. In other words, it is only during runtime that unchecked exceptions manifest themselves.

Figure 3.5 Exception occurs during run-time

```
Exception in thread "main" java.lang.ArithmeticException: / by zero
    at UncheckedException.main(UncheckedException.java:5)
```

How to Handle Checked Exception

Checked exception is so named, because it causes syntax error if the condition that warrants it is not present in the code during the compilation of the program. That is, the compiler expects your program to contain procedure for dealing with such exception. Checked exceptions are outside the scope of the programmer. For example, the programmer cannot know in advance whether or not a file would exist. Therefore embedded in the program should be a safeguarding mechanism so that the program does not halt during execution.

Checked exceptions can be handled in one of two ways: either implement the **try – catch** mechanism around the code that may cause the exception, or refer the exception to the point from which the method was called. In applying the first method, the compiler is expecting to see try - catch block handling the exception, as shown in **Listing 3.4**.

```
1.  // Listing 3.4 – handling exception within a method
2.
3.  import java.io.FileReader;
4.  import java.io.FileNotFoundException;
5.
```

```
6.    class CheckedException
7.    {
8.        public static void main(String[] arg)
9.        {
10.               try
11.               {
12.                       FileReader f = new FileReader("input.txt");
13.               }
14.               catch(FileNotFoundException e)
15.               {
16.                       // Handle exception the way you see fit
17.               }
18.        }
19. }
```

The second approach requires the use of the throws clause. The throws clause indicates to the compiler two things – that method in which the exception may occur will not handle the exception, it will rely on the method which calls it. Secondly, it announces the type of exception(s) that it is capable of throwing. This is indicated in the method header. The general format of using the throws clause is as follows:

```
return_type  methodName( <parameter> ) throws E1, E2, E3, ...
{
    // try-catch is not used
}
```

Where E1, E2, E3, ... represents the types of exception that is method is capable of throwing. **Listing 3.5** shows this alternate approach of handling checked exceptions.

```
// Listing 3.5 refererng the exception to the point from which method was called
1.
2.    import java.io.FileReader;
3.    import java.io. FileNotFoundException;
4.
5.    class CheckedException {
6.        public static void main(String[] arg) throws FileNotFoundException
7.        {
8.               FileReader f = new FileReader("input.txt");
9.        }
10. }
```

More will be said about checked exception when we discuss the throws clause.

All exceptions other than RuntimeException and its subclasses are checked exceptions. All exceptions in packages **java.io** and **java.net** are checked exception; also the first six listed under **java.lang** are checked exception. We continue the discussion on checked exceptions.in chapter 4.

How to Handle Unchecked Exception

Unchecked Exception is the set of exceptions that is not verified during compilation time. However, the exception manifests itself during execution time, as we have seen in **Figure 3.6**. Unchecked exceptions are generally as a result of poor programming logic, and can be dealt with without exception handling technique. For instance, when Listing 3.2 is re-arranged, as shown in **Listing 3.6** there is no execution error.

```
1. // Listing 3.6 – Unchecked exception - caused by poor program logic
2.
3.    class UncheckedException {
4.         public static void main(String [ ] arg)
5.         {
6.              int denom = 0;
7.
8.              if (denom != 0)
9.                   int x = 20/denom;
10.        }
11. }
```

Unchecked exceptions can be handled in one of two ways – either implement the try/catch mechanism around the code that may cause the exception, or simple say nothing. If you say nothing the compiler will automatically refer the exception to the point from where the method was called, allowing that segment of the program to handle the exception. If no handler is there to deal with the exception, then the program will fail, as we saw in Figure 3.6.

In applying the first method, the compiler is expecting to see the try - catch block handling the exception, as shown in **Listing 3.7**. When the exception is raised, the JVM automatically throws the exception which gets caught by the catch block.

```
1.    // Listing 3.7 Use try-catch to deal with exception
2.
3.    class UncheckedException {
4.         public static void main(String [ ] arg) {
5.              try
6.              {
7.                   int x = 20/0;
8.              }
9.              catch(ArithmeticException e)
10.             {
11.
12.             }
13.        }
14. }
```

Self-Check

1. What happens if an exception is thrown and is not caught?

2. What class is the superclass of all types of exceptions?

3. Name the two exception classes that are direct subclass of the class Throwable, and differentiate between these two categories of exceptions.

4. What is the difference between checked exception and unchecked exception?

5. True or false – Some unchecked exception classes are subclasses of the class RuntimeException.

6. True or false – Some checked exception classes are subclasses of the class RuntimeException.

7. Explain how the try-catch exception feature works in Java. You may use examples to assist in your explanation.

8. True or false – When an exception is thrown by code in a try block, all of the statements in the try block are always executed.

9. True/False. The Java Virtual Machine will throw all RuntimeExceptions automatically, when executing a program.

Handling Multiple Exceptions

A single try block could have the potential of generating multiple types of exceptions. When this happens the program should reflect separate catch blocks to handle each kind of exception; or in some cases, you may use a single catch block with multiple parameters, each parameter reflecting one of these possible exceptions that must be caught.

Although a try block could raise multiple possibilities of exceptions, and although there may be multiple catch block, only one exception can be raised at a time; likewise, one one catch block can also be activated to catch an exception.

Handling Multiple Unrelated Exceptions

When there are multiple unrelated exceptions to be caught, separate catch blocks are required. In this case the parameter of each block must be unique; otherwise this would give rise to syntax error. The order in which the catch blocks are arranged does not matter.

Listing 3.8 shows a class called Division. The critical point in this class is the arithmetic expression, **arr[i]/arr[i+1]** on **Line 12**. The two critical issues to look for are – an index that could exceed the the limit of the array; and a denominator whose value could be zero. Against this background it would be appropriate to apply the exception handling technique to prevent the program from terminating abruptly when it is executing. The exception objects as you see are ArithmeticException and ArrayIndexOutOfBoundsException. These objects are not related; hence the order of specifying them does not make any difference to the result.

```
1.   // Listing 3.8 Class Division demonstrates unrelated exceptions
2.
3.   public class Division {
4.        int arr[];
5.
6.        Division(int a[]) {
7.             arr = a;
8.        }
9.        public void divide(int i) {
10.            try
11.            {
12.                 System.out.println(" i + 1 = " + (i+1) + "  result = " + arr[i]/arr[i+1]);
13.                 System.out.println("No exception occured\n");
14.            }
15.            catch(ArithmeticException e)
16.            {
17.                 System.out.print("index i+ 1 = " + (i+1) + " arr[" + (i+1) + "] = " + arr[i+1] + "\n");
18.                 e.printStackTrace();
19.                 System.out.println();
20.            }
21.            catch(ArrayIndexOutOfBoundsException e)
22.            {
23.                 System.out.print(" i + 1 = " + (i+1) + "\n");
24.                 e.printStackTrace();
25.                 System.out.println();
26.            }
27.        }
28.  }
```

The test class MyException, shown in **Listing 3.9**, creates an array of three integer values. See **Line 5**. It uses that array to create an object from the class Division, as shown in **Line 4**. The for-loop calls the method divide, using the index value *i*, as parameter.

```
// Listing 3.9 Test class

1.   public class MyException {
2.        public static void main(String[] args) {
3.             int[] arr = {10, 5, 0};
4.             Division d = new Division(arr);
5.
6.             for (int i = 0; i < arr.length; i++) {
7.                  System.out.print("Index i = " + i + " ");
8.                  d.divide(i);
9.             }
10.       }
11.  }
```

As we have seen in **Figure 3.6,** that when the program is executed, it produces the correct value for the array at index 0. That is, arr[0]/arr[0+1] = 10/5, which is 2. No exception occurred. However, when the index is 1, the expression arr[1]/arr[1+1] = 10/0, which results in ArithmeticException being raised. Finally, when index is 2, the denominator, arr[2+1], results in ArrayIndexOutOfBoundsException.

Figure 3.6 Unrelated exceptions thrown caused by arithmetic expression arr[i]/arr[i+1]

```
General Output

Index i = 0     i + 1 = 1   result = 2
No exception occured

Index i = 1   index i+ 1 = 2 arr[2] = 0
java.lang.ArithmeticException: / by zero
    at Division.divide(Division.java:15)
    at MyException.main(MyException.java:12)

Index i = 2     i + 1 = 3
java.lang.ArrayIndexOutOfBoundsException: 3
    at Division.divide(Division.java:15)
    at MyException.main(MyException.java:12)
```

Handling Multiple Related Exceptions

When exception objects are related by inheritance, the catch blocks should be arranged in reverse order of how the classes were inherited. For example, consider **Listing 3.10**. This code appears to be fine; however, upon attempting to compile it, the compilation fails as shown in **Figure 3.7**.

```
// Listing 3. 10 Catch blocks are improperly arranged

1.    class ExceptionOrder {
2.        public static void main(String[] arg) {
3.            int arr[] = {20, 10, 50, 40, 25};
4.
5.            try{
6.                System.out.println(arr[arr.length]);
7.            }
8.            catch(RuntimeException e) {
9.                e.printStackTrace();
10.           }
11.           catch(ArrayIndexOutOfBoundsException e) {
12.               e.printStackTrace();
13.           }
14.       }
15.   }
```

The syntax error shown in **Figure 3.7** happens as result of the catch blocks being improperly arranged. The parameter ArrayIndexOutOfBoundsException, **Line 11**, is a subclass of the class RuntimeException. This means that an ArrayIndexOutOfBoundsException is also a RuntimeException. Therefore when the compiler sees the second catch block, it declares that it has already seen an ArrayIndexOutOfBoundsException object.

Figure 3.7 Syntax error - catch blocks are improperly arranged

Message	Folder	Location
Resource: ExceptionOrder.java		
error: exception ArrayIndexOutOfBoundsException has already been caught	C:\JAS...	line 14

Because of the inheritance hierarchy, ArrayIndexOutOfBoundsException must be caught before specifying RuntimeException catch blocks; if we switch the order of the catch block, the code compiles.

Alternate Handling of Multiple Exceptions

If unrelated exceptions are involved, and that they share the same message, then they can be combined as one list of parameters in a catch block. These parametric objects can be viewed as alternate exception choices. The format for this option is as follows:

```
try {
      <throw new ExceptionObject>
}
catch(E1 | E2 | E3 .... e) {
      <handle exception>
}
```

Where E1, E2, E3 are alternate exception choices. When alternate choices are involved, the choices must be unique; they must not be related by inheritance. Consider **Listing 3.11**.

// Listing 3.11 Catch arguments are related through inheritance

```
1.   class ExceptionOrder
2.   {
3.       public static void main(String[] arg)
4.       {
5.       int arr[] = {20, 10, 50, 40, 25};
6.
7.          try{
8.              System.out.println( arr[arr.length] );
9.          }
10.        catch(RuntimeException | ArrayIndexOutOfBoundsException e )
```

```
11.        {
12.              e.printStackTrace();
13.        }
14.    }
15. }
```

As seen in the listing the classes RuntimeException and ArrayIndexOutOfBoundsException are related by inheritance. As a result the code does not compile, as seen in **Figure 3.8**. The only correction to this situation would be to use the tradition method, and by specifying the parameters in the reverse order of the inheritance hierarchy, as described earlier.

Figure 3.8 Improper parametric combinations

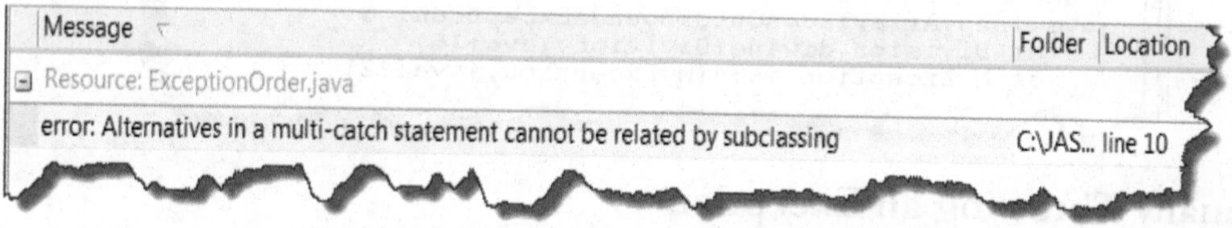

Message	Folder	Location
⊟ Resource: ExceptionOrder.java		
error: Alternatives in a multi-catch statement cannot be related by subclassing	C:\JAS... line 10	

This format for catching exceptions is best used when the same kind of information is required from any of the objects. For instance, if we are simply requiring information from the method printStackTrace, then it would be quite appropriate use alternate choice method. **Listing 3.12** uses the alternate approach of catching the exceptions as shown in Listing 3.8.

```
1.  // Listing 3.12  Exception handling using the alternate method
2.
3.  public class Division {
4.        int arr[];
5.
6.        Division(int a[]){
7.            arr = a;
8.        }
9.        public void divide(int i) {
10.            try {
11.                System.out.println(" i + 1 = " + (i+1) + "  result = " + arr[i]/arr[i+1]);
12.                System.out.println("No exception occured\n");
13.            }
14.            catch(ArithmeticException | ArrayIndexOutOfBoundsException e)
15.            {
16.                System.out.print("index i+ 1 = " + (i+1) + " arr[" + (i+1) + "] = " + arr[i+1] + "\n");
17.                e.printStackTrace();
18.                System.out.println();
19.            }
20.        }
21. }
```

Figure 3.9 shows that with the exception of the indexing information, the printStackTrace output is the same as that of Listing 3.8.

Figure 3.9 Result is the same as before

```
General Output

Index i = 0    i + 1 = 1   result = 2
No exception occured

Index i = 1  index i+ 1 = 2 arr[2] = 0
java.lang.ArithmeticException: / by zero
     at Division.divide(Division.java:15)
     at MyException.main(MyException.java:12)

Index i = 2    i + 1 = 3
java.lang.ArrayIndexOutOfBoundsException: 3
     at Division.divide(Division.java:15)
     at MyException.main(MyException.java:12)
```

Manually Throwing an Exception

So far we having been catching exception objects that were created and were thrown automatically by the JVM. There are times when it would best for the programmer to manually create and throw an exception. For example, if we want to make a more informed report about an exception, it would be best to create an exception object with a tailor made message. In this case the exception object would have to be manually thrown, using the **throw** clause. In the current example about arrays, if a negative value is supplied as index value, or a value that is larger than the allowable index, the program will throw a default ArrayIndexOutOfBoundsException message. If we wish to differentiate between the two indices value – negative value or oversize value – we would have to create and throw the ArrayIndexOutOfBoundsException object with the tailor made message. See **Listing 3.13**.

```
1.   // Listing 3.13 Throwing exceptions manually
2.
3.   public class Division {
4.       int arr[];
5.
6.       Division(int a[]) {
7.           arr = a;
8.       }
9.       public void divide(int i) {
10.          try
11.          {
12.              if ( i < 0 )
13.                  throw new ArrayIndexOutOfBoundsException("\nIndex -" + i + "
                     cannot be used as index\n");
14.              if (i >= arr.length || (i+1 >= arr.length ))
15.                  throw new ArrayIndexOutOfBoundsException("\nIndex " + i + " is
                     beyond the array index\n");
```

```
16.              if (arr[i+1] == 0)
17.                  throw new ArithmeticException("The value of arr[i+1] is 0,\nwill
                     cause division problem\n");
18.              System.out.println("The index  i + 1 = " + (i+1) + ",  result = " +
                 arr[i]/arr[i+1]);
19.              System.out.println("No exception occured\n");
20.          }
21.          catch(ArithmeticException e)
22.          {
23.              System.out.println(e.toString());
24.          }
25.          catch(ArrayIndexOutOfBoundsException e)
26.          {
27.              System.out.println(e.toString());
28.          }
29.      }
30.  }
```

In Listing 3.13 there are three conditions that warrant creating and throwing exceptions with tailor made messages. **Line 13** causes a ArrayIndexOutOfBoundsException object to be created and thrown with tailor made message. Likewise if the index exceeds the maximum limit of the array, an ArrayIndexOutOfBoundsException object with a different message is created and thrown in **Line 15.** On the other hand, **Line 17** creates and throws an ArithmeticException with a unique message if the value of the array at a given index is zero. In all three cases cited above the programmer creates the exception object and throws them explicitly. **Listing 3.14** shows a test class that utilizes the class Division.

```
// Listing 3.14 Test class

1.    public class MyException
2.    {
3.        public static void main(String[] args)
4.        {
5.            int[]  arr = {10, 5, 0};
6.
7.            Division d = new Division(arr);
8.
9.            for (int i = -1; i < arr.length; i++)
10.                d.divide(i);
11.       }
12.   }
```

Figure 3.10 shows the output generated from the program. Notice the uniqueness of the exception messages.

Figure 3.10 Output with tailor made exception messages

```
java.lang.ArrayIndexOutOfBoundsException:
Index -1 cannot be used as index

The index  i + 1 = 1,  result = 2
No exception occured

java.lang.ArithmeticException: The value of arr[i+1] is 0,
will cause division problem

java.lang.ArrayIndexOutOfBoundsException:
Index 2 is beyond the array index
```

Self-Check

1. True or False – if a try block has several catch blocks associated with it, all only one catch block can be activated at a time.

2. True or False – if E1 and E2 are sibling exception classes, the order of specifying them in a series of catch blocks does not matter.

3. If you attempt to compile the following segment of code, will this code compile? Explain.

```
try {

}
catch (Exception e) {

}
catch (ArithmeticException a) {

}
```

4. If you attempt to compile the following segment of code, will this code compile? Explain.

```
try {

}
catch (Exception | ArithmeticException e) {

}
```

5. If you attempt to compile the following segment of code, will this code compile? Explain.

```
try {

}
catch (NullPointerException | ArithmeticException e) {

}
```

In Listing 3.8 if we were to switch the order of the catch blocks, what would be the result when we run the program? Explain.

Using finally Block

When the JVM begins executing a block of code, it can exit the block by executing all the statements within the block, thereby executing beyond the closing curly brace. Other ways that it can exit the block is by using the **break** statement, the **continue** statement, or the **return** statement. In the latter three ways where the program block can be exited, the implication is that there may be statements within the block that would not be executed. Likewise, if an exception is thrown that isn't caught inside the block, the block could be exited while a catch clause is being searching for.

Given that a block can be exited in any of the many ways outlined above, it is important to ensure that all secured measures are taken so that the program does not generate any unintended results, no matter how the block is exited. For example, if the program opens a file in a method, you may want to ensure the file gets closed, no matter how the method completes.

In a practical sense, if you go to an ATM to withdraw cash, once you have entered your loin information, your file is opened. Now if the withdrawal transaction is successful you would hope that the system closes your file. If on the other hand the transaction was not successful, in the sense that there were insufficient funds, you would hope that the system protects you file by closing it. Thirdly, since a program can exit a block in so many anomalous ways as we saw earlier, the program should also close your file, just as if the transaction was normally executed. In other words the desirable thing for the program to do in this case, is to make sure that all open files be closed, whether the transaction was successful or not. In Java, you express such a desire with a finally clause.

How The finally Block Works

When using the finally clause, you simply place the code that must be executed when the try block is exited in a finally block. An exit point of a try block, other than the normal flow to the end of a block can either be a **break** statement, a **continue** statement, or a **return** statement.

try-catch Without Transfer of Control

When the JVM enters a try-catch block of codes, if no exception occurs and no transfer of control is executed in the try block, then the finally block is executed, and the statement that follows the try-catch-finally block is executed.

On the other hand, if an exception occurs during the execution of a try block; and if there is a catch block for that exception; and if the catch block does not issue a transfer of control, then the catch block is executed, followed by the finally block, followed by the first statement (if any), after the try-catch-finally construct. **Listing 3.15** shows the class called FinallyBlock. This class receives an array of string values. The method **test** receives an integer value, which it uses to call the method display. As you will notice, the method **test** has two sets of codes – the first is the try-catch- finally, and the second is the single print statement of **Line 24**. The method has no exit flow of control point. Hence, **Line 24** is guaranteed to be executed after the competition of the try-catch-finally block. With respect to the try-catch-finally, the try block and the finally blocks are guaranteed to be executed, but not the catch block.

// Listing 3.15 How the finally block works

```
1.    class FinallyBlock
2.    {
3.        String s[ ];
4.
5.        FinallyBlock(String []s)
6.        {
7.            this.s = s;
8.        }
9.        void test(int i)
10.       {
11.           try
12.           {
13.               display(i);
14.               System.out.println("in try block - no exception caught");
15.           }
16.           catch(ArrayIndexOutOfBoundsException e)
17.           {
18.               System.out.println( e.toString());
19.           }
20.           finally
21.           {
22.               System.out.println("Finally is executed!!");
23.           }
24.           System.out.println("Outside the try-catch-finally construct ....!!\n");
25.       }
26.       void display(int i) {
27.           System.out.print(s[i] + " - ");
28.       }
29.   }
```

Listing 3.16 shows a test class that implements the class FinallyBlock. As seen Line 6 establishes a string array of one value, which is used to create the FinallyBlock, referenced by **fb**, as shown in **Line 7**. The method test is called with the integer value 0, as shown in **Line 8**.

```
1.    // Listing 3.16 Test class
2.
3.    public class TestFinallyBlock {
4.        public static void main(String[ ] args)
5.        {
6.            String s[ ] = {"Hi"};
7.            FinallyBlock fb = new FinallyBlock(s);
8.            fb.test(0);
9.            fb.test(1);
10.       }
11. }
```

Tracing the code in the method test, we see that the method **display** is called with the value 0. At this point the value in the array, **s**, is extracted and is displayed. Thereby, no exception has been raised, and so control returns to **Line 14** for it to be executed. That is the end of the try block. No exception is raised; hence the catch block is bypassed. However, the finally block is executed. Once the finally block is executed the next statement (**Line 24**) is executed; and control goes back to main. The first section of **Figure 3.11** shows that the finally block was executed although no exception was thrown.

Figure 3.11 No exception raised; however, finally block is executed

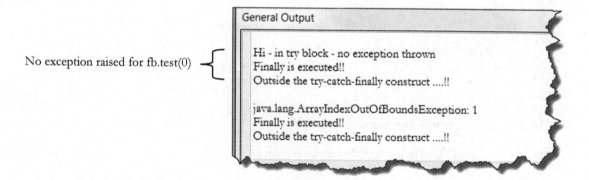

No exception raised for fb.test(0)

General Output

Hi - in try block - no exception thrown
Finally is executed!!
Outside the try-catch-finally construct ....!!

java.lang.ArrayIndexOutOfBoundsException: 1
Finally is executed!!
Outside the try-catch-finally construct ....!!

Referring to the test class TestFinallyBlock, **Listing 3.16**, when **Line 8** is executed, the method test accepts the value 1, and calls the method display with this value. It should be evident at this point that **s[1]** does not exists, hence ArrayIndexOutOfBoundsException is thrown and is caught by the catch block, **Line 16**, of the class FinallyBlock. Once the exception is thrown the rest of the try block is skipped, and the catch block is executed, after which the finally block is executed. After the finally block is executed then next statement **Line 24** is executed; and control goes back to main. The second section of **Figure 3.12** shows the result when a catch-finally combination is executed without transfer flow of control.

Figure 3.7 Exception is raised, remainder of try block is dead; finally is executed

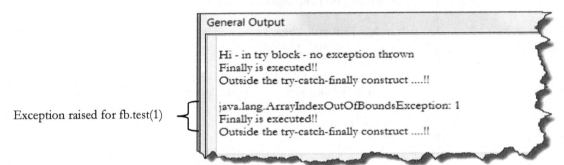

Exception raised for fb.test(1)

General Output

Hi - in try block - no exception thrown
Finally is executed!!
Outside the try-catch-finally construct ....!!

java.lang.ArrayIndexOutOfBoundsException: 1
Finally is executed!!
Outside the try-catch-finally construct ....!!

The try-catch **With Transfer of Control**

If a try block and a catch block each has a flow of control statement, if the try block does not throw an exception, then the finally block will be executed before the catch block. See **Listing 3.17**.

```
1.    // Listing 3.17 try-catch With transfer of control
2.
3.    class FinallyBlock
4.    {
5.        String s[];
6.
7.        FinallyBlock(String []s)
8.        {
9.            this.s = s;
10.       }
11.       String test(int i)
12.       {
13.           try
14.           {
15.               display(i);
16.               return "No exception caught\n";
17.           }
18.           catch(ArrayIndexOutOfBoundsException e)
19.           {
20.               return e.toString();
21.           }
22.
23.           finally
24.           {
25.               System.out.println("Finally is executed!!");
26.           }
27.   }
```

```
28.        void display(int i)
29.        {
30.            System.out.println("First statement in method display ...");
31.            System.out.print(s[i] + " second statement in method display\n");
32.        }
33.  }
```

As you have seen in the listing, there are two exit points – the return statement on **Line 14** and the return statement on **Line 18**.

Listing 3.18 shows the test class, TestFinallyBlock. When Line 7 is executed, the method *test* calls the method *display* in the class FinallyBblock, and both lines of codes are executed without any exception being thrown. Hence, the catch block is not executed. That being the case, one would have thought that the return statement on Line 14 would have been executed; instead the finally block is executed first.

```
1.    // Listing 3.18
2.
3.    public class TestFinallyBlock
4.    {
5.        public static void main(String[] args)
6.        {
7.            String s[] = {"Hi"};
8.            FinallyBlock fb = new FinallyBlock(s);
9.            System.out.println("Report to main - " + fb.test(0));
10.           System.out.println("Report to main - " + fb.test(1));
11.       }
12.  }
```

In **Figure 3.13** the first four statements shows that the finally block is executed before the return statement comes into effect.

Figure 3.13 – Finally block executes before return statement takes effect

When flow of control is involved, and no exception raised finally block is executed first.

```
First statement in method display ...
Hi second statement in method display
Finally is executed!!
Report to main - No exception caught

First statement in method display ...
Finally is executed!!
Report to main - java.lang.ArrayIndexOutOfBoundsException: 1
```

Pitfall: finally **Block – with Transfer of Control**

You should never use **return**, **break**, **continue**, or throw statements within a finally block. When program execution enters a try block that has a finally block, the finally block, as we have seen, always executes, regardless of whether the try block or any associated catch blocks executes to normal completion. Therefore if the finally block contains any of these statements, these statements will cause the finally block to complete abruptly, which will also cause the try block to terminate abruptly and consequently bypass any exception thrown from the try or catch blocks. **Listing 3.19** shows that the finally block has a return statement. See **Line 25.**

```
1.    // Listing 3.19 Return statement in finally block circumvents catch block
2.
3.    class FinallyBlock
4.    {
5.        String s[];
6.
7.        FinallyBlock(String []s)
8.        {
9.            this.s = s;
10.       }
11.       String test(int i)
12.       {
13.           try
14.           {
15.               display(i);
16.               return "No exception caught\n";
17.           }
18.           catch(ArrayIndexOutOfBoundsException e)
19.           {
20.               return e.toString();
21.           }
22.           finally
23.           {
24.               System.out.println("Finally is executed!!");
25.               return "Do not issue return statement in the finally block\n";
26.           }
27.       }
28.       void display(int i)
29.       {
30.           System.out.println("First statement in method display ...");
31.           System.out.print(s[i] + " second statement in method display\n");
32.       }
33. }
```

When the statement is executed:

System.out.println("Report to main - " + fb.test(1));

the value 1 causes an ArrayOutOfBoundsException to be thrown from Line 29 in the display method of **Listing 3.19**. Because the finally block is executed before the catch block, the return statement in the finally block returns control back to main. As a result the catch block was never executed. See **Figure 3.14**.

Figure 3.14 Return statement in finally caused the catch block not to be executed

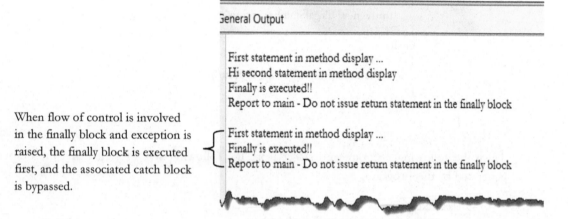

When flow of control is involved in the finally block and exception is raised, the finally block is executed first, and the associated catch block is bypassed.

General Output

First statement in method display ...
Hi second statement in method display
Finally is executed!!
Report to main - Do not issue return statement in the finally block

First statement in method display ...
Finally is executed!!
Report to main - Do not issue return statement in the finally block

Self-Check

1. If the finally block is coded in a try-catch block, which of the following responses that is (are) true?
    (a) The finally block is executed only if no exception is thrown
    (b) The finally block can come anywhere within the scope of the try-catch block.
    (c) There MUST be a finally block for each try-catch block.
    (d) The finally block will always be executed, regardless if an exception was thrown or not.
    (e) The finally block must come after the catch blocks.

2. What would happen if you attempt to compile the following segment of code?

```
try {

}
finally {

}
```

3. True or false - As it pertains to Exception handling in Java, the **finally** block gets executed only if no exception is caught.

4. True or false – When coding a try-catch block, it is mandatory to code the **finally** block.

5. Comment on the following program code. Which will or will not be executed? Explain.

```
class TryFinally
{
    void test()
    {
        try
        {
            throw new IllegalStateException();
        }
        finally
        {
            System.out.println("testing is done");
        }
    }
}
```

6. Trace the following program and select from the following sets of statements the output generated by this program.

```
class Exception {
    public static void main(String[] arg)
    {
        int i[] = {2, 4, 6};
        method(i[0], i);
        method(i[2], i);
    }
    static void method(int i, int[] arr)
    {
        try
        {
            System.out.println(arr[i] / ( arr[i] - 6));
        }
        catch(ArrayIndexOutOfBoundsException e)
        {
            System.out.println("ArrayIndexOutOfBoundsException caught");
        }
        catch(ArithmeticException e)
        {
            System.out.println("ArithmeticException caught");
        }
        finally
        {
            System.out.println("Yes it is true");
        }
    }
}
```

7. Study the following program carefully.

```
class Except
{
    void test(String []s)
    {
        try
        {
            method(s);
            System.out.println("No exception caught");
        }
        catch (NullPointerException e)
        {
            System.out.println("Null pointer");
        }
        catch(ArrayIndexOutOfBoundsException e)
        {
            System.out.println("Array index is out of bounds");
        }
        finally
        {
            System.out.println("Program is fine!!");
        }
    }
    void method(String[] a)
    {
        a[1] = "hello world";
        System.out.println(a[1]);
    }
}
```

What will be outputted if the following two statements are executed on the class Except?

```
Except a = new Except();
String s[] = {"Hi"};
a.test(s);
```

8. Comment on the following program code. Which will or will not be executed? Explain.

```
class TryFinally {
    boolean test() {
        try
        {
            throw new IllegalStateException();
        }
        catch(IllegalStateException e) {
```

```
                System.out.println("IllegalStateException caught");

            return false
            }
            finally
            {
                System.out.println("Testing is done");
                return true;
            }
        }
    }
```

The *try-with-resources* Statement

The finally block as we know is designed to execute its codes, regardless of the outcome of the try block. With this expectation, Java 7 implements what is referred to as the try-with-resources statement to automatically close resources that have been opened. The try-with-resources statement is a try statement that declares one or more resources. When the resource is no longer in use, it is automatically closed, just as if the finally block was implemented.

A *resource* is an object that must be closed after the program is finished with it. That is, the try-with-resources statement ensures that each resource is closed at the end of the statement. The general format of this statement is as follows:

```
try( Resource r = new Resource(<parameter> ) {
    <throw new E>
}
catch(E₁ e) {
    <handle exception>
}

        ⋮

catch(Eₙ e) {
    <handle exception>
}
```

A resource is defined as objects from the following packages - io, nio, net, and sql. Typical among the resources are files, streams, sockets, and database connections.

User Defined Exception Classes

Although Java defines several exception classes to handle a wide array of exceptions, there are cases where none of those classes reflect situations that are unique to some problems. Consider for instance the quadratic formula for finding the root of quadratic equations, where the formula is given by:

$$x = \frac{-b \pm \sqrt{b^2 - 4ac}}{2a}$$

The inexperience programmer may go straight ahead to plug in the values for a, b, and c, without considering whether or not the values are representative of a quadratic equation; or, if they do, whether or not the equation has real roots. In an attempt to finding the root of quadratic equations, using the quadratic formula, two things must be taken into consideration:

1. If the co-efficient a = 0, then the three values do not represent a quadratic equation. This should be noted as an exception.
2. If the discriminant, ($b^2 - 4ac < 0$) the equation has no real root. A condition of this kind should also be viewed as an exception.

As we have seen, conditions 1 and 2 above make the case for exception to be raised. However, Java does not have any predefined exception classes for either of these situations. Against this background it would be appropriate to design our own exception class to handle these extraneous cases.

When designing an exception class, such a class must be a subclass of the class Throwable, or one of its subclasses. The general format for a user defined exception class is as follows:

```
class UserDefinedException extends ThrowableObject
{
        UserDefinedException (<parameter> )
        {
            // code for the constructor
        }
        data_type method( <parameter>)
        {
            // code to handle exception
        }
}
```

When defining your own exception class you may define your own exception message. Also, you may define methods that handle the exception. In the case of the quadratic equation problem, we could provide exception messages for when a = 0, and when the discriminant is. If the quadratic has no real root, then we could provide a method that finds the imaginary root. An exception class of the kind would be more informative than if the program would throw some form of default exception message. **Listing 3.20** shows a user defined exception class called QuadraticException.

```
1.   // Listing 3.20 User defined exception
2.
3.   class QuadraticException extends Throwable
4.   {
5.       double a, b, discriminant;
```

```
6.
7.         QuadraticException(String message)
8.         {
9.              super(message);
10.        }
11.        QuadraticException(String message, double a, double b, double d)
12.        {
13.             this(message);
14.             this.a = a;  // Co-efficient of x square
15.             this.b = b;  // Co-efficient of x
16.             discriminant = d;
17.        }
18.        public String imaginaryRoots()
19.        {
20.             double x1 = (-b + Math.sqrt(-discriminant))/(2 * a);
21.             double x2 = (-b - Math.sqrt(-discriminant))/(2 * a);
22.             return "Imaginary roots: " + x1 + "i" + " and " + x2 + "i";
23.        }
24. }
```

In the listing the fields **a** and **b** represent the co-efficient of x^2 and **x**, respectively. The field called discriminant represents the value:

$$b^2 - 4ac$$

The overloaded constructors accept the user defined message; the second constructor accepts also the values for a, and b, and the discriminant, respectively. The method imaginaryRoots actually finds the imaginary roots of the equation when the discriminant is negative. **Listing 3.21** shows the class Quadratic that solves quadratic equations for either real or imaginary roots.

```
1.   // Listing 3.21 Solution to the Quadratic equation
2.
3.   class Quadratic{
4.        double a, b, c, discriminant, root1, root2;
5.        String s;
6.
7.        Quadratic(double x[ ]) {
8.             s = "";
9.             a = x[0];
10.            b = x[1];
11.            c = x[2];
12.        }
13.        boolean isZero(){
14.             try{
15.                  if ( a == 0.0)
16.                       throw new QuadraticException("Coefficient of x square is zero, hence no
```

```
                        quadratic");
17.                 return false;
18.             }
19.             catch(QuadraticException e) {
20.                 s = s + e.toString();
21.                 return true;
22.             }
23.         }
24.     void calculateDiscriminant() {
25.         discriminant = Math.pow(b, 2) - 4 * a * c;
26.         try{
27.             if (discriminant < 0)
28.                 throw new QuadraticException("No real root", a, b, discriminant);
29.             calculateDoubleRoots();
30.             s = s + "Root 1 = " + root1 + "\tRoot 2 = " + root2;
31.         }
32.         catch(QuadraticException e) {
33.             s = s + e.toString() +": " + e.imaginaryRoots();
34.         }
35.     }
36.     void calculateSingleRoot() {
37.         s = s + (-b / (2 * a));
38.     }
39.     void calculateDoubleRoots() {
40.         root1 = (-b + Math.sqrt(discriminant))/(2 * a);
41.         root2 = (-b - Math.sqrt(discriminant))/(2 * a);
42.     }
43.     boolean singleRoot(){
44.         return discriminant == 0;
45.     }
46.     String getResult(){
47.         return s;
48.     }
49. }
```

The class accepts an array of the three values representing the values a, b, and c of the equation. The method isZero determines if the expression is quadratic. If it is not, an exception of the user defined type QuadraticException is created and thrown, as shown in **Line 16**. Notice that the tailor made exception message is passed on to the constructor of the class QuadraticException. In addition, the parameter of the catch block is of type QuadraticException. See **Line 19**. Also, **Line 20** extracts the exception message via the toString method, and appends it to the values of the imaginary roots by calling the method imaginaryRoots.

Listing 3.22 shows the test class. Line 5 shows a two dimensional array of four sets of values; each set of values represents the co-efficient values for a quadratic equation.

```
1.  // Listing 3.22 Test class gives no indication of exception handling
2.
```

```
3.   class TestQuadratic
4.   {
5.       public static void main(String[] arg)
6.       {
7.           double arr[][] = {{1, 0, -9}, {1, 0, 9}, {2, -8, 8}, {0, 4, 12}, {1, -1, -6}};
8.
9.           for (int i = 0; i < arr.length; i++)
10.          {
11.              String s = "a = " + arr[i][0] + "  b = " + arr[i][1] + "  c = " + arr[i][2] + "\n";
12.              Quadratic q = new Quadratic(arr[i]);
13.
14.              if (!q.isZero())
15.              {
16.                  q.calculateDiscriminant();
17.                  if (q.singleRoot())
18.                      q.calculateSingleRoot();
19.                  else
20.                      q.calculateDoubleRoots();
21.              }
22.              System.out.println(s + q.getResult() + "\n");
23.          }
24.      }
25.  }
```

This module is designed so that all the arrays are evaluated. As such no exception is made to be raised in it; because once an exception is raised the remainder of the block is dead. As seen, each set of values is used to create a Quadratic object – **Line 12**. The method isZero determines whether or not the values represent those of a quadratic function. If they do, the discriminant is found in order to determine single or double root solution. Notice that no mention is made of exception in this class. As a matter of fact, by looking at the code you could never tell if exception had occurred – it is fully **Figure 3.15** shows the result from the five sets of values.

Figure 3.8

```
a = 1.0  b = 0.0  c = -9.0
Real roots are 3.0  and -3.0

a = 1.0  b = 0.0  c = 9.0
QuadraticException: No real root:Imaginary roots: 3.0i and -3.0i

a = 2.0  b = -8.0  c = 8.0
Single root 2.0

a = 0.0  b = 4.0  c = 12.0
QuadraticException: Coefficient of x^2 is zero, not a quadratic

a = 1.0  b = -1.0  c = -6.0
Real roots are 3.0  and -2.0
```

The values used in the program were taken from these equations.

a) $x^2 - 9 = 0$ d) $4x + 12 = 0$

b) $x^2 + 9 = 0$ e) $x^2 - x - 6 = 0$

c) $2x^2 - 8x + 8 = 0$

Using the throws Clause

As mentioned earlier, checked exceptions must be reported, otherwise the program will not compile. A method that has the potential of raising an exception but does not prepare to handle the exception, must announce its intention in its header by using the throws clause. This means that the exception must be handled by the segment of code that called the method, or some point higher up. Re-call the general format for using the throws clause:

```
data_type methodName(< parameter> ) throws E1, E2, ...
{
        // program code - try catch is not applicable here
}
```

Where **E1, E2**, etc. are exception objects.

The throws clause is only relevant to checked exceptions and user defined exceptions, since unchecked exceptions would be thrown regardless. This means that if the throws clause is not used for these two categories of exceptions, the code will generate syntax error. **Listing 3.23** shows an alternate version of the class Quadratic.

```
1.   // Listing 3.23 Using the throws clause
2.
3.   class Quadratic{
4.          double a, b, c, discriminant, root1, root2;
5.          String s;
6.
7.          Quadratic(double x[ ]){
8.                s = "";
9.                a = x[0];
10.               b = x[1];
11.               c = x[2];
12.          }
13.         boolean isZero() throws QuadraticException
14.         {
15.               if ( a == 0.0)
16.                     throw new QuadraticException("Coefficient of x^2 is zero, not a quadratic");
17.               return false;
18.         }
19.         void calculateDiscriminant() throws QuadraticException
20.         {
21.               discriminant = Math.pow(b, 2) - 4 * a * c;
```

```
22.              if (discriminant < 0)
23.                  throw new QuadraticException("No real root", a, b, discriminant);
24.
25.              calculateDoubleRoots();
26.              s = s + "Real roots are " + root1 + "\tand " + root2;
27.          }
28.      void calculateSingleRoot()
29.          {
30.              s = "Single root " +(-b / (2 * a));
31.          }
32.      void calculateDoubleRoots()
33.          {
34.              root1 = (-b + Math.sqrt(discriminant))/(2 * a);
35.              root2 = (-b - Math.sqrt(discriminant))/(2 * a);
36.          }
37.      boolean singleRoot(){
38.              return discriminant == 0;
39.          }
40.      String getResult(){
41.              return s;
42.          }
43. }
```

In the listing the methods isZero and calculateDiscriminant use the throws clause to indicate that they are not prepared to handle the exception if one is ever raised by using the throws class, and by creating the exception object and throw it. Notice that the try-catch construct is not used.

Listing 3.24 shows the modified version of the test class which prepares to catch the QuadraticException object and to handle it if one is ever thrown.

```
1.   // Listing 3.24Test class catches and handles exceptions
2.
3.   class TestQuadratic
4.   {
5.       public static void main(String[] arg)
6.       {
7.           double arr[][] = {{1, 0, -9}, {1, 0, 9}, {2, -8, 8}, {0, 4, 12}, {1, -1, -6}};
8.
9.           for (int i = 0; i < arr.length; i++)
10.          {
11.              String s = "a = " + arr[i][0] + " b = " + arr[i][1] + " c = " + arr[i][2] + "\n";
12.              Quadratic q = new Quadratic(arr[i]);
13.
14.              try
15.              {
16.                  if (!q.isZero())
17.                  {
18.                      try
```

```
19.                           {
20.                                q.calculateDiscriminant();
21.                           }
22.                           catch(QuadraticException e)
23.                           {
24.                                s = s + e.toString() + ":" + e.imaginaryRoots();
25.                           }
26.
27.                           if (q.singleRoot())
28.                                q.calculateSingleRoot();
29.                           else
30.                                q.calculateDoubleRoots();
31.                      }
32.                 }
33.            catch (QuadraticException e)
34.            {
35.                 System.out.println( e.toString() + "\n");
36.            }
37.            System.out.println( s + q.getResult() + "\n");
38.       }
39.  }
40. }
```

Nesting try-catch - blocks

Sometimes there are situations where a segment of a block may cause one error; as well as the entire block itself may cause another error. In situations of this kind, it is best to handle the errors by nesting the exception handlers. That is, a *try* statement can be inside the block of another *try*. The general format for nesting the try-catch-finally block is as follows:

```
try{
    // Java statement
    try{
        <throw new ExceptionObject>
    }
    catch(ExceptionObject e){
        <handle exception>
    }
    :
    finally {
        <handle exception>
    }
    // Java statement
}
catch(ExceptionObject e){
    <handle exception>
}
    :
finally {
```

```
        <handle exception>
    }
```

When nested try blocks are used, the inner try block is executed first. Any exception thrown in the inner try block is caught by one of its corresponding catch blocks. If a corresponding catch block is not found, then catch blocks of the outer try block are inspected until all nested try statements are exhausted. If no matching blocks are found, the JVM search up to the point where the method was called in search of a handler. If an exception occurs in the outer *try* before reaching the inner *try* block, then the inner *try* will never be executed. **Listing 3.24** shows the concept of using nested try-catch block.

When nesting try-catch blocks, each try block must have its own associated catch-finally block. In other words, two or more try blocks cannot share the same catch block. For example, the try blocks of **Line 14** and **Line 18** of **Listing 3.24** cannot share the catch block of Line 33 of the same listing.

Rethrowing Exception

When throwing exception, there are times when you would prefer the associated catch block not to handle the exception, but rather re-throw it so that some exception handler in the next higher level in the hierarchy to deal with the exception. Any further **catch** clauses for the same **try** block are then ignored.

Approaching exception handling this way can be useful if the method that catches the exception needs to take some additional action upon seeing the Exception, before re-throwing it. Re-throwing causes the Exception to be propagated to the caller, so that the caller can handle it. If you simply re-throw the exception, the information that you print about that exception in **printStackTrace( )** will pertain to the exception's origin, and not the place where you re-throw it. See **Listing 3.25**.

```
// Listing 3.25 Re-throwing exception

1.   public class TryRethrow
2.   {
3.        public static void rethrowIt(boolean x)
4.        {
5.            try
6.            {
7.                if (x)
8.                    throw new ArithmeticException(" ");
9.                else
10.                   throw new NullPointerException();
11.           }
12.           catch(Exception e)
13.           {
14.               System.out.println("Do some handling\nand then rethrow to " + e.getMessage());
```

```
15.                    throw e;
16.              }
17.        }
18.        public static void main( String[] args )
19.        {
20.            try
21.            {
22.                rethrowIt(true);
23.            }
24.            catch(NullPointerException | ArithmeticException e)
25.            {
26.                System.out.println("main .. " + e.toString());
27.            }
28.        }
29. }
```

Figure 3.16 shows the output of re-throwing an exception. Notice that when the method, rethrowIt is called from main the catch block of rethrowIt catches the exception, **Line 14**, and then re-throws the exception. See **Line 18**. This call causes the catch block of main, **Line 24**, to catch the ArithmeticException where it is handled.

Figure 3.16

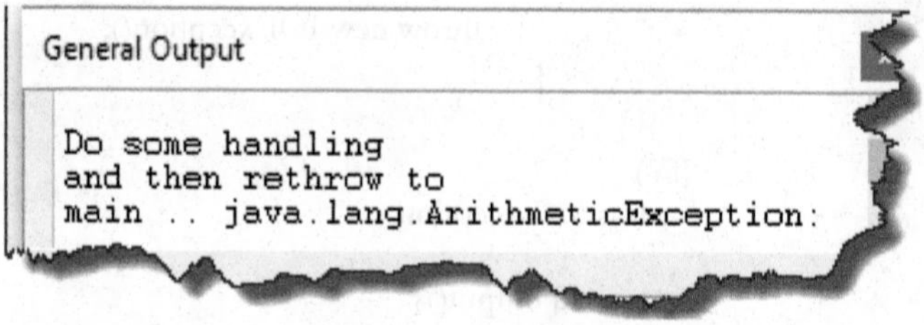

```
General Output

Do some handling
and then rethrow to
main .. java.lang.ArithmeticException:
```

Self-Check

1. Which of the following are true about exception and exception handling?
   (a) Only some user defined exception classes are derived from the class Throwable or any of its subclasses.
   (b) A programmer can define an exception class without deriving it from the class Throwable or any of its subclasses.
   (c) All user-defined exceptions are unchecked exceptions.
   (d) Exceptions cannot be nested. This arrangement of code would compile, but it would not execute.

2. As it pertains to programming, what does the term exception means?

3. What is the significance of using the keyword *throws* in Java?

4. Assume that the method *display()* for the class MyException might throw either of the two exceptions: IOexception or RuntimeException. Assume that the appropriate import statement has been declared. Which of the following class(es) will compile? Explain.

(I)
```
class MyException {
    void output()
    {
        try
        {
            display();
        }
        catch(IOException e)
        {

        }
    }
    void display()throws IOException
    {
        throw new IOException();
    }
}
```

(II)
```
class MyException{
    void output()
    {
        try
        {
            display();
        }
        catch(IOException e){

        }
        catch(RuntimeException e){

        }
    }
    void display()throws RuntimeException{
        throw new IOException();
    }
}
```

(III)
```
class MyException
{
    void output(){
        try
        {
            display();
        }
        catch(IOException e){

        }
    }
    void display()
    {
        throw new IOException();
    }
}
```

(IV)
```
class MyException
{
    void output(){
        try
        {
            display();
        }
        catch(IOException | RuntimeException e){

        }
    }
    void display() throws IOException
    {
        throw new IOException();
    }
}
```

5. Consider the statement:

```
int x = .....;

double y = Math.sqrt(x);
```

Define an exception class of your own that would catch an exception if x is a negative value.

6. With respect to the topic exception and exception handling, differentiate between the keywords *throw* and *throws*.

7. When attempting to run a certain program, the compiler gave the following runtime error. Analyze the error message, and explain as much information you can about the error.

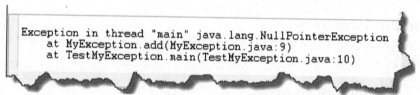

```
Exception in thread "main" java.lang.NullPointerException
    at MyException.add(MyException.java:9)
    at TestMyException.main(TestMyException.java:10)
```

Chapter Summary

- An exception in Java is a segment of code that if not handled appropriately can cause the entire program to terminate abnormally.

- Exception must be differentiated from syntax error and logic error. Whereas syntax error will cause the program not to compile, logic error will generate erroneous results when the program executes.

- When a method encounters an exception, it creates an exception object and throws it, hoping that there is a segment of code that will catch the exception and handle it.

- Java uses the try-throw-catch-finally model to address exception.

- The Java programming language provides an inheritance hierarchy of class to deal with the more common types of exception. These classes are defined as either checked exception or unchecked exception.

- **Unchecked** exceptions are so named because the compiler does not check the code to see if the exception objects are created and thrown during compilation time.

- **Checked** exceptions are so named because the compiler checks the code to make sure that the exception objects are created and thrown during compilation time.
- The class RuntimeException and all of its subclasses are unchecked exception. All other exceptions are checked exceptions.

- A single try block may throw multiple exceptions, in which case separate catch blocks are required.

- Where multiple catch blocks are involved, the alternate catch format may be used if the parameters are unrelated by inheritance.

- The *throw* clause may be used if the programmer wishes to define a unique exception message.

Programming Exercises

1. Write a program that can be used to determine if an email address is of a valid form. To begin, the format of email addresses is:

> local-part@domain-part

Where **local-part** may be up to 64 characters long, and the **domain-part** may have a maximum of 254 characters. For this exercise, let us limit the local part of an email address to the following ASCII characters:

- Uppercase and lowercase letters A to Z and a to z
- Digits 0 to 9
- Special characters ! # $ % & ' * + - / = ? ^ _ ` { | } ~
- Period/Dot ., provided that it is not the first or last character, and provided also that it does not appear consecutively.

Also, let us limit the domain-part of the address to at most three trunks, each trunk an alphanumeric string, each separated by a period (.). In your solution write a class called EmailAddress that accepts a string, and determines if the string represents a valid email address in form. If a string does not have the form of a valid address, the program should throw an exception to that effect, and alert the user with information pertaining to the formation of an email address.

> Note: validation of the form of an email address does not mean that such an email address exists.

Chapter 4 Input ■ Output using Files and Streams

Objectives

After reading this chapter you will:

- Have an in-depth understanding of the java.io package.
- Know the difference between byte oriented streams and character oriented streams.
- Understand the input-output hierarchy for byte streams as well as character streams.
- Know the purpose and function of the input stream called StreamTokenizer.
- Understand the principle of a random access file.
- Know the purpose and function of the input – output stream called RandomAccessFile.
- Know the procedure for handling input-output exceptions.

Introduction

Java programming language supports input-output operations through the concept of streams. A stream is an abstraction that either produces data, or consumes data. The consumption of data refers to input, and the production of data refers to output. A stream is linked to a physical input-output device by the JVM. Because of inheritance, most streams behave alike, since they use the same method names.

Input is any data that is needed by a program during execution. There are many forms that input may take - graphical forms like input dialog boxes; by clicking the mouse in a areas of the screen; by typing the data at the console (as we have done using the scanner class); by hard coding the data (as we have done); by network connections; or by files stored on external devices such as the hard drive. There are other methods such as the microphone, scanners, and digital cameras, also.

Output is any information that the program conveys to the user, or data that is sent to another device such as the transfer of digital data to another computer. The information you see on the computer screen is one form of output. The printing of a document is another form of output; and the sound that the computer's audio speaker produces is a form of output.

Standard Input and Output

Input from the keyboard is referred to as standard input; likewise, output to the display screen is referred to as standard output. The class System provides support for standard input and output. There are three streams that are associated with standard Input/Output. These streams are:

- **err**   Standard error output stream.
- **out**   Standard output stream
- **in**   Standard input stream

err

The standard output stream, **err**, is used to display messages concerning errors about program execution. The typical usage is as follows:

    System.err.println(" message string ...");

out

The standard output stream, **out**, works similar to the *err* output stream, except that the output produced is intended for normal expected use. The typical usage is as follows:

    System.out.println(" Expected output" + id);

in

The standard **in**, input stream reads character data from the keyboard. The way that this works is that the data is inputted from the standard input device (the keyboard) by calling Java's System.in.read() method. In the class System the reference variable **in** – calls the read() which belongs to a member of the class called InputStream. System.in.read() takes no arguments. However it returns the integer representation of the character that it reads.

By default **in** is a **buffered** input stream. This means that input from the keyboard is kept in a buffer until the program reads it. The value that is read is returned as an integer. In order to know its char representation it must be converted by casting it to *char*. **Listing 4.1** shows a class called StandardInput that reads data from the keyboard and displays the integer value of the character that it reads, along with the character itself value itself.

```
1.  // Listing 4.1 Reading from the keyboard
2.
3.  class StandardInput {
4.      public static void main (String [] args) throws java.io.IOException {
```

```
5.              int ch;
6.              System.out.print ("Enter text --> ");
7.
8.              while ((ch = System.in.read ()) != '\n')
9.                  System.out.println (ch + "\t\t" + (char)ch );
10.         }
11. }
```

As shown in **Figure 4.1**, the first line represents the input. In the succeeding lines, the first column represents the integer that is associated with each character shown in the second column. In the output, notice that digits are characterized as chars, and also show their respective ASCII value.

Figure 4.1 Output from the program

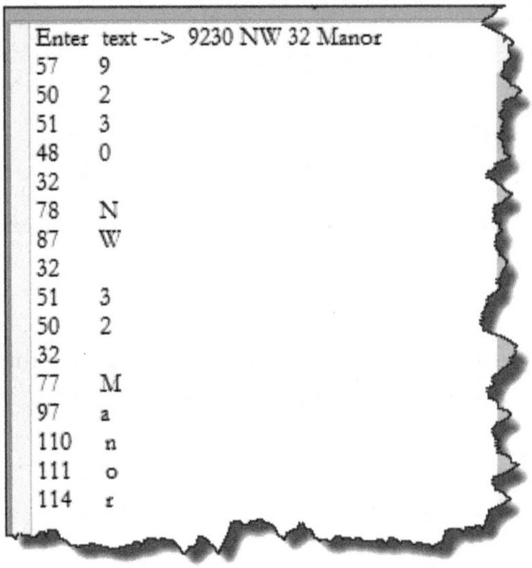

```
Enter text --> 9230 NW 32 Manor
57      9
50      2
51      3
48      0
32
78      N
87      W
32
51      3
50      2
32
77      M
97      a
110     n
111     o
114     r
```

Reading data from the keyboard and writing information to the screen are temporary means for input and output. In the real world data are inputted and outputted from and to other devices such as the disk. In these situations the data must be stored in files. When data are stored in files, each file must be given a name; likewise, most times one would like to know about the properties of a file. The following section details the class called **File**, which is part of the Java I/O system.

Self-Check

1. Consider the following two sets of statements and tell the effects of each of them.

    System.in.read()   Scanner s = new Scanner(System.in);

                                        s.readInt()

2. Select (true or false). The statements - System.in and System.out - are ways of temporarily handle data in primary memory.

3. Study the program below. What output is generated when it reads the following number: 1250?

```java
class StandardInputAppend {
    public static void main (String [] args) throws java.io.IOException {
        int ch;
        String s = "";
        System.out.print ("Enter  text --> ");

        while ((ch = System.in.read ()) != '\n')
            s = s + (char)ch + "+";
        System.out.println (s );
    }
}
```

4. Explain the similarities and differences between **System.out** and **System.err**.

The class File Class

The class **File** represents the name of a file or directory on the host file system. The class does not handle file manipulation such as reading or writing; instead it provides information about the properties of a file. Three of its four overloaded constructors are as follows:

- File(String directoryPath)   Creates a new File instance by converting the given pathname string into an abstract pathname.

- File(String directoryPath, String filename)   Creates a new File instance from a parent pathname string, and a child pathname string.

- File(File directoryObject, String filename)   Creates a new File instance from a parent abstract pathname, and a child pathname string.

The following two Java statements have the same results:

- File f = new File ("C:\\encryption\\Cipher.java");
- File f = new File ("C:\\encryption", "Cipher.java");

The string representing directory separator is system dependent. Whereas Windows uses the double backslash as shown in the above examples, Unix and Mac use a single forward slash (/).

The class File has several methods. These methods can be divided into two groups – one group that tests and reports on the nature of the file object, and the other group that accesses file objects for file attributes.

Methods for Testing File Objects

Once you have a file object, you can ask questions about some properties of the file such as the following:

Methods		Description
boolean	exists()	returns true/false about the existence/non-existence of file or directory object.
boolean	isDirectory()	returns true if the object is directory and false otherwise
boolean	isFile()	returns true if the object is file and false otherwise
boolean	isAbsolute()	returns true if the file object refers to an absolute path name, and false otherwise.
boolean	canRead()	returns true if you are permitted to read from the file and false otherwise.
boolean	canWrite()	returns true if you are permitted to write to the file and false otherwise
boolean	equals()	compare two file object if their names are the same. If they are equal, true is returned and false otherwise

Methods for Accessing File Objects

The methods for accessing information file object are as follows:

Methods	Description
String getName()	Returns a string object containing the name of the file, but not the path. If the file Represents a directory, only the directory name is returned.
String getPath()	Returns a string object containing the path of the file object, including the file or directory name.
String getAbsolutePath()	Returns the absolute path of the file or directory referenced by the current file object
String getParent()	Returns a string object containing the parent directory of the file or directory represented by the file object.
String[] list()	This method returns a list of the files in the directory named by this file
long length()	Returns a value of type long that is the number of bytes in the file
String toString()	This method returns a string representation of the current file object, and it is called automatically with a string object.
boolean delete()	Deletes the file specified by this object. If the file name is the name of a directory, the directory must first be emptied before it can be deleted.
boolean mkdir()	Creates a directory whose pathname is specified by this file object. It returns true if the directory was made.
boolean mkdirs()	Creates all directories whose pathnames are specified by this file object, including any necessary parent directories. It returns true if all the directories were made

boolean renameTo(File)   This method renames this file specified by this File object to the new file destination, given by the File argument

Listing 4.2 shows a class called FileAttributes. This class uses the class, File, to exhibit directories and ordinary files along the path **"C:\\answer\\"**.

```
1.   // Listing 4.2 Recursively list the contents of a directory
2.
3.   import java.io.File;
4.
5.   public class Directory_File
6.   {
7.     public static void main(String[] args)
8.     {
9.        File dir = new File("c:\\assgn1\\");
10.       listRecursive(dir);
11.    }
12.
13.    public static void listRecursive(File dir)
14.    {
15.      if (dir.isDirectory())
16.      {
17.        File[] f = dir.listFiles();
18.        for (File i : f)
19.        {
20.          if (i.isFile())
21.            System.out.println("\tFile: " + i.getAbsoluteFile() + "\t" + i.length()+ " bytes");
22.          else // (i.isDirectory())
23.          {
24.            System.out.println("Directory: " + i.getName());
25.            listRecursive(i);  // Recursive call
26.          }
27.        }
28.      }
29.    }
30. }
```

In the Listing, **Line 9** shows the creation of a File object using the given string that represents the path of the file. Notice that it uses the first constructor to create the object. **Line 15** determines those strings that represent directories. **Line 17** returns an array of the string of names along the current path. The body of the for loop determines those strings which represent ordinary files, or if they represent directories. If the string does not represent an ordinary file but instead a directory, the method is called again to perform the same test on this new directory.

Figure 4.2 shows the output from the program.

Figure 4.2 A list of the files and directories within the path C:\\assign1

```
                              General Output
------------------Configuration: <Default>-------------------
      File: c:\assgn1\Assignment_2.rar    25744 bytes
Directory: Cryptograph
Directory: build
Directory: classes
      File: c:\assgn1\Cryptograph\build\classes\.netbeans_automatic_build 0 bytes
      File: c:\assgn1\Cryptograph\build\classes\.netbeans_update_resources    0 bytes
Directory: cryptograph
      File: c:\assgn1\Cryptograph\build\classes\cryptograph\Caesar.class  1467 bytes
      File: c:\assgn1\Cryptograph\build\classes\cryptograph\CaesarCipher.class    1021 bytes
      File: c:\assgn1\Cryptograph\build\classes\cryptograph\Cipher.class  1620 bytes
      File: c:\assgn1\Cryptograph\build\classes\cryptograph\Constants.class   438 bytes
      File: c:\assgn1\Cryptograph\build\classes\cryptograph\Cryptograph.class 1984 bytes
      File: c:\assgn1\Cryptograph\build\classes\cryptograph\Reverser.class   1383 bytes
      File: c:\assgn1\Cryptograph\build\classes\cryptograph\Transpose.class   882 bytes
      File: c:\assgn1\Cryptograph\build.xml    3618 bytes
      File: c:\assgn1\Cryptograph\manifest.mf 85 bytes
Directory: nbproject
      File: c:\assgn1\Cryptograph\nbproject\build-impl.xml     79335 bytes
      File: c:\assgn1\Cryptograph\nbproject\genfiles.properties    475 bytes
Directory: private
      File: c:\assgn1\Cryptograph\nbproject\private\private.properties    114 bytes
      File: c:\assgn1\Cryptograph\nbproject\project.properties    2445 bytes
      File: c:\assgn1\Cryptograph\nbproject\project.xml    519 bytes
Directory: src
Directory: cryptograph
      File: c:\assgn1\Cryptograph\src\cryptograph\Caesar.java 2333 bytes
      File: c:\assgn1\Cryptograph\src\cryptograph\Cipher.java 1518 bytes
      File: c:\assgn1\Cryptograph\src\cryptograph\Constants.java  404 bytes
      File: c:\assgn1\Cryptograph\src\cryptograph\Cryptograph.java    1682 bytes
      File: c:\assgn1\Cryptograph\src\cryptograph\Reverser.java   1012 bytes
      File: c:\assgn1\Cryptograph\src\cryptograph\Transpose.java  547 bytes
      File: c:\assgn1\Cryptograph.7z  15655 bytes
```

In the figure, notice that the absolute path and the size of each file are outputted as dictated by Line 21 of the codes i,getAbsoluteFile() and i.length().

Self-Check

1. Which of the following methods of the class File is used to test if a file or directory exists?
    (a) isFileOrDirectory()
    (b) isFile()
    (c) isDirectory()
    (d) exists()

2. True or False. Does creating a file object automatically create a disk file?
    (a) True
    (b) False

3. What File method creates a new disk directory?
    (a) mkdir()
    (b) dir()
    (c) makeDirectory()

    (d) new File("c:\\\\example\\\\input.txt");

    (e) createDirectory()

4.   What is the output of the following program?

```
import java.io.File;

class files
{
        public static void main(String args[])
        {
                File f = new File("c:\\java\\crse\\system.txt");
                System.out.print(f.getParent() + "\t" + f.getName());
        }
}
```

    (a) c:\java   system.txt
    (b) c:\java\crse   system.txt
    (c) java\crse   system.txt
    (d) c:\java\   crse\system.txt

5.   True or False. The class File can be used to read data from an external storage such as the hard drive.

6.   What is the output of the following program, given that the only files in the current directory are the two shown in the diagram to the right? Explain the reason for your choice.

```
import java.io.File;

class files
{
    public static void main(String args[])
    {
        File f = new File("system.txt");
        System.out.println(f.canRead() + "\t" + f.canWrite());
    }
}
```

    (a) true   false
    (b) false   true
    (c) true   true
    (d) false   false

7. What does a File object represent?
   (a) The name and path of a physical file or directory
   (b) A file or directory
   (c) A file or directory and its contents
   (d) All the data in a file

Customized File Class using JFileChooser

When selecting a file from the host file system, it is customary that we either specify the name of the file by typing it, or select it via some form of dialog box. While the former is simple enough, with today's volume of files on a storage medium, this method is losing its practicality. In addition, almost all application programs today use some form of graphical user interface program to select files. Using the second approach, Java provides the class **JFileChooser** that can be used to select files.

The class JFileChooser found the swing package provides a graphical user interface (GUI) for choosing files - by navigating the file system, and then either choosing a file or directory from a list, or entering the name of a file or directory. It cannot be over emphasized that a JFileChooser object only presents the GUI for choosing files. Once the file is selected it is the responsibility of the program to determine what must be done with the chosen file, such as opening or saving it, for reading and writing, respectively.

In this section we will use the JFileChooser class to define a customized class for selecting files. First we will examine some constants, constructors, and methods that are applicable to our design. To keep things simple, of the six overloaded constructors, we will create a JFileChooser object which points at the current working directory, represented by the string "**.**". When working with dialog boxes, in most cases the user is required to make confirm or reject a selection by pressing the **Yes/OK** button, or the **No/Cancel** button. The class provides the constant **APPROVE_OPTION** - for clicking the **Yes/OK** button. Likewise it uses the constant **CANCEL_OPTION** for clicking **No/Cancel**.

Of the several methods in the class, we will focus on only two of them:

    int showOpenDialog(null)

for bringing up the dialog box for selecting a file or directory; and

    File getSelectedFile()

that returns the name of the file object that was selected when the **OK** button was clicked.

In an attempt to selecting a file, two mishaps could happen – the **OK** button was not selected, or the file name was typed wrongly. In either case we would want to protect the program from crashing by applying exception handing. In the first case we could throw an instance of IOException, and in the second we could throw an instance of FileNotFoundException.

Listing 4.3 shows the customized class for selecting files. As you will notice, it uses the JFileChooser class as the focal point. The core of the class is bringing up the file dialog box for the purpose of selecting a file, as shown in **Line 16**.

```
1.   // Listing 4.3 Using the class JFileChooser select a files
2.
3.   import javax.swing.JFileChooser;
4.   import javax.swing.JOptionPane;
5.   import java.io.File;
6.   import java.io.FileNotFoundException;
7.   import java.io.IOException;
8.
9.   public class BasicFile
10.  {
11.      File f;
12.
13.      public BasicFile()
14.      {
15.          JFileChooser choose = new JFileChooser(".");
16.          int status = choose.showOpenDialog(null);
17.
18.          try
19.          {
20.              if (status != JFileChooser.APPROVE_OPTION)
21.                  throw new IOException();
22.
23.              f = choose.getSelectedFile();
24.
25.              if (!f.exists())
26.                  throw new FileNotFoundException();
27.
28.                          display(f.getName(), "FIle has been choosen",
                                    JOptionPane.INFORMATION_MESSAGE);
29.          }
30.          catch(FileNotFoundException e)
31.          {
32.              display("File not found ....", e.toString(), JOptionPane.WARNING_MESSAGE);
33.          }
34.          catch(IOException e)
35.          {
36.              display("Approve option was not selected", e.toString(),
                                        JOptionPane.ERROR_MESSAGE);
37.          }
38.      }
39.      void display(String msg, String s, int t)
40.      {
41.          JOptionPane.showMessageDialog(null, msg, s, t);
42.      }
43.  }
```

When attempting to select a file from the file dialog box, if the button marked **Open** is not chosen then IOException is thrown, and no further operation takes place. See Lines **20** and **21**. If no exception is raised, at this point the program goes on to **Line 23** to obtain a reference (**f**) to the (supposedly) selected file. If on the other hand, the user types the filename and then click the **Open** button, an IOException will not be thrown, even if the filename has been misspelled. In either case, if no exception is thrown the program goes on to **Line 23** to obtain the reference, **f**. Now, since **f** is a file object, it can be used it to interrogate the file, as shown on **Line 25** where it is used to determine if the actual file exists, and if not, it throws FileNotFoundException. At this point the exception is thrown, and no further operation takes place.

Listing **4.4** shows a typical test class. The class is designed to run continuously until the option 4 is selected, which terminates the program. The program simply brings up the open file dialog box when option 1 is selected, as shown in **Figure 4.3**.

```
1.    // Listing 4.4 The test class
2.
3.    import javax.swing.JOptionPane;
4.
5.    class TestFile
6.    {
7.        public static void main(String[] arg)
8.        {
9.            boolean done = false;
10.           BasicFile f;
11.
12.           String menu = "Enter option\n1. Open File\n2. ....\n4. Quit";
13.           while(!done)
14.           {
15.               String s = JOptionPane.showInputDialog( menu);
16.               try
17.               {
18.                   int i = Integer.parseInt(s);
19.                   switch(i)
20.                   {
21.                       case 1:
22.                           f = new BasicFile();
23.                       break;
24.                       case 4:
25.                           done = true;
26.                       break;
27.                       default:
28.                           display("This option is underfined", "Error");
29.                       break;
30.                   }
31.               }
32.               catch(NumberFormatException | NullPointerException e)
33.               {
34.                   display(e.toString(), "Error");
35.               }
36.           }
37.       }
```

```
38.        static void display(String s, String err)
39.        {
40.            JOptionPane.showMessageDialog(null, s, err, JOptionPane.ERROR_MESSAGE);
41.        }
42. }
```

The output shown in **Figure 4.3** opens a file dialog box for selecting a file. In this case the file called **BasicFile.java** is highlighted as the selected file. Notice the file name is reflected in the text field for the filename.

Figure 4.3 File dialog box for selecting file

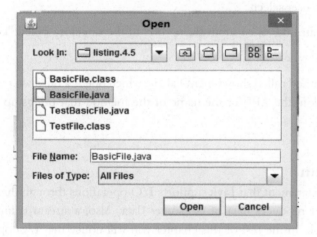

Now that our program can select files, we can improve on the class BasicFile to provide us more information about the selected file, by incorporating methods from the class **File**. Below are some methods that are added to the class BasicFile.

```
String getPath(){
    return f.getAbsolutePath();
}

long getFileSize(){
    return f.length();
}

String canRead(){
    return (f.canRead())? "This file can be opened for reading": "Cannot read this file";
}

String directoryOrFile(){
    return (f.isDirectory())? "This is a directory and not an ordinary file": "This is a file and not
    a directory";
```

```
      }

String exists(){
    return (f.exists())? "The physical file exists": "The physical file does not exists";
}
```

Self-Check

1. What is the purpose of the JFileChooser class?

2. Given that **jfc** is a reference variable to a JFileChooser. Use this variable to write a java statement that will retrieve the file that the user selects.

3. Write a Java statement that creates the open input dialog box in the directory called "computer science" on drive C.

4. The class JFileChooser has a method called showOpenDialog() which opens a file dialog box from which you can select files. Look in the API for the name of the method that brings up the save dialog box for saving file.

Java Input ▪ Output System

We began the chapter with the statement that **Java** supports I/O operations through the concept of streams, and that a stream either produces data or consumes data. Also, a stream is linked to a physical device such as the hard disk. In the rest of this chapter you will notice that I/O operations involve three basic steps, taken in order:

1. Open an input/output stream associated with a physical device by constructing an appropriate I/O stream objects.

2. Read from the opened input stream until end-of-stream is encountered, or write to the opened output stream.

3. Close the stream, especially the output streams. If output streams are not closed, then chances are that any data remaining in the stream may not be outputted, or worst nothing gets written to the file.

The **java.io** system can be divided into two broad categories, namely – character streams and byte streams: Character stream classes allow the program to read characters of data from character input streams, and to write characters of data to character output streams. Byte stream classes on the other hand allow the program to read bytes of data from byte input streams, and to write bytes of data to byte output streams. IO classes that end with the word **Stream** are byte oriented streams, as in the case of the class FileInputStream. Character stream classes on the other hand end with the word **reader** and writer for input and for output, respectively. In summary, the class InputStream and its subclasses are meant for reading streams of bytes such as image data. The classes **Reader** and **Writer**, and their subclasses are meant for reading and writing text.

Byte Oriented Input Streams

Byte stream classes use two class hierarchy structures – one for reading and the other for writing. The class InputStream, used for reading, is the super class for all byte input stream classes. **Figure 4.4** shows the hierarchy of byte input stream classes.

Figure 4.4 Byte Input stream classes

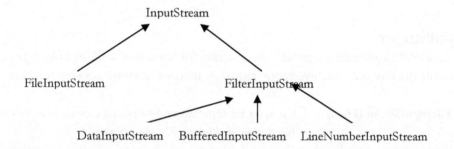

InputStream

The class **InputStream** is the superclass of all byte input streams. As an abstract class it provides the basic input methods for reading bytes from an input stream. Subclasses of this class override some of these basic methods for their implementation. The class has a single parameter less constructor and ten methods. The methods are described below:

Input methods	Description
int read() throws IOException	Reads the next byte of data from the input stream and returns the integer representation of the byte in the range 0 to 255.
int read(byte[] array) throws IOException	Reads some number of bytes from the input stream and stores them into the array b.
int read(byte[] array, int begin, int n) throws IOException	Reads up to **n** bytes of data from the input stream into an array of bytes

Mark and Reset Methods	Description
void mark(int limit)	Marks the current position in this input stream.
boolean markSupported()	Tests if this input stream supports the mark and reset methods
void reset() throws IOException	Repositions this stream to the position at the time the mark method was last called on this input stream.

Other methods	Description
int available() throws IOException	Returns an estimate of the number of bytes that can be read (or skipped over) from this input stream
long skip(long n) throws IOException	Skips over and discards **n** bytes of data from this input stream.
void close()throws IOException	Closes this input stream and releases any system resources associated with it.

The class InputStream is an abstract class; in addition, its read methods are not class methods, hence we are not able to use them directly to read data. Instead, we use its subclasses to read data. For example we can use the subclass FileInputStream to read data.

FileInputStream

The class FileInputStream constructs a byte stream for input from a file in a file system, or a string that represents the filename. The two more frequently used, of the three constructors are:

- **FileInputStream(File f)**   Creates a FileInputStream by opening a connection to an actual file, represented by the File object named **f**.
- **FileInputStream(String s)**   Creates a FileInputStream by opening a connection to an actual file, represented by the path named **s** in the file system.

In either case, if the file is nonexistent Java will throw FileNotFoundException. In addition, the class does not provide any new methods. It uses the methods inherited from InputStream.

FilterInputStream

The class **FilterInputStream** accepts some other input stream object, and transform this stream so that newly created stream can be read in a specialized way such as the case of its subclasses DataInputStream, BufferedInputStream, and LineNumberInputStream. This is made possible by it overriding all methods of InputStream. In addition, the subclasses themselves do not only include additional methods, but further override some of the methods that they inherit.

DataInputStream

The DataInputStream class enables you to read Java primitives instead of bytes only, from InputStream. This is useful if the data you want to read consists of Java primitive types including boolean values. The class has only one constructor as shown below.

DataInputStream(InputStream in)   Creates a DataInputStream that uses the specified underlying InputStream.

The following methods are unique to the class. In addition, they all throw IOException.

Methods		Description
boolean	readBoolean()	Reads returns the next boolean value.
byte	readByte()	Reads returns the next byte value.
char	readChar()	Reads returns the next character value.
double	readDouble()	Reads returns the next double value.
float	readFloat()	Reads returns the next float value.
int	readInt()	Reads returns the next int value.
long	readLong()	Reads returns the next long value.
short	readShort()	Reads returns the next short value.
int	readUnsignedByte()	Reads returns the next unsigned byte value.
int	readUnsignedShort()	Reads returns the next unsigned short value.
String	readUTF()	Reads returns the next Unicode character value.

BufferedInputStream

BufferedInputStream reads data from an InputStream by using a buffer to optimize the reading speed. It also reduces disk or network access. When a BufferedInputStream is created, an internal buffer array is created. As bytes from the stream are read, the buffer is refilled as necessary. So, whenever the program calls for data, the data is now read out of the buffer rather directly from the source – the disk, for example. The two constructors of the class are shown below:

- **BufferedInputStream(InputStream** in)   Creates a BufferedInputStream with a default buffer of 8KB (8192 bytes)

- **BufferedInputStream(InputStream** in, int size)   Creates a BufferedInputStream with a specified buffer size.

As you would have noticed, the default buffer size is 8 kilobytes. The recommended user defined buffer size should be in multiplies of 1 KB (1024 bytes). The class does not have any additional methods as in the case of the FilterInputStream class.

Listing **4.5** illustrates by contrast the advantage of using buffering as opposed to not using buffering, when reading data. As you will noticed, the method **unbufferedTime()** creates an unbuffered object using the class FileInputStream, which is not a buffered stream. It simply uses the while loop to read the file until it is empty. While the reading is being performed it is being timed as shown by **Lines 44** and **49**. The method **bufferedTime()** on the other hand, creates a buffered object using the class BufferedInputStream, and a buffer size of 4 KB (4096 bytes). See **Line 56**. Similar to the previous method, the reading is also timed.

```
1.   // Listing 4.5 Buffering vs. Unbuffering
2.
3.   import javax.swing.JFileChooser;
```

```
4.    import java.io.File;
5.    import java.io.FileNotFoundException;
6.    import java.io.IOException;
7.    import javax.swing.JOptionPane;
8.    import java.io.FileInputStream;
9.    import java.io.BufferedInputStream;
10.
11.   public class BasicFile
12.   {
13.       File f;
14.
15.       public BasicFile()
16.       {
17.           JFileChooser choose = new JFileChooser(".");
18.           int status = choose.showOpenDialog(null);
19.
20.           try
21.           {
22.               if (status != JFileChooser.APPROVE_OPTION) throw new IOException();
23.               f = choose.getSelectedFile();
24.               if (!f.exists()) throw new FileNotFoundException();
25.           }
26.           catch(FileNotFoundException e)
27.           {
28.               display(e.toString(), "File not found ....");
29.           }
30.           catch(IOException e)
31.           {
32.               display(e.toString(),  "Approve option was not selected");
33.           }
34.       }
35.
36.       void display(String msg, String s)
37.       {
38.           JOptionPane.showMessageDialog(null, msg, s, JOptionPane.ERROR_MESSAGE);
39.       }
40.
41.       void unbufferedTime() throws IOException
42.       {
43.           FileInputStream fis = new FileInputStream(f);
44.           System.out.println(f.getName() + " - " + f.length() + " bytes");
45.
46.           long startTime = System.nanoTime();
47.
48.           while(fis.read() != -1)
49.               ;
50.
51.           long endTime = System.nanoTime();
52.           System.out.println("Time elapse when unbuffered " + (endTime -
               startTime)/1000000.0 + " msec");
53.       }
```

```
54.        void bufferedTime() throws IOException
55.        {
56.            BufferedInputStream bis = new BufferedInputStream(new FileInputStream(f), 4096);
57.
58.            System.out.println(f.getName() + " - " + f.length() + " bytes");
59.            long startTime = System.nanoTime();
60.
61.            while(bis.read() != -1)
62.                ;
63.
64.            long endTime = System.nanoTime();
65.            System.out.println("Time elapse when buffered " + (endTime - startTime)/1000000.0
                + " msec");
66.        }
67. }
```

Listing 4.6 shows the test class which simply creates a BasicFile object for selecting a file. See **Line 11**. After selecting a file, you have the option of selecting one of the methods - unbufferedTime() or bufferedTime(). The time difference of these methods determines the efficiency of the classes - FileInputStream and BufferedInputStream.

```
1.   // Listing 4.6
2.
3.   import javax.swing.JOptionPane;
4.   import java.io.IOException;
5.
6.   class TestFile
7.   {
8.       public static void main(String[] arg)
9.       {
10.          boolean done = false;
11.          BasicFile f = new BasicFile();
12.
13.          while(!done)
14.          {
15.              String menu = "Enter option\n1. Unbuffered reading\n2. Buffered reading\n4.Quit";
16.              String s = JOptionPane.showInputDialog( menu);
17.              try
18.              {
19.                  int i = Integer.parseInt(s);
20.                  switch(i)
21.                  {
22.                      case 1:
23.                          f.unbufferedTime();
24.                      break;
25.                      case 2:
26.                          f.bufferedTime();
27.                      break;
28.                      case 4:
```

```
29.                              done = true;
30.                          break;
31.                      default:
32.                          System.out.println("This option is undefined");
33.                      break;
34.                  }
35.              }
36.              catch(NumberFormatException | NullPointerException | IOException e)
37.              {
38.                  System.out.println(e.toString());
39.              }
40.          }
41.      }
42.  }
```

The output shows a remarkable difference in the time it took to read the file when no buffering was applied, in comparison to when buffering was applied. See **Figure 4.5.** As you can see, the time it took to read the file when buffering was used was negligible compared to when no buffering was used.

Figure 4.5

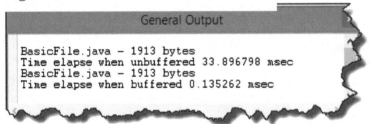

```
General Output

BasicFile.java - 1913 bytes
Time elapse when unbuffered 33.896798 msec
BasicFile.java - 1913 bytes
Time elapse when buffered 0.135262 msec
```

Self-Check

1. What class is the super class of all streams that input byte-oriented data?
    (a) ByteInputStream
    (b) BufferedInputStream
    (c) InputStream
    (d) FilterInputStream

2. Which of the following opens the file "input.txt" for input?
    (a) FileInputStream fis = new FileInputStream(new File("input.txt"));
    (b) FileInputStream fis = new FileInputStream(new File("input.txt"), true);
    (c) FileInputStream fis = new FileInputStream(new BufferedInputStream("input.txt"));
    (d) FileInputStream fis = new FileInputStream("input.txt");

3. Name the class that allows reading of binary representations of Java primitives from a byte input stream.

4. Name the exception thrown by the read method defined in InputStream class.

5. Which of the following class is inherited by FilterInputStream?
   (a) InputStream
   (b) FileInputStream
   (c) BufferedInputStream
   (d) BufferedFileInputStream

6. What happens when the constructor for the class FileInputStream fails to open a file for reading?
   (a) It throws IOException
   (b) It throws FileNotFoundException
   (c) It returns null
   (d) It throws DataFormatException
   (e) It creates the file

Byte Oriented Output Streams

Just as byte oriented input streams read data byte per byte, byte oriented outputs streams write data in terms of bytes. The class OutputStream, used for writing, is the super class for all byte output stream classes. **Figure 4.6** shows the hierarchy of byte output stream classes.

Figure 4.6 Byte Output stream classes

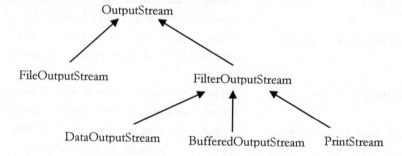

OutputStream

The class OutputStream is the superclass of all byte output streams. It is an abstract class that provides the basic output methods for writing bytes to an output stream. Subclasses of this class override some or all of these basic methods for their implementation. The class has a single parameter less constructor. The class has only five methods as shown below.

Methods	Description
• void close()	Closes the output stream and releases any system resources associated with it.
• void flush()	Flushes this output stream and forces any buffered output bytes to be written out.
• void write(byte[ ] b)	Writes **b**.length number of bytes from the specified array to this output stream.
• void write(byte[] b, int off, int n)	Writes **n** bytes from the specified array starting at offset off to this output stream.
• void write(int b)	Writes the specified byte to this output stream.

All these methods throw IOException. Because the class is an abstract class, we look to its subclasses to provide appropriate functionality to these methods.

FileOutputStream

A FileOutputStream object is an output stream for writing bytes of data to a file. That is, the class is designed to write streams such as image (which are non-text) data. If the file exists the data is written to it. If the file does not exist, it will be created, and the data is written to it. Four of the more popular constructors are shown below:

Constructor	Description
FileOutputStream(File f)	Creates a file output stream to write to the file represented by the specified File object.
FileOutputStream(File f, boolean append)	Creates a file output stream to which data can be appended to the file represented by the specified File object.
FileOutputStream(String f)	Creates a file output stream to write to the file with the specified name represented by the given string.
FileOutputStream(String f, boolean append)	Creates a file output stream to which data can be appended to the file by the specified name.

The program shown in **Listing 4.7** reads data from the file **a.txt,** and writes it to the file **a2.txt**. The class DataInputStream is used to read the data, and the class FileOutputStream writes the data to the file a2.txt.

```
1.   // Listing 4.7 Appending data to a file
2.
3.   import java.io.DataInputStream;
4.   import java.io.FileInputStream;
5.
6.   import java.io.FileOutputStream;
```

```
7.
8.    import java.io.IOException;
9.    import java.io.FileNotFoundException;
10.
11.   public class AppendToFile
12.   {
13.        public static void main(String[] args)
14.        {
15.             FileOutputStream fos = null;
16.             try
17.             {       // Create DataInputStream object
18.                  DataInputStream dis = new DataInputStream(new FileInputStream("a.txt"));
19.
20.                  fos = new FileOutputStream("a2.txt", true);
21.
22.                  int length = dis.available();  // available stream to be read
23.                  byte[] buf = new byte[length]; // create buffer
24.                  dis.readFully(buf); // read the full data into the buffer
25.
26.                  fos.write(buf, 0, buf.length);
27.             }
28.             catch(FileNotFoundException e)
29.             {
30.                  System.out.println("Error: while opening file:\n" + e);
31.             }
32.             catch( IOException e)
33.             {
34.                  System.out.println("Error while reading stream:\n" + e);
35.             }
36.        }
37.   }
```

In the listing, line 18 shows where a DataInputStream object is created with the source file **a.txt**, a text file. It also creates a FileOutputStream object that data can be appended to it at some other times when the program runs. See Line 20. As you would have noticed, **Line 22** gets the size of the file; **Line 23** creates an array of the size of the file; and Line 24 reads the data in one go. Line 26 simply writes the data to the output file with write operation.

Figure 4.7 shows the input file, a.txt.

Figure 4.7

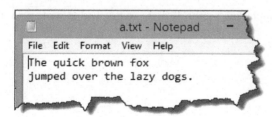

Figure 4.8 shows the output from the program. Notice that the file contains twice the input. This happens because of two things. First, the output file was created as an appendable file. **See Listing 4.5, Line 20**; by setting the second parameter to true, sets the stage for data to be appended to the file on subsequent execution of the program. Secondly, the program was executed two separate times; the file was not over written, but instead the data was simply appended. If the parameter was set to false, or if the single parameter constructor was used, the contents of the file would have been over written on subsequent execution of the program.

Figure 4.8

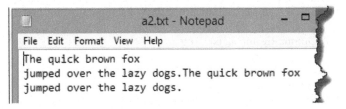

These two classes, DataInputStream and DataOutputStream are perfect candidates for copying text files as well as image files[1].

FilterOutputStream

The class **FilterOutputStream** accepts an OutputStream object, and transforms this stream so that newly created stream can be written to it, in a specialized way such as in the case of its subclasses – BufferedOutputStream, DataOutputStream, and PrintStream. This is made possible by it overriding all methods of OutputStream. In addition, the subclasses themselves do not only override some of the methods that they inherit, but they also include additional methods of their own.

DataOutputStream

The DataOutputStream class enables you to write Java primitive types, instead of only bytes, to an outputStream. This is useful if the data you want to write consists of Java primitive types including boolean values. The class has only one constructor as shown below.

DataOutputStream(InputStream out)   Creates a DataOutputStream that uses the specified underlying OutputStream.

As mentioned, the class has several methods, including methods that can be used to write primitive data types. See below.

---

[1] Copying image files will be left as an exercise.

Method		Description
void	writeBoolean(boolean b)	Writes a boolean value to the underlying output stream as a 1-byte value.
void	writeByte(int b)	Writes out a byte value to the underlying output stream as a 1-byte value.
void	writeBytes(String s)	Writes out the string to the underlying output stream as a sequence of bytes.
void	writeChar(int ch)	Writes a char to the underlying output stream as a 2-byte value. The high byte is written first.
void	writeChars(String ch)	Writes a string to the underlying output stream as a sequence of characters.
void	writeDouble(double d)	Converts the double argument **d** to a long using the doubleToLongBits method in class Double, and then writes that long value to the underlying output stream as an 8-byte quantity. The high byte is written first.
void	writeFloat(float f)	Converts the float argument **f** to an int, using the floatToIntBits method in class Float, and then writes that int value to the underlying output stream as a 4-byte quantity. The high byte is written first.
void	writeInt(int i)	Writes an int to the underlying output stream as four bytes. The high byte is written first.
void	writeLong(long l)	Writes a long to the underlying output stream as eight bytes. The high byte is written first.
void	writeShort(int s)	Writes a short to the underlying output stream as two bytes. The high byte is written first.
void	writeUTF(String s)	Writes a string to the underlying output stream using modified UTF-8 encoding in a machine-independent manner.

All of these methods have one thing in common. They all throw IOException, which must be taken into account when used in a program.

In **Listing 4.8** we will create a **.dat** file called **employee.dat** to store data. A **.dat** file stores arbitrary data. A file with this extension is not associated with any one particular program, or application, such as **.docx**, or **.java**. In this case you have to figure out how to open it, because different **.dat** files may be opened with different programs. The best way to open a **.dat** file is to use the program that created it. In this case we will use DataOutputStream to create it, and DataInputStream to open and read it. See **Lines 16** and **42**, respectively.

```
1.   /* Listing 4.8
2.   * This program:
3.   * Firstly, creates a DataOutputStream and writes data of different types to it.
4.   * Secondly, it reades back the data using a DataInputStream and display it.
5.   */
6.   import java.io.DataInputStream;
7.   import java.io.FileInputStream;
8.   import java.io.DataOutputStream;
9.   import java.io.FileOutputStream;
10.  import java.io.IOException;
11.
12.  public class InputOutputStream
13.  {
14.      public static void main(String[] args) throws IOException {
15.          boolean done = false;
16.          DataOutputStream dos = new DataOutputStream(
                                 new FileOutputStream("employee.dat"));
17.          dos.writeUTF("ABC Employees"); // Write a String value to the output stream
18.
19.          while (!done) {
20.              int s = GetData.getInt("Select\n1. To enter more data\n2. If you are done");
21.              if (s == 2)
22.                  done = true;
23.              else {
24.                  // Collecting data via JOptionPane
25.                  String id = GetData.getString("Enter Id number");
26.                  String name = GetData.getString("Enter name");
27.                  int age = GetData.getInt("Enter age in years");
28.                  int married = GetData.getInt("Enter marital status: [1]
                                 Married [2] Unmarried");
29.                  boolean marital_status = (married == 1);
30.                  double money = GetData.getDouble("Enter salary");
31.
32.                  // Write the data to a DataOutputStream
33.                  dos.writeUTF(id); // String
34.                  dos.writeUTF(name); // String
35.                  dos.writeInt(age); // int value
```

```
36.                         dos.writeBoolean(marital_status); // boolean value
37.                         dos.writeDouble(money); // double value
38.                     }
39.                 }
40.             try {
41.                     // Create a DataInputStream
42.                     DataInputStream dis = new DataInputStream(
                                        new FileInputStream("employee.dat"));
43.                     // Read and display the data from the input stream
44.                     System.out.println(dis.readUTF()); // Read the first line - the title
45.
46.                     while(dis != null)  {
47.                             System.out.println("Id    : " + dis.readUTF());
48.                             System.out.println("Name   : " + dis.readUTF());
49.                             System.out.println("Age   : " + dis.readInt());
50.                             System.out.println("Married: " + dis.readBoolean());
51.                             System.out.println("Salary : " + dis.readDouble());
52.                             System.out.println();
53.                         }
54.                 }
55.             catch(IOException e) {
56.
57.                 }
58.         }
59. }
```

As you would have seen, the data is gathered as type String, int, and double. See **Lines 25** thru **27** and **Line 30**. Line 33 thru 37 show the data being written to the output stream in the form of String, int, double, and boolean. Once the file is created, it is opened and read back. Its contents is then displayed on the console. See **Lines 44**, and **48** thru **51**.

Figure 4.9 shows what is supposed to be the contents of the file when Notepad was used to open it. As you may know, Notepad can open any kind of file, even image and video files and display them as text. Almost all of the contents of the file will most likely be gibberish, but sometimes at the beginning or at the end of the file, you will see some useful information, as you notice in the Figure.

Figure 4.9

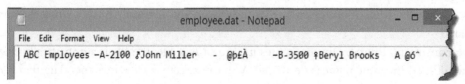

Instead of using Notepad or any such program, we will use the class DataInputStream to open and read the file. Referring to **Listing 4.8**, Line **42** opens the file **employee.dat**. **Line 44** reads the title of the file. Likewise, **Lines 48** thru **52** read the respective data value from the file and displays in on the screen. See **Figure 4.10**.

Figure 4.10

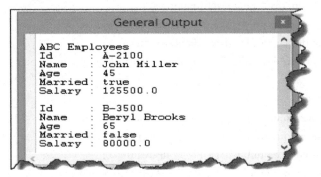

```
                    General Output                    ×

  ABC Employees
  Id      : A-2100
  Name    : John Miller
  Age     : 45
  Married : true
  Salary  : 125500.0

  Id      : B-3500
  Name    : Beryl Brooks
  Age     : 65
  Married : false
  Salary  : 80000.0
```

BufferedOutputStream

BufferedOutputStream writes data to an OutputStream by using a buffer to optimize the writing speed. It also reduces disk or network access. When a BufferedOutputStream is created, an internal buffer array is created. As bytes from the stream are written, the buffer is refilled as necessary. So, whenever the program is ready to write data, the data is moved out of the buffer to the destination – the disk, for example. The constructors of the class are as follows:

BufferedOutputStream(OutputStream out)	Creates a BufferedOutputStream with a default buffer of 8KB (8192 bytes)
BufferedInputStream(OutputStream out, int size)	Creates a BufferedOutputStream with a specified buffer size.

The class does not have any additional methods as in the case of the FileOutputStream class. In addition, it is best to use buffer sizes that are multiples of 1024 bytes. For example the specification can be written as follows: **n * 1024**, where **n** is an integer value.

PrintStream

The class PrintStream is used for character output to a text file as well as to standard output. The class prints formatted output of every primitive types, as well as string values. This stream can be designated as "autoflush" when it is created so that the stream automatically flushes when the current line is terminated.

When you construct a PrintStream that writes its output to a file, the file is automatically created. Any pre-existing file by the same name is destroyed. You can specify a character encoding that it must use to construct the object. The file closes automatically when the program ends without using the close() method. However, it is recommended you close the file before terminating the program.

The class has several overloaded constructors as shown below.

Constructors	Description
PrintStream(File file)	Creates a print stream, without automatic line flushing, with the specified file.
PrintStream(File file, String charset)	Creates a print stream, without automatic line flushing, with the specified file and charset.
PrintStream(OutputStream out)	Creates a print stream.
PrintStream(OutputStream out, boolean autoFlush)	Creates a print stream.
PrintStream(OutputStream out, boolean autoFlush, String charset)	Creates a print stream
PrintStream(String fileName)	Creates a print stream, without automatic line flushing, with the specified file name.
PrintStream(String fileName, String charset)	Creates a print stream, without automatic line flushing, with the specified file name and charset.

As mentioned, the class has several overloaded methods for each primitive type and arrays of types. If we re-call the variable, **out**, in the class **System**, this variable is of type PrintStream. Hence the statement, **System.out** was used to call any of these overloaded print(), println() and write() methods.

	Method	Description
void	close()	Closes the stream and releases any system resources associated with it.
void	flush()	Flushes the stream.
void	print(boolean b)	Prints a boolean value.
void	print(char c)	Prints a character.
void	print(char[] s)	Prints an array of characters.
void	print(double d)	Prints a double-precision floating-point number.
void	print(float f)	Prints a floating-point number.
void	print(int i)	Prints an integer.
void	print(long l)	Prints a long integer.
void	print(Object obj)	Prints an object.
void	print(String s)	Prints a string.

void	println()	Terminates the current line by writing the line separator string.
void	println(boolean x)	Prints a boolean value and then terminates the line.
void	println(char x)	Prints a character and then terminates the line.
void	println(char[] x)	Prints an array of characters and then terminates the line.
void	println(double x)	Prints a double-precision floating-point number and then terminates the line.
void	println(float x)	Prints a floating-point number and then terminates the line.
void	println(int x)	Prints an integer and then terminates the line.
void	println(long x)	Prints a long integer and then terminates the line.
void	println(Object x)	Prints an Object and then terminates the line.
void	println(String x)	Prints a String and then terminates the line.
void	setError()	Indicates that an error has occurred.
void	write(char[] buf)	Writes an array of characters.
void	write(char[] buf, int off, int len)	Writes A Portion of an array of characters.
void	write(int c)	Writes a single character.
void	write(String s)	Writes a string.
void	write(String s, int off, int len)	Writes a portion of a string.

Listing 4.9 and Listing **4.10** show two programs. With the exception of Line 15, these two programs are identical. In Listing 4.9 the output is directed to the standard output, and in Listing 4.10 the output is directed to the file, **printstream.txt**.

```
1.   // Listing 4.9
2.
3.   import java.io.PrintWriter;
4.   import java.io.IOException;
5.
6.   public class MyPrintWriter
7.   {
8.       public static void main(String[] args) throws
         IOException
9.       {
10.          int x = 15;
11.          double y = 2.5;
12.          String s = "Hello there!!";
13.
14.          // create Printstream object
15.          PrintWriter pw = new
             PrintWriter(System.out);
16.          // Write to standard output
```

```
1.   // Listing 4.10
2.
3.   import java.io.PrintWriter;
4.   import java.io.IOException;
5.
6.   public class MyPrintWriter
7.   {
8.       public static void main(String[] args)
         throws IOException
9.       {
10.          int x = 15;
11.          double y = 2.5;
12.          String s = "Hello there!!";
13.
14.          // create Printstream object
15.          PrintWriter pw = new
             PrintWriter("printstream.txt");
16.          // Write to standard output
```

17.	pw.println(s + " \t");	17.	pw.println(s + " \t");
18.	pw.print("x is: ");	18.	pw.print("x is: ");
19.	pw.println(x);	19.	pw.println(x);
20.	pw.println("\t&");	20.	pw.println("\t&");
21.	pw.println("y is: " + y);	21.	pw.println("y is: " + y);
22.	pw.print("The End");	22.	pw.print("The End");
23.	pw.flush(); // flush the stream	23.	pw.flush(); // flush the stream
24.	}	24.	}
25. }		25. }	

Figure 4.11 and **Figure 4.12** show the output from these programs. If it were not for the title of each frame you could not tell which of the two outputs was generated by Listing 4.7(a) or which was generated by Listing 4.7(b), because both programs use the same methods. The difference is that the outputs are directed at two different output media..

Figure 4.11

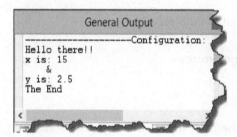

Figure 4.12

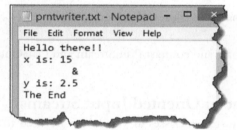

Self-Check

1. Which of these packages contain classes and interfaces used for input and output operations of a program?
   (a) java.util
   (b) java.lang
   (c) java.io
   (d) javax.swing

2. Which stream does Java application uses to read data from a peripheral source such as a file?

   (a) OutputStream

   (b) Input/OutputStream

   (c) InputStream

   (d) None of the above

3. Which of the following classes is the super class of all byte output stream classes?
   (a) OutputStream
   (b) ByteOutputStream

(c) ByteStream

(d) BinaryOutputStream

4. Which of the following opens the file "output.txt" for output by first deleting any file with that name?

(a) FileOutputStream fos = new FileOutputStream("output.txt", true);

(b) FileOutputStream fos = new FileOutputStream("output.txt");

(c) FileOutputStream fos = new FileOutputStream(new BufferedOutputStream("output.txt");

(d) FileOutputStream fos = new FileOutputStream(new File("output.txt", true));

5. What method does the class DataOutputStream has that determines the number of bytes in a file?

(a) length()

(b) available()

(c) size()

(d) getSize()

6. Compare and contrast FileOutputStream and DataOutputStream.

7. Compare and contrast PrintStream and DataOutputStream

Character Oriented Input Streams

Byte stream classes as you know are used to perform input and output of 8-bit bytes, but the character stream classes are used to perform input and output for 16-bit Unicode characters. **Figure 4.13** shows the hierarchy of the more frequently used classes from both sets of stream classes. The class Reader, used for reading, is the super class for all character input stream classes; and the class Writer, is the superclass for all character output streams. The Reader family reads two bytes at a time, and the Writer family writes two bytes at a time.

Figure 4.13 Character Input stream classes

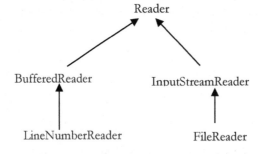

The class Reader

As mentioned, the **character input** stream classes read data from a stream as Unicode characters. The class **Reader**, an abstract class, is the base class for all character input stream classes. Its methods and their functionalities are shown below:

Input methods	Description
int read() throws IOException	Reads the next character of data from the input stream and returns the integer representation of the characters in the range 0 to 65535.
int read(char[] array) throws IOException	Reads some number of characters from the input stream and stores them into the array b.
abstract int read(char[] array, int begin, int n) throws IOException	Reads up to **n** characters of data from the input stream into an array of characters
int read(CharBuffer b)	Attempts to read characters into the specified character buffer.

Mark/reset methods	Description
void mark(int limit)	Marks the current position in this input stream.
boolean markSupported()	Tests if this input stream supports the mark and reset methods
void reset() throws IOException	Repositions this stream to the position at the time the mark method was last called on this input stream.

Other methods	Description
int available() throws IOException	Returns an estimate of the number of bytes that can be read (or skipped over) from this input stream
boolean ready()	Tells whether this stream is ready to be read.
long skip(long n) throws IOException	Skips over and discards **n** bytes of data from this input stream.
void close()throws IOException	Closes this input stream and releases any system resources associated with it.

InputStreamReader

The class InputStreamReader is a bridge from byte streams to character streams. It reads bytes and converts them into characters. The constructors for this class are shown below.

Constructors	Description
InputStreamReader(InputStream in)	Creates an InputStreamReader that uses the default charset.
InputStreamReader(InputStream in, Charset cs	Creates an InputStreamReader that uses the given charset.

InputStreamReader(InputStream in, CharsetDecoder dec)	Creates an InputStreamReader that uses the given charset decoder.
InputStreamReader(InputStream in, String ch)	Creates an InputStreamReader that uses the named charset.

Charset

Just like how there are different classifications of numbers, so there are different classifications of encoding schemes for the characters, defined in the class **Charset**. The first encoding standard was the ASCII scheme. This encoding scheme defines 127 different alphanumeric characters that could be used on the internet. This character set included the following: the digits (0-9), letters of the alphabet (A-Z, a- z), and some special characters like ! $ + - ( ) @ < >. Of the various encoding schemes, the UTF-8 covers almost all of the characters and symbols in the world. The table below shows the Charset set to which the class InputStreamReader refers.

Charset	Description
US-ASCII	Seven-bit ASCII of the Unicode character set
ISO-8859-1	ISO Latin Alphabet No. 1, a.k.a. ISO-LATIN-1
UTF-8	Eight-bit UCS Transformation Format
UTF-16BE	Sixteen-bit UCS Transformation Format, big-endian byte order
UTF-16LE	Sixteen-bit UCS Transformation Format, little-endian byte order
UTF-16	Sixteen-bit UCS Transformation Format, byte order identified by an optional byte-order mark

Just as there is Charset, there is the class CharsetDecoder, which is used to determine the encoding and Charset of a text.

FileReader

The class FileReader creates a Reader that is used to read 16-bits characters from a file. Its two most commonly used constructors are as follows:

Constructor	Description
FileReader(**File** file)	Creates a new FileReader, given the File to read from.
FileReader(**String** fileName)	Creates a new FileReader, given the name of the file to read from.

These constructors do not throw IOException, instead they throw FileNotFoundException. The class has no additional method of its own.

The method, fileReader seen in **Listing 4.11**, accepts a file object, and reads the contents of that file using the class FileReader. As you would have noticed, the method uses the reference variable, f, to create a FileReader object. See **Line 3**. Next, an array, the size of the file, is created. See **Line 4**. The entire file is then read all at once, as shown on **Line 6**. The contents of the array, which represents the contents of the file is displayed on the console.

// **Listing 4.11**

```
1.   void fileReader(File f) throws IOException
2.   {
3.        FileReader fr = new FileReader(f); //Creates a FileReader Object
4.        char arr[] = new char[(int)f.length()];
5.
6.        fr.read(arr); // Reads the content of the file into the array
7.
8.        for(char c : arr)
9.           System.out.print(c); // Displays the characters one by one
10.       fr.close();
11.  }
```

Figure 4.14 shown the output when displayed on the console. Notice that although we have used System.out.**print**, and not System.out.**println**, the output maintains end of line format as the input.

Figure 4.14

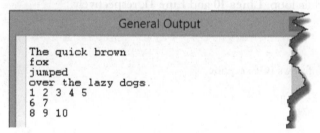

```
General Output

The quick brown
fox
jumped
over the lazy dogs.
1 2 3 4 5
6 7
8 9 10
```

BufferedReader

The class BufferedReader reads text from a character-input stream, buffering characters so as to provide for efficient reading. It provides efficiency in two ways – creating a buffer that speeds up the reading, and providing a method that reads entire lines of test at a time. The buffer size may be specified, or the default size may be used. The default is 8,192 characters. Its two constructors are as follows:

Constructor	Description
BufferedReader(**Reader** r)	Creates a buffering character-input stream that uses a default-sized input buffer.
BufferedReader (**Reader** r, int size)	Creates a buffering character-input stream that uses an input buffer of the specified size..

Neither constructor throws FileNotFoundException, nor IOException. However, the second throws IllegalArgumentException, if the specified buffer size is negative or zero.

The class, as mentioned, has an additional method, **readLine**. This method reads texts, line by line. A line is terminated by any one of the following: a line feed - ('\n'), a carriage return ('\r'), or a carriage return followed immediately by a linefeed. This method throws IOException.

LineNumberReader

The class LineNumberReader, a subclass of BufferedReader, does not only creates a buffer for reading text, or being able to read the text line by line, but it also keeps track of the line number in a file, and allows for setting line number. That is, the class defines two additional methods - setLineNumber(int) and getLineNumber() for setting and getting the current line number, respectively.

By default, line numbering begins at 0. This number increments at every line terminator as the data is read, and can be changed with a call to setLineNumber(int). The method, setLineNumber(int) does not actually change the current position in the stream; it only changes the value that will be returned by getLineNumber().

Listing 4.12 shows a method called readLineByLine which accepts a reference variable, **f**, which it uses to create a LineNumberReader object. See **Line 7**. The file is read one line at a time. As each line is read, it is displayed. See the while loop, **Lines 10** and **Line 11**, respectively.

```
// Listing 4.12

1.    void readLineByLine(File f) throws IOException
2.    {
3.         LineNumberReader lnr = null;
4.
5.         try {
6.              //Construct the LineNumberReader object
7.              lnr = new LineNumberReader(new FileReader(f));
8.              String line = "";
9.
10.             while ((line = lnr.readLine()) != null)
11.                  System.out.println("Line " + lnr.getLineNumber() + ": " + line);
12.        }
13.        finally {
14.             try //Close the LineNumberReader {
15.                  lnr.close();
16.             }
17.             catch (IOException e)
18.             {
19.                  e.printStackTrace();
20.             }
21.        }
22.   }
```

Figure 4.15 shows the contents of the file. Each line is preceded with identifying the line that was read, by displaying the line number. Notice also that the call lnr.getLineNumber(), returns the actual line number from the file.

Figure 4.15

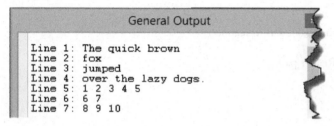

```
                        General Output

Line 1: The quick brown
Line 2: fox
Line 3: jumped
Line 4: over the lazy dogs.
Line 5: 1 2 3 4 5
Line 6: 6 7
Line 7: 8 9 10
```

Self-Check

1. What is the super class of all character-oriented input streams?
    (a) BufferedReader
    (b) FileReader
    (c) LineNumberReader
    (d) Reader

2. Which of the following opens the file "input.txt" for input?
    (a) InputStreamReader isr = new InputStreamReader (new File("input.txt"));
    (b) InputStreamReader isr = new InputStreamReader ("input.txt");
    (c) InputStreamReader isr = new InputStreamReader (new FileInputStream("input.txt"));
    (d) InputStreamReader isr = new InputStreamReader (FileReader("input.txt"));

3. What happens when the constructor for the class FileReader fails to open a file for reading?
    (a) It throws IOException
    (b) It throws FileNotFoundException
    (c) It returns null
    (d) It throws DataFormatException
    (e) It creates the file

5. Which class is more appropriate to determine the number of lines read in a file?
    (a) (a) FileChooser
    (b) BufferedReader
    (c) LineNumberReader
    (d) LineReader
    (e) BufferedLineReader

6.   The following code has syntax errors. Find the errors and fix them.

```
import java.io.Reader;

class MyReader
{
    BufferedReader br;
    MyReader(String path) throws new IOException
    {
        br = new BufferedReader(path);
    }
    void read()
    {
        br.readLine();
    }
}
```

Character Oriented Output Streams

The outputting of characters to a stream involves the automatic conversion of the data to the character set found on the host computer.   Unlike byte output streams which do not carry out conversion, these classes convert each character, a 16-bit value, to the corresponding character. In this regard you use character stream classes if you want to write ordinary text. All character output stream classes are derived from the abstract class called **Writer**; and all streams must be closed, otherwise the data may not be written to the file. **Figure 4.16** shows the class hierarchy of the character output stream classes.

Figure 4.16 Character Output stream classes

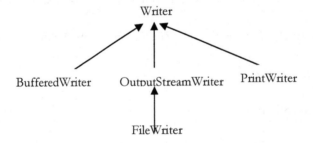

The class Writer

The class Writer, as shown in Figure 4.5 is the super class of all character output streams. As mentioned, it is an abstract that class that provides the basic output methods for writing characters to an output stream. Subclasses of this class override some or all of these basic methods for their implementation. Files that are opened must be closed in order for the contents of the buffer to be place in it.

The class has a single parameter less constructor. Its methods are shown below.

• Writer	append(char ch)	Appends the specified character to this writer.
• Writer	append(CharSequence ch)	Appends the specified character sequence to this writer.
• Writer	append (CharSequence ch, int start, int end)	Appends a subsequence of the specified character sequence to this writer.
• void	close()	Closes the output stream and releases any system resources associated with it.
• void	flush()	Flushes this output stream and forces any buffered output bytes to be written out.
• void	write(char[ ] b)	Writes b.length number of bytes from the specified array to this output stream.
• void	write(char[] b, int off, int len)	Writes n bytes from the specified array starting at offset off to this output stream.
• void	write(int b)	Writes the specified byte to this output stream.
• void	write(String str, int off, int len)	Writes a portion of a string.

All of these methods throw IOException. Since the class is an abstract class, we look to the subclasses to provide appropriate functionality to these methods.

OutputStreamWriter

The class OutputStreamWriter is a bridge from character streams to byte streams. That is, characters that are to be written to it are encoded into bytes using a specified Charset. The charset that it uses may be specified by name, or may be given explicitly, or the platform's default charset may be accepted. Each call to a write() method causes the character(s) to be encoded into its corresponding two bytes. A summary of its constructors are as follows:

Constructors	Description
• OutputStreamWriter(OutputStream out)	Creates an OutputStreamWriter that uses the default character encoding.
• OutputStreamWriter(OutputStream out, Charset cs)	Creates an OutputStreamWriter that uses the given Charset.
• OutputStreamWriter(OutputStream out, CharsetEncoder enc)	Creates an OutputStreamWriter that uses the given Charset encoder.
• OutputStreamWriter(OutputStream out, String charsetName)	Creates an OutputStreamWriter that uses the named Charset.

The only method that is added to this class the method **getEncoding()**, which returns a string representing the name of the character encoding being used by this stream.

FileWriter

The FileWriter class makes it possible to write a sequence of characters to a file. It works much like the FileOutputStream except that a FileOutputStream writes sequence of bytes, whereas a FileWriter writes a sequence of character. In addition, the class accepts file objects as well as file name represented by a string; and it allows appending to the file, or the over writing of a file. The four most used constructors are as follows:

Constructors	Description
FileWriter(File f)	Constructs a FileWriter object given a File object.
FileWriter(File f, boolean append)	Constructs a FileWriter object given a File object that allows appending to the file rather than over writing the file.
FileWriter(String fileName)	Constructs a FileWriter object given a file name.
FileWriter(String fileName, boolean append)	Constructs a FileWriter object given a file name with a boolean indicating whether or not to append data to the file, or write the file.

Listing 4.13 below shows three methods – getFile, readLineByLine and saveFile. The method getFile returns the file that was selected for reading the data. The second, readLineByLine, simply opens an input file, if it exists and reads the contents of the file into a string and returns this value. The third method saves the contents of the string in the file referenced by the variable, **f.**

```
// Listing 4.13

1.    File getFile()
2.    {
3.        return f;
4.    }
5.   String readLineByLine(File f) throws IOException
6.   {
7.        //Construct the LineNumberReader object
8.        LineNumberReader lnr = new LineNumberReader(new FileReader(f));
9.        String line = "", s = "";
10.
11.       while ((line = lnr.readLine()) != null)
12.           s = s + "Line : " + lnr.getLineNumber() + " " + line + "\n";
13.       return s;
14. }
15.
16. void saveFile() throws IOException
17. {
```

```
18.      JFileChooser choose = new JFileChooser(".");
19.      int status = choose.showSaveDialog(null);
20.
21.      if (status != JFileChooser.APPROVE_OPTION)
22.          throw new IOException();
23.      File f = choose.getSelectedFile();
24.
25.      FileWriter fw = new FileWriter(f);
26.      String s = readLineByLine(getFile());
27.      fw.write(s, 0, s.length());
28.      fw.flush();
29.      fw.close();
30. }
```

In the above listing, **Line 23** selects a file, represented by **f**, from the file dialog box, and uses this variable to create a FileWriter object to which the contents of **s** will be written. First we should note that if the file does not already exists, it will be created. If the name on the other hand represents a directory that exists, then it will point to that location, otherwise, it will throw IOException.

In this example the name of the selected file is **pqr.txt**. **Figure 4.17** shows the contents of the file when opened by Notepad. Notice that the newline feature was not observed.

Figure 4.17

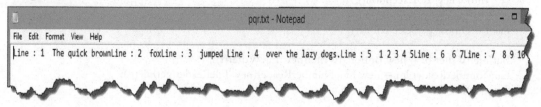

BufferedWriter

In general, a FileWriter sends its output immediately to the underlying character stream. Unless prompt output is required, it is advisable to use the BufferedWriter class, which buffers the text in order make sets of data to be released to the output stream. This class parallels the class BufferedOutputStream. Whereas the former outputs characters, the latter outputs bytes. The constructors of this class are shown below.

Constructor	Description
BufferedWriter(Writer out)	Creates a buffered character-output stream that uses a default-sized output buffer.

| BufferedWriter(Writer out, int size) | Creates a new buffered character-output stream that uses an output buffer of the given size. |

Like BufferedInputStream, BufferedWriter creates a new buffered character-output stream that uses an output buffer of the given size. If the specified buffer size is not positive, then **IllegalArgumentException** is thrown. The class recognizes new line separator, by implementing the method newLine, as shown below.

Method	Description
void newLine()	Writes a line separator. The line separator string is defined by the system property **line.separator**, which may be one or more newline ('\n') character.

Listing 4.14 shows the method saveFile which copies the contents of a file, using the class BufferedWriter to write the data into a file.

// Listing 4.14

```
1.   void saveFile() throws IOException
2.   {
3.       JFileChooser choose = new JFileChooser(".");
4.       int status = choose.showSaveDialog(null);
5.
6.       if (status != JFileChooser.APPROVE_OPTION)
7.           throw new IOException();
8.
9.       File f = choose.getSelectedFile();
10.
11.      BufferedWriter bf = new BufferedWriter(new FileWriter(f));
12.      LineNumberReader lnr = new LineNumberReader(new FileReader(getFile()));
13.      String line = "";
14.
15.      while ((line = lnr.readLine()) != null)
16.      {
17.          bf.write(line, 0, line.length());
18.          bf.newLine();
19.      }
20.      bf.flush();
21.      bf.close();
22.  }
```

In the listing **Line 11** creates a BufferedWriter with the reference of the file variable, **f**, by first creating a FileWriter object. As the lines are read (**Line 15**), they are written to the output file. See **Line 17**. The new line is appended as shown in **Line 18**.

Figure 4.18 and **Figure 4.19** show the result of the program. **Figure 4.9** shows the input and **Figure 4.10** shows the copied result.

Figure 4.18

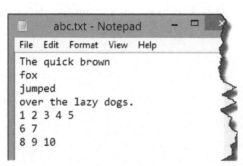

Figure 4.19

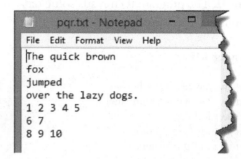

This segment of code can be adopted for copying a textfile.

PrintWriter

The class PrintWriter parallels the class PrintStream. Whereas PrintStream directs the output to the console, PrintWriter directs its output to a file. This means that the output from PrintStream is temporary, whereas the output from PrintWriter is permanent on the device on which the output is written. In this regard PrintStream should be used to display information when developing a program, and PrintWriter should be used for formatted output on a permanent basis.

PrintWriter defines eight overloaded constructors, of which the six most popular ones are shown below.

Constructors	Description
PrintWriter(File file)	Creates a PrintWriter, without automatically flushing the line.
PrintWriter(OutputStream out)	Creates a PrintWriter, without automatic line flushing, from an existing OutputStream.
PrintWriter(OutputStream out, boolean auto)	Creates a PrintWriter from an existing OutputStream, when **auto** is set to true.
PrintWriter(String fileName)	Creates a PrintWriter, without automatic line flushing, with the specified file name.
PrintWriter(Writer out)	Creates a PrintWriter, without automatic line flushing.
PrintWriter(Writer out, boolean auto)	Creates a PrintWriter with automatic flushing when **auto** is set to true

PrintWriter supports the print( ) and println( ) methods that are used by System.out for all types, including Object. That is, you can use these methods in the same way as they have been used with System.out. If an argument is not a primitive type, the PrintWriter methods call the object's toString( ) method and then prints the result.

Listing 4.15 shows the class BasicFile again. This time it includes a method called printWriter. The method first uses the selected file, represented by the file variable **f**, to create a PrintWriter object pw. See **Line 31**. The program then reads some data; see **Lines 39** thru **42**; then writes this data to the selected output file. See **Line 44**.

```java
1.    // Listing 4.15
2.
3.    import javax.swing.JFileChooser;
4.    import javax.swing.JOptionPane;
5.    import java.io.File;
6.    import java.io.IOException;
7.    import java.io.PrintWriter;
8.    import java.text.NumberFormat;
9.
10.   public class BasicFile {
11.       File f;
12.
13.       BasicFile(){
14.           try{
15.               JFileChooser choose = new JFileChooser(".");
16.               choose.setDialogTitle("Select or type file name to store database") ;
17.               int status = choose.showSaveDialog(null);
18.
19.               if (status != JFileChooser.APPROVE_OPTION)
20.                   throw new IOException();
21.               f = choose.getSelectedFile();
22.           }
23.           catch(IOException e) {
24.               JOptionPane.showMessageDialog(null, e.toString(), "Sorry - change my mind",
                  JOptionPane.WARNING_MESSAGE);
25.               System.exit(0);
26.           }
27.       }
28.
29.       void printWriter() throws IOException {
30.           NumberFormat nf = NumberFormat.getCurrencyInstance();
31.           PrintWriter pw = new PrintWriter(f);
32.           pw.println("Last name\tFirst name\tAge\tSalary");
33.           boolean done = false;
34.
35.           while (!done) {
36.               int option = GetData.getInt("More data\n1. Yes\n2. No");
37.               switch(option) {
38.                   case 1: // Read the data
39.                       String lname = GetData.getString("Enter last name");
40.                       String fname = GetData.getString("Enter first name");
41.                       int age = GetData.getInt("Enter age");
42.                       double salary = GetData.getDouble("Enter salary");
43.                       // Write data to the file
```

```
44.                        pw.print(lname + "\t" + fname + "\t\t" + age + "\t" + nf.format(salary));
45.                        pw.println();
46.                   break;
47.                   case 2:
48.                        done = true;
49.                   break;
50.                   default:
51.
52.                   break;
53.              }// switch
54.         } // while
55.         pw.flush();
56.         pw.close();
57.    }
58. }
```

The test class, **Listing 4.16**, creates a PrintWriter object by calling the method printWriter() in the class BasicFile. **Line 21** calls the method printWriter that generates the text that is to be written to the file.

```
1.    // Listing 4.16
2.
3.    import javax.swing.JOptionPane;
4.    import java.io.IOException;
5.
6.    class TestFile {
7.        public static void main(String[] arg) {
8.             boolean done = false;
9.             BasicFile f = new BasicFile();
10.
11.            String menu = "Enter option\n1.Collect an save data using PrintWriter..\n2... \n4. Quit";
12.            while(!done) {
13.                 String s = JOptionPane.showInputDialog( menu);
14.                 try {
15.                     int i = Integer.parseInt(s);
16.                     switch(i) {
17.                         case 1:
18.                             f.printWriter();
19.                         break;
20.                         case 4:
21.                             done = true;
22.                         break;
23.                         default:
24.                             display("This option is underfined", "Error");
25.                         break;
26.                     }
27.                 }
28.            catch(NumberFormatException | NullPointerException | IOException e)
```

```
29.              {
30.                   display(e.toString(), "Error");
31.              · }
32.          }
33.      }
34.      static void display(String s, String err)
35.      {
36.          JOptionPane.showMessageDialog(null, s, err, JOptionPane.ERROR_MESSAGE);
37.      }
38. }
```

When the program is executed, the file dialog box shows only six files – three Java files, and the compiled version of each file. See **Figure 4.20**. The output file as you would have noticed is non-existent in the file dialog box, but is being shown in the textfield for file name, while it is being typed ("prq.txt").

Figure 4.20

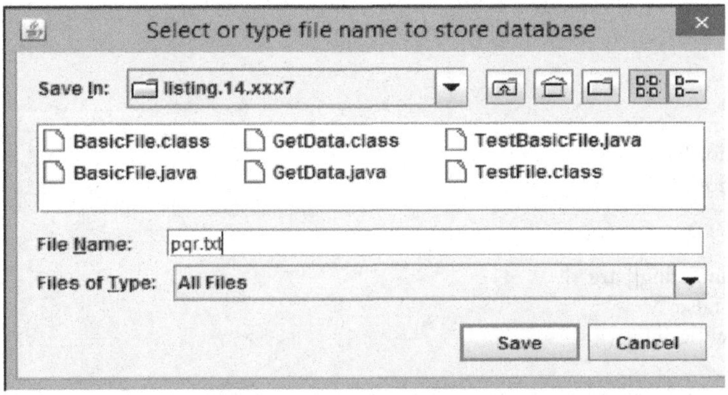

When the program runs, the data file "pqr.txt" is created. See **Figure 4.21**. This proves that FileWriter creates the output file if it did not already exists.

Figure 4.21

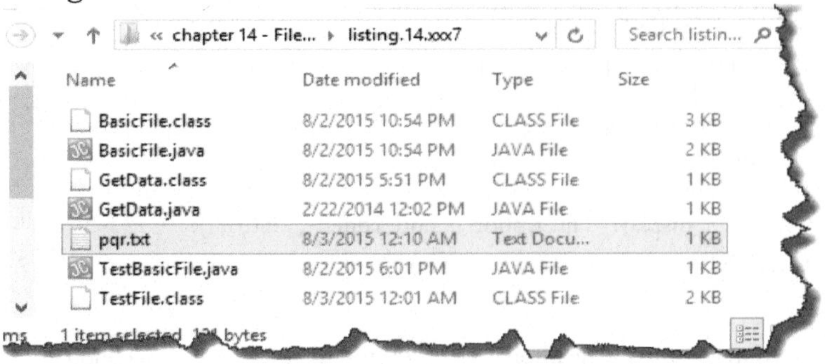

Figure 4.22 shows the contents of "pqr.txt" when opened in notepad. Notice that this output is similar to the output generated by System.out.

Figure 4.22

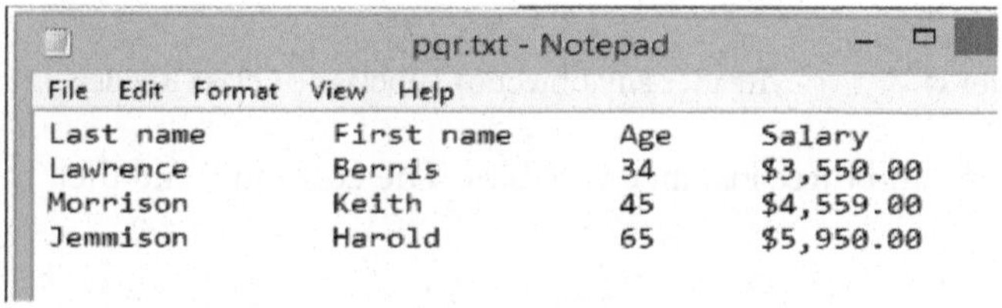

```
pqr.txt - Notepad                    –  □
File  Edit  Format  View  Help
Last name        First name     Age     Salary
Lawrence         Berris         34      $3,550.00
Morrison         Keith          45      $4,559.00
Jemmison         Harold         65      $5,950.00
```

Self-Check

1. What is the abstract superclass of character output streams called?
   (a) OutputStream
   (b) Writer
   (c) File
   (d) FileWriter
   (e) None of the above

2. What is the abstract superclass of character input streams called?
   (a) InputStream
   (b) Reader
   (c) File
   (d) FileReader
   (e) None of the above

3. What are the two types of I/O streams supported by Java?
   (a) byte and short
   (b) Short and character
   (c) byte and character
   (d) byte and int

4. Why is a PrintWriter object also needed in addition to a FileOutputStream object to save integers into a file?
   (a) Because a FileOutputStream object cannot write anything directly into a file. It must use the PrintWriter to write something to the file.
   (b) Because the PrinterWriter first print to the FileOutputStream.
   (c) The FileOutputStream is the input for the PrinteWriter.
   (d) FileOutputStream can write any data type that is supplied by the PrintWriter class.

The Class StreamTokenizer

The class **StreamTokenizer** is a character based input stream that parses its input into units of elements called tokens. The tokens are read one at a time. The tokenizer can recognize identifiers, numbers, quoted strings, and various comment styles. The way to tokenize an input stream is to first convert the input stream into a character stream, shown by the constructor below:

StreamTokenizer(Reader r)   - Reader any object of subclass of class Reader

A token is governed by four constants, and three instance variables. The constants and their meanings are shown below.

Constants	Description
TT_WORD	The token is a string that is stored in the variable **sval**.
TT_NUMBER	The token is a number (double) that is stored in the variable **nval**.
TT_EOF	The token is the end of file marker – the end of file has been reached.
TT_EOL	The token is an end of line marker – the end of a line has been read.

The three instance variables and their meanings are shown below.

Instance Variables	Description
sval	The token is a string values and it is stored in this variable.
nval.	The token which is a double value is stored in this variable.
ttype	This field contains the type of the token just read - . **TT_WORD, TT_NUMBER, TT_EOF, or TT_EOL**

The class also has several instance methods that parse characters/words, parse numbers, determine types of flags, and determine letter case as shown below.

Method		Description
void	commentChar(int ch)	Specified that the character argument starts a single-line comment.
void	eolIsSignificant(boolean flag)	When set to **true**, end of line is recognized.
int	lineno()	Return the current line number.
void	lowerCaseMode(boolean fl)	When set to **true** case sensitivity is ignored.
int	nextToken()	Parses the next token from the input.
void	ordinaryChar(int ch)	Specifies that the character argument is "ordinary" int. It removes any significance to the value of **ch**.

void	ordinaryChars(int low, int hi)	Specifies that all characters c in the range [low, high] are "ordinary" values. It removes any significance to any value in that range.
void	parseNumbers()	Specifies that numbers should be parsed digit by digit, except for floating point numbers.
void	pushBack()	Causes the next call to the nextToken method of this tokenizer to return the current value in the ttype field, and not to modify the value in the nval or sval field.
void	quoteChar(int ch)	Specifies that matching pairs of this character delimit string constants in this tokenizer.
void	resetSyntax()	Resets this tokenizer's syntax table so that all characters are "ordinary."
void	slashSlashComments(boolean flag)	When set to **true**, it recognizes C++-style comments.
void	slashStarComments(boolean flag)	When set to **true**, it recognizes C-style comments.
String	toString()	Returns the string representation of the current stream
void	whitespaceChars(int low, int high)	Specifies that all characters in the range [low, high] are white space characters.
void	wordChars(int low, int hi)	Specifies that all characters in the range [low, high] are word constituents.

The following example performs lexical analysis, or tokenization on a file of text containing strings, numbers, and punctuation symbols. Firstly the analysis will be performed using the default syntax. Secondly, the syntax is reset, and the analysis is performed again. An analysis will be performed on both outputs.

Figure 4.23 shows the file of text that will be parsed using the default parser. Notice that in addition to having strings, there are also double quotation mark, single quotation mark, comma, period, the @ symbol, the exclamation symbol, and number.

Figure 4.23

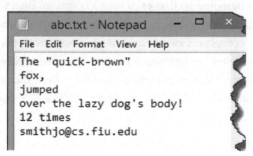

In **Listing 4.17** the StreamTokenizer class creates a tokenized stream with the FileReader object it gets. See **Line 9**. The while loop attempts to recognized the four types of default tokens – TT_EOF, TT_WORD, TT_NUMBER, and TT_EOLN, as shown on **Lines 11, 13, 16,** and **19**, respectively. Any token element that is not recognized is passed on to the default statement, **Line 24**. As you will notice, **Line 11** parses the next token, the value of the then stored in the **ttype**. Action is taken by the switch statement.

```
1.   // Listing 4.17
2.
3.   import java.io.StreamTokenizer;
4.   import java.io.FileReader;
5.   import java.io.IOException;
6.
7.   class TokenizeStream {
8.     public static void main(String[] args) throws IOException {
9.        StreamTokenizer st = new StreamTokenizer(new FileReader("abc.txt"));
10.
11.       while (st.nextToken() != StreamTokenizer.TT_EOF) {
12.         switch(st.ttype){
13.            case StreamTokenizer.TT_WORD: // Test for string
14.               System.out.println(st.sval);
15.            break;
16.            case StreamTokenizer.TT_NUMBER: // Test for number
17.               System.out.println(st.nval);
18.            break;
19.            case StreamTokenizer.TT_EOL: // Test for end of line
20.               System.out.print( "\tNew line ++> " + st.sval + (char) st.ttype);
21.            break;
22.            default: // Display any other values
23.               System.out.println((char) st.ttype + " --> not recognized" );
24.            break;
25.         }
26.       }
27.     }
28. }
```

As shown in **Figure 4.24**, the program is designed so that each token is written on a separate line. Notice there were tokens that were not recognized – double quote, comma, the single quote, the (@) symbol, and end of line. By default the parser recognizes case sensitivity as shown with the word **The**. Also, although there are several lines of texts, the end of line was not detected, sine statement 23, when executed, did not recognize those tokens. Lastly, after each non-recognized token, the remainder of the line is ignored, as shown after the first double quote ("), the comma (,), the single quote ('), and the ampersand (@).

Figure 4.24

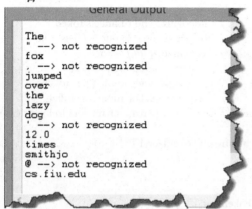

As was mentioned, StreamTokenizer breaks the input stream into tokens using whitespace as a delimiter. By default, Unicode characters '\u0000'through '\u0020' are considered whitespaces. This takes into consideration space, tab, and newline. You can change this list by invoking the method:

whitespaceChars(int low, int high);

This means that all characters having Unicode values between low and high are considered whitespaces, in addition to the default set. You can call whitespaceChars() any number of times - each invocation will add to the list of whitespace characters. In general, to clear out the list of non-default delimiter is to set those characters to be something other than whitespace by using methods such as:

ordinaryChar(int ch),
ordinaryChars(int low, int high),
wordChars(int low, int high),
resetSyntax()

Listing 4.18 shows the modifications that causes all tokens in the file to be recognized. For instance, the method eolIsSignificant, when its parametric value is set to true, end of line is recognized. Likewise, the overloaded method wordChars, which accepts a range of values will cause all values in that range to be considered ordinary characters. Also, the parametric value of the method lowerCaseMode is set to true, uppercase characters are converted to lowercase.

```
1. // Listing 4.18
2.
3. import java.io.StreamTokenizer;
4. import java.io.FileReader;
5. import java.io.IOException;
6.
7. class TokenizeStream  {
8.      public static void main(String[] args) throws IOException
```

```
9.        {
10.            StreamTokenizer st = new StreamTokenizer(new FileReader("abc.txt"));
11.
12.            st.eolIsSignificant(true);     // Recognize end of line as token
13.            st.wordChars('"', '"');        // Recognize double quote (") as token
14.            st.wordChars('@', '@');        // Recognize at (@) as token
15.            st.wordChars(',', ',');        // Recognize comma (,) as token
16.            st.wordChars('\'', '\'');      // Recognize single quote (') as token
17.            st.wordChars('!', '!');        // Recognize exclamation(!) as token
18.            st.lowerCaseMode(true); // Convert uppercase characters to lower case
19.
20.            while (st.nextToken() != StreamTokenizer.TT_EOF)
21.            {
22.                switch(st.ttype)
23.                {
24.                    case StreamTokenizer.TT_WORD:
25.                        System.out.println(st.sval + " ");
26.                    break;
27.                    case StreamTokenizer.TT_NUMBER:
28.                        System.out.println(st.nval);
29.                    break;
30.                    case StreamTokenizer.TT_EOL:
31.                        System.out.print( "\tNew line --> " + st.sval + (char) st.ttype);
32.                    break;
33.                    default:
34.                        System.out.println((char) st.ttype + " ++> not recognized");
35.                    break;
36.                }
37.            }
38.        }
39. }
```

Figure 4.25 shows the output from the program. First you will notice that the uppercase **T** in the word **The** has been converted to lowercase. Secondly, the string within the double quote has been recognized. The new line features has also been recognized; and all of the remaining characters have been recognized.

Figure 4.25

```
                      General Output

the
"quick-brown"
        New line --> null
fox,
        New line --> null
jumped
        New line --> null
over
the
lazy
dog's
body!
        New line --> null
12.0
times
        New line --> null
smithjo@cs.fiu.edu
```

Self-Check

1. What is the purpose of the class StreamTokenizer?
   - (a) It accumulates sequences of files into tokens.
   - (b) It accumulates sequences of integers into tokens.
   - (c) It accumulates sequences of non-white-space characters into tokens.
   - (d) It accumulates sequences of doubles into tokens.

2. Select ALL possible things that a token might be:
   - **(a)** A word
   - **(b)** A single character.
   - **(c)** A number.
   - **(d)** A while space

3. How does the class StreamTokenizer indicate that a number value has been read?
   - (a) It will automatically converts every string it reads into a number.
   - (b) It uses the method called nextNumber to read only numbers.
   - (c) It has a method called nextToken that returns the int defined as StreamTokenizer.NUMBER.
   - (d) It has a method called nextToken that returns the int defined as StreamTokenizer.TT_NUMBER

4. What is the superclass of the class StreamTokenizer?

5. Name the constants found in the class StreamTokenizer, and tell the purpose of each.

6. Name the instance variables found in the class StreamTokenizer, and tell the purpose of each.

7. Given the following program and the input file (abc.txt), what output is generated from the program?

```
import java.io.StreamTokenizer;
import java.io.FileReader;
import java.io.IOException;

class TokenizeStream
{
    public static void main(String[] args) throws IOException
    {
        StreamTokenizer st = new StreamTokenizer(new FileReader("abc.txt"));
        st.eolIsSignificant(true);
        while (st.nextToken() != StreamTokenizer.TT_EOL)
```

```
            {
                switch(st.ttype)
                {
                    case StreamTokenizer.TT_WORD:
                        System.out.println(st.sval);
                    break;
                    case StreamTokenizer.TT_NUMBER:
                        System.out.println(st.nval);
                    break;
                    case StreamTokenizer.TT_EOL:
                        System.out.println(st.nval);
                    break;
                    default:
                        System.out.println("Unknown token");
                    break;
                }
            }
        }
    }
```

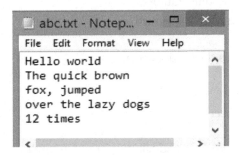

8. Given the following string "input.txt" representing name of a text file, write a method called sumNumbers. The method is required to use the class StreamTokenizer, and return the sum all numbers, if any, in the file.

Random Access File Stream

The file structures that we have studied so far are referred to as sequential files, where to access data at any position in the file you start searching from the first record in the file. Another way of structuring data is referred to as random access file. Unlike sequential file organization, random access file organization allows non-sequential, or random access to any location in file. This means you do not have to start from first line if you want to read, let's say, line number 10. You can go directly to line 10 and read. This is made possible by what is called the file pointer, similar to using the index of an array.

Java provides the class RandomAccessFile which gives you the ability to read and write into any random access file. The way that this works is as follows - when reading from a file, the reading starts at the current position of file pointer, and the pointer is moved past the number of bytes that were read. Similarly when writing data into random access file, writing begins from current location of file pointer and then advances the file pointer past number of bytes written. Random access is achieved by setting file pointer to any arbitrary location using the method called **seek()**. You can get the current file pointer location by calling the method, **getFilePointer()**. The table below shows two overloaded constructors in the class.

Constructors	Description
RandomAccessFile(File f, String mode)	Create a random access file stream to read from, and optionally to write to, the file specified by the File argument.
RandomAccessFile(String f, String mode)	Create a random access file stream to read from, and optionally to write to, a file with the specified name.

A random access file can be created in one of four access modes. In order to write data into random access file, you first need to create an instance of RandomAccessFile class in read and write modes. This is done by passing the string "rw" as the read/write access mode of the file. The access mode value is a string, as shown below:

Mode	Meaning
"r"	The file is opened in a read-only mode
"rw"	The file is opened in a read-write mode. The file is created if it does not exist.
"rws"	The file is opened in a read-write mode. Any modifications to the file's content and its metadata are written to the storage device immediately.
"rwd"	The file is opened in a read-write mode. Any modifications to the file's content are written to the storage device immediately

On closer examination, this is the only file structure that allows reading and writing to the same file during execution of the program.

The class has several methods including those named in the class PrintWriter that you can use to read and write in various types.

Listing 4.19 shows a class called DealerShip which creates a random access file object in read/write access mode, using the data file "dealership.txt". See **Line 11**. Following this, three pieces of information were read from the keyboard for some vehicle. These values were written to the random access file, using the methods writeUTF(s), to write the string value; writeInt(q); and, writeDouble(p), to write integer value, and the double value, respectively. See **Lines 22, 24**, and **26** respectively.

After writing data to the file, the same file is prepared to be read from, by re-setting the file pointer to the beginning of the file. **See Line 29**. Next, the values are read back from the file, and are displayed on the console.

```
1.   // Listing 4.19
2.
3.   import java.io.IOException;
4.   import java.io.RandomAccessFile;
5.
6.   public class DealerShip
7.   {
8.       public static void main(String[] args)  throws IOException
9.       {
10.          // Get the number of vehicle records to be stored
11.          int i = GetData.getInt("Enter number of vehicle records");
12.          // Create a random access file for reading and writing
13.          RandomAccessFile raf = new RandomAccessFile("dealership.txt", "rw");
14.
15.          for (int indx = 0; indx < i; indx++)
16.          {   // Entering the data that is to be stored
17.              String s = GetData.getString("Enter name of vehicle");
18.              int q = GetData.getInt("Enter quantity");
19.              double p = GetData.getDouble("Enter price");
20.              // Display the file pointer, then write the data
21.              System.out.println("Loc " + raf.getFilePointer() + ": \t\t" + s);
22.              raf.writeUTF(s);
23.              System.out.println("Loc " + raf.getFilePointer() + ": \t" + q);
24.              raf.writeInt(q);
25.              System.out.println("Loc " + raf.getFilePointer() + ": \t" + p);
26.              raf.writeDouble(p);
27.              System.out.println("The file pointer is now " + raf.getFilePointer());
28.          }
29.          raf.seek(0); // Reset the file pointer to the beginning of the file
30.          System.out.println("\nThe data and its location");
31.          /*
32.          * While the raf pointer is less than the raf length, read the next
33.          * strings of data raf from the current position of the raf pointer.
34.          */
35.          while (raf.getFilePointer() < raf.length())
36.          {
37.              System.out.println("Loc " + raf.getFilePointer() + ": \t\t" + raf.readUTF()+ "\t" );
38.              System.out.println("Loc " + raf.getFilePointer() + ": \t\t" +  raf.readInt() + "\t");
39.              System.out.println("Loc " + raf.getFilePointer() + ": \t\t" + raf.readDouble() + "\n");
40.              System.out.println("The file pointer is now " + raf.getFilePointer());
41.          }
42.      }
43. }
```

The result from the program is seen in **Figure 4.26**.

Figure 4.26

```
Loc  0:          Toyota Corolla
Loc 16:          10
Loc 20:          18000.0
The file pointer is now 28
Loc 28:              Ford Mustang
Loc 42:          25
Loc 46:          34000.0
The file pointer is now 54
Loc 54:              Hyundai Sonata
Loc 70:          15
Loc 74:          21000.0
The file pointer is now 82
Loc 82:              Dodge Caravan
Loc 97:          28
Loc 101:         28000.0
The file pointer is now 109

The data and its location
Loc  0:          Toyota Corolla
Loc 16:          10
Loc 20:          18000.0

The file pointer is now 28
Loc 28:          Ford Mustang
Loc 42:          25
Loc 46:          34000.0

The file pointer is now 54
Loc 54:          Hyundai Sonata
Loc 70:          15
Loc 74:          21000.0

The file pointer is now 82
Loc 82:          Dodge Caravan
Loc 97:          28
Loc 101:         28000.0

The file pointer is now 109
```

In the output notice the following:

- The location where the first value was written in the file was location 0.
- The location of the file pointer when the file was reset, was also location 0, the beginning of the file.
- Each time that the file was written to, the file pointer was advanced to a new available position in the file where information can be written. For instance, when the value, 1800.0 was written at location 20, the file pointer advanced to location 28 awaiting for data to be written; and surely it did, because the next value "Ford Mustang" was written at that location.
- Similarly, when data was read from a location, the file pointer advanced to the succeeding location for the next quantum of data to be read back. For instance, when the data was read from location 20, the file pointer advanced to location 28, awaiting for the next item, "Ford Mustang" to be read.

Figure 4.27 shows the behavior of a random access file. That is, the location for writing data to a random access file is not uniform, as such we cannot be predict the location where the next piece of data will be written. Notice that the path that the graph takes is not uniform – you cannot ascribe a line nor a uniform curve to it.

Figure 4.27

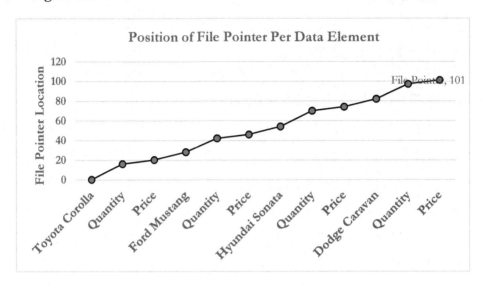

Exercises

1. What is RandomAccessFile?

2. Compare and contrast random access file with sequential access file in Java.

3. True/False. A rendoma access file can also be a sequential access file.

4. Write Java statement(s) that indicates how to create a random access file for reading and for writing data.

5. What is an IO stream?

6. Explain the similarities of the classes PrintStream and PrintWriter.

7. What is the necessity of two types of streams – byte streams and character streams?

8. What is the difference between the Reader/Writer class hierarchy and the InputStream and OutputStream hierarchy?

9. Which abstract class is the super class of all classes used for reading bytes? Select the one correct answer.
    (a) Reader
    (b) FileReader
    (c) ByteReader
    (d) InputStream
    (e) FileInputStream

10. Which abstract class is the super class of all classes used for writing characters? Select the one correct answer.
    (a) Writer
    (b) FileWriter
    (c) CharWriter
    (d) OutputStream
    (e) FileOutputStream

11. Name the exception, if any, that is thrown by the class, FileReader.

12. Why is it important to close an output file?
    (a) Because if you don't close it, some extra garbage information will be written into the file.
    (b) Because failure to do so will often result in some of the text you think you have written not winding up in the file.
    (c) Because the program will not actually write to the file unless you close it. Failure to close the file will result in an empty file.
    (d) Because if you don't close it, some error may occur the next time this file is opened and written.

Chapter Summary

- Java supports the inputting and outputting of data via standard input (keyboard) and standard output (display screen) and also external storage devices such as the hard disk.

- There are several classes in the java.io package for reading and for writing data in various forms.

- The class called File found in the java.io package does not carry out I/O operations on data, instead it mainly provides attribute information about files.

- The class JFileChooser, found in the swing package provides a dialog box that enables the user to conveniently select a file.

- Java uses the concept of stream to read data from a file and to write data to a file. The reading of the data represents data being streamed into the program, and the writing of data represents streaming information from the program onto the output device.

- Java I/O streaming classes are divided into two categories – byte oriented streams, and character oriented streams.

- Classes that end with the word "stream" represent byte oriented streams. Except for the class StreamTokenizer which is a character oriented stream, classes that end the "Reader" or "Writer" represent character streams.

- The super class of all byte input streams is the class InputStream, and the super of all output streams is the class OutputStream.

- The super class of all character input stream (except StreamTokenizer) is the class Reader, and the super class of all character output streams is the class Writer.

- All classes that are descendants of InputStream, OutputStream, Reader, and Writer access their data serially.

- Java introduces the class RandomAccessFile which has the ability to read from any location in a file, and to write into any location in a file at random. Random access file uses access permission, "r", for read only operation, and "rw", for read and write permission to the same file.

- The class StreamTokenizer is a character based input stream class that parses its contents into distinct character, or groups of characters called tokens. The class has no output stream as counter-part.

Programming Exercises

1. Given that "input.txt" is the name of a text base input file, write a Java program that can be used to replicate the contents of the file. Place this copied version in a file called "input2.txt"

2. Given that "input.jpg" is a file containing an image such as the following image:

Write a Java program that makes a duplicate of the file.

3. Write a java program that will use the following data to create a random access file that can be read at some later date.

Product	Origin	Day	Sales
Apples	Local	Monday	$100.00
Bananas	imported	Monday	$120.00
Grapes	Local	Monday	$200.00
Mangoes	imported	Monday	$230.00
Oranges	Local	Monday	$250.00
Peaches	Local	Monday	$350.00
Pine Apples	Local	Monday	$300.00
Apples	Local	Tuesday	$300.00
Bananas	imported	Tuesday	$400.00
Grapes	Local	Tuesday	$350.00
Mangoes	imported	Tuesday	$450.00
Oranges	Local	Tuesday	$400.00
Peaches	Local	Tuesday	$120.00
Pine Apples	Local	Tuesday	$300.00
Apples	Local	Wednesday	$300.00
Bananas	imported	Wednesday	$250.00
Grapes	Local	Wednesday	$250.00
Mangoes	imported	Wednesday	$120.00
Oranges	Local	Wednesday	$250.00
Peaches	Local	Wednesday	$350.00
Pine Apples	Local	Wednesday	$200.00
Apples	Local	Thursday	$120.00
Bananas	imported	Thursday	$300.00
Grapes	Local	Thursday	$400.00
Mangoes	imported	Thursday	$350.00
Oranges	Local	Thursday	$200.00
Peaches	Local	Thursday	$250.00
Pine Apples	Local	Thursday	$120.00
Apples	Local	Friday	$200.00
Bananas	imported	Friday	$250.00
Grapes	Local	Friday	$350.00
Mangoes	imported	Friday	$500.00
Oranges	Local	Friday	$300.00
Peaches	Local	Friday	$300.00
Pine Apples	Local	Friday	$250.00
Apples	Local	Saturday	$250.00
Bananas	imported	Saturday	$200.00

Grapes	Local	Saturday	$200.00
Mangoes	imported	Saturday	$400.00
Oranges	Local	Saturday	$250.00
Peaches	Local	Saturday	$350.00
Pine Apples	Local	Saturday	$120.00
Apples	Local	Sunday	$1,200.00
Bananas	imported	Sunday	$250.00
Grapes	Local	Sunday	$300.00
Mangoes	imported	Sunday	$200.00
Oranges	Local	Sunday	$250.00
Peaches	Local	Sunday	$250.00
Pine Apples	Local	Sunday	$450.00

Using the data above, generate tow reports of the following form – one that displays this output on screen, and the other that stores this report on an external device such as the hard disk.

Row Labels	Sunday	Monday	Tuesday	Wednesday	Thursday	Friday	Saturday
Apples	$600.00	$100.00	$300.00	$300.00	$120.00	$200.00	$250.00
Bananas	$250.00	$120.00	$400.00	$250.00	$300.00	$250.00	$200.00
Grapes	$300.00	$200.00	$350.00	$250.00	$400.00	$350.00	$200.00
Mangoes	$200.00	$230.00	$450.00	$120.00	$350.00	$500.00	$400.00
Oranges	$250.00	$250.00	$400.00	$250.00	$200.00	$300.00	$250.00
Peaches	$250.00	$350.00	$120.00	$350.00	$250.00	$300.00	$350.00
Pine Apples	$450.00	$300.00	$300.00	$200.00	$120.00	$250.00	$120.00
Grand Total	$2,300.00	$1,550.00	$2,320.00	$1,720.00	$1,740.00	$2,150.00	$1,770.00

4. Write a Java program to imitate a file system of an operating system.

In your solution, design a class called BasicFile with options to carry out the following operations:
(a) Select and open an input file using a file dialog box.

(b) Make a copy of the file, whether it is a text file or an image file.

(c) Write to an output file with the option of either appending to the file, or over-writing the contents of the file.

(d) Display the following attributes of the input file in a scrollable screen:
   i.   The absolute path of the file
   ii. Files and directories that are in the path of the file.

iii. The size of the file in kilobytes.

iv. The number of lines in the file, if the is a text file.

(e) Display the contents of the input file in a scrollable pane.

(f) Search the input file line by line for a given string. The output must contain the line number, followed by the contents of the line that contains the search argument. For instance given the following the search string: **Java**, the program would search the file line by line generating a result such as the following:

    50: on the island of Java

    95: The people of JAVA loves jaVa.

Use recursion to search the file.

(g) Tokenize the input file so that program recognizes all printable characters on the keyboard.

You may utilize the classes BasicFile and TestBasicFile as a source of reference.

5. Consider the following program.

```
1.   import java.io.StreamTokenizer;
2.   import java.io.FileReader;
3.   import java.io.IOException;
4.
5.   class TokenizeStream
6.   {
7.       public static void main(String[] args) throws IOException
8.       {
9.           StreamTokenizer st = new StreamTokenizer(new FileReader("abc.txt"));
10.          while (st.nextToken() != StreamTokenizer.TT_EOF)
11.          {
12.              switch(st.ttype)
13.              {
14.                  case StreamTokenizer.TT_WORD:
15.                      System.out.println(st.sval + " ");
16.                  break;
17.                  case StreamTokenizer.TT_NUMBER:
18.                      System.out.println(st.nval);
19.                  break;
20.                  case StreamTokenizer.TT_EOL:
21.                      System.out.print( "\t\tnew line ---> " + st.sval + (char) st.ttype);

22.                  break;
23.                  default:
24.                  break;
25.              }
```

```
26.              }
27.        }
28.  }
```

When the program run using the using the data on the left, it produces output shown on the right.

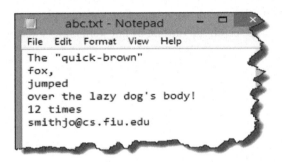   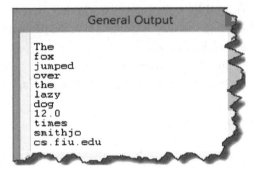

Modify the program so that it produces the following output.

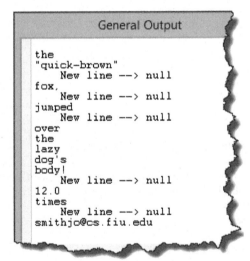

6.   This is a two-part exercise.

Part I

Write a program to create a text file containing an inventory of items. Each item has the following format:

Inventory code	Name of Item	Quantity	Unit price
xxxxxxxxxx	xxxxxxxxxx	xxxx	xxx.xx

- Call this file inventory.txt.

- Generate a printed report pertaining to this file with the following information:
  (a) The name of the file.
  (b) The directory in which the file is stored.
  (c) The number of records in the file (Lines of information)
  (d) The approximate number of bytes in the file.
  (e) The date and time when the file was created.

Note:
- Use the JOptionPane to enter the data.
- This file will be used as a scratch pad. That is, if the file already exists, its contents will be over written.
- Use the PrintWriter and the FileWriter classes to write the information to the file and to the screen, respectively.

Part II

Write a second program that updates a master file called **master.txt** using the data from the inventory file. Before carrying out the update however, make a backup copy of the master file, if one exists.

When attempting to carry out the update, if the master file does not exists, create it, by reading the data from the inventory file and writing it in the master file. If a master file exists, however, first read its contents into a vector before doing the update. To do the update, read one record at a time from the inventory file, compare it with each record in the vector (the master file records). Use the field called **code** as the key field upon which the comparison must be based. If there is a match, update the quantity field in the master file. A negative quantity in the inventory file reduces the amount field in the master file; a positive quantity in the inventory file increases the amount field in the master file. Any record in the inventory file that does not appear in the master file must be added to the master file.

- Generate a printed report pertaining to new master file. The report must contain the following information:
  o The name of the file.
  o The directory in which the file is stored.
  o The number of records in the file
  o The number of bytes in the file.
  o The time and date when the file was created

7. Create a random access file for storing student records. A student record must be comprised of the following attributes:
   - Last name
   - First name

- Date entered the institution
- The courses taken
- The current grade point average.

Display the contents of the file on the screen.

Chapter 5 Recursion

Objectives

After reading this chapter you will be able to:

- Develop an understanding and appreciation about the concept of recursion.
- Differentiate between recursion and iteration.
- Write recursive definitions.
- Determine when to use recursion instead of iteration.
- Develop and appreciate the trade-offs between recursion and iteration.

Introduction

In this chapter you will learn about another type of programming technique that causes, not only a statement or a block of statements to be executed, but the entire method is called to repeat itself. This concept is called recursion. Recursion can be seen all around us. When the reflective surfaces of two mirrors are placed parallel to each other, they form an endless series of images. In this situation, one mirror calls upon the other to produce the image it sees, likewise the other mirror. Consider the song:

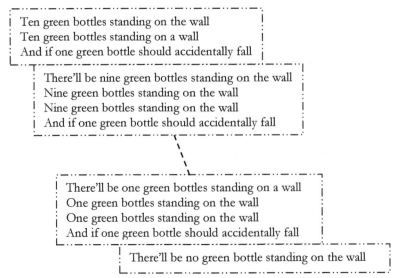

Ten green bottles standing on the wall
Ten green bottles standing on a wall
And if one green bottle should accidentally fall

There'll be nine green bottles standing on the wall
Nine green bottles standing on the wall
Nine green bottles standing on the wall
And if one green bottle should accidentally fall

There'll be one green bottles standing on a wall
One green bottles standing on the wall
One green bottles standing on the wall
And if one green bottle should accidentally fall

There'll be no green bottle standing on the wall

This song by definition is recursive, since it is made to repeat word for word, except the count of the number of green bottles, and the last line that ends it.

Whereas in the first case the process seems not to end, in the second it does end. In programming we prefer the recursive definition that has a finite number of calls – hence the recursion must end.

Recursion

By definition, recursion is a process that repeats itself a finite number of times, until a given condition is met, then the process stops. The desired result of the process is realized only when the continuous call stops. The condition that causes the process to terminate is referred to as the base case, and the condition for the continuous call is referred to as the inductive step. The inductive step specifies the set of rules that causes the process to move towards the base case.

The bottle song above can be modeled as a recursive definition, as shown the flowchart of **Figure 5.1**.

Figure 5.1 Recursive definition for "*Ten green bottle*" song

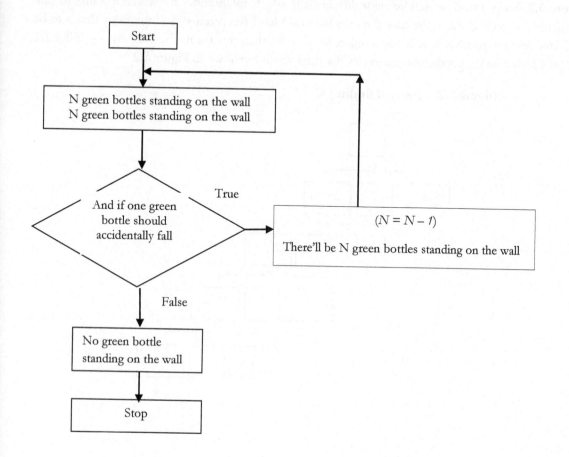

To understand how recursion works, it is useful to visualize what happens when a recursive definition is invoked. Let us consider the Mathematical concept called factorial, written **n!**. By definition:

$$n! = \begin{cases} 1, \text{if } n = 0 \\ n * (n\text{-}1)! \text{, where } \mathbf{n} \text{ is an integer, and } \mathbf{n} > 0 \end{cases}$$

This reads:

n factorial = 1, if n is zero;

Otherwise it is, n times the factorial of $(n - 1)$. This occurs when n > 0.

Example 5.1 Find the value of 4!

According to the definition of factorial, inductive step, produces three terms:

1. The number for that factorial
2. The operator that is involved (in this case the operator is multiplication), and
3. The call to repeat the process (which in this case is factorial (n - 1).

Figure 5.2 shows a trace of 4! The algorithm actually asks if the number for which it wants to find the factorial is zero. If this is the case then the base case has been reached, and the value that is to be generated and stored must is 1. If the number is not zero, then this forms the basis for the inductive step, in which case the production generates the three terms as shown in Figure 5.2.

Figure 5.2 A trace of finding 4!

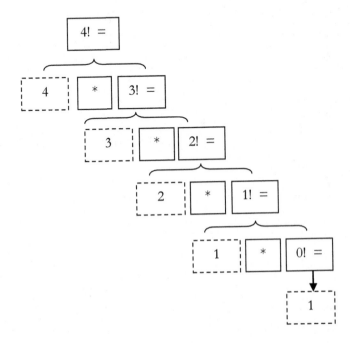

Once the base case has been reached, it is time for the actual multiplication to take place. The way that this works is as follows. Starting with the last value that was generated, by the base case, this value gets multiplied by its predecessor, and its predecessor, all the way back to the first value that was generated. In the end, the value (24 in this case) is generated. See **Figure 5.3**.

Figure 5.3 Calculation done in reverse of how numbers were generated

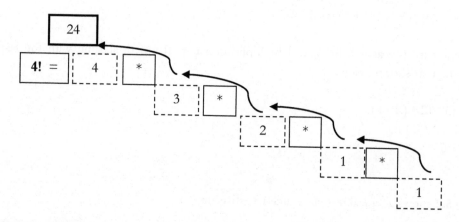

Although this process looks complicated, the programming is very simple. One of the first things to recognize when dealing with recursion is that the principle is based on the selection construct **if/else**. The only stipulation in the test is to first ascertain if the base case has been reached. If it has been reached, the result will automatically be generated. If not, the process is called again.

Revisiting the factorial problem, n! can be expressed as a method definition as follows:

$$\text{factorial}(n) = \begin{cases} 1, \text{ if } n = 0 \\ n * \text{factorial}(n-1), \text{ where is an integer, and } n > 0 \end{cases}$$

The above algorithm converted to program code as shown in **Listing 5.1**.

```
1.  // Listing 5.1 Class Recursion
2.
3.  class Recursion
4.  {
5.      long factorial(int n)
6.      {
7.          if ( n == 0)
8.              return 1;
9.          else
10.             return n * factorial(n - 1);
11.     }
12. }
```

In the listing, notice that the method definition follows exactly as the algorithm. The effect of this algorithm is:

factorial(4) =

$$4 * factorial(3)$$
$$4 * (3 * factorial(2))$$
$$4 * (3 * (2 * factorial(1)))$$
$$4 * (3 * (2 * (1 * factorial(0))))$$
$$4 * (3 * (2 * (1 * (1))))$$

Once the base case is reached, the actual multiplication is performed, starting with the last value down to the first, as shown below.

$$4 * (3 * (2 * (1 * (1))))$$
$$= 4 * (3 * (2 * (1)))$$
$$= 4 * (3 * (2))$$
$$= 4 * (6)$$
$$= 24$$

Listing 5.2 shows a typical test class called TestRecursion.

```
1.   // Listing 5.2
2.
3.   class TestRecursion
4.   {
5.        public static void main(String[] arg)
6.        {
7.              Recursion r = new Recursion();
8.              System.out.println("The value of 4! is " + r.factorial(4));
9.        }
10. }
```

Example 5.2 Find the value of $\Sigma n!$

Solution
By definition, $\Sigma n! = n! + \Sigma(n - 1)!$, $n \varepsilon$ Integer, $n > 0$
This expression looks intimidating at first, but we already know what n! is.

$$n! = \begin{cases} 1, \text{if } n = 0 \\ n * (n-1)! \text{ , where is an integer, and } n > 0 \end{cases}$$

Therefore this solution is simplified to be

$$\Sigma n! = \begin{cases} 1, \text{if } n = 0 \\ n! + \Sigma(n-1)!, \text{where is an integer, and } n > 0 \end{cases}$$

The above algorithm is easily coded as a recursive construct, as shown below.

```
int sumFactorial(int n)
{
    if ( n == 0)
        return 1;
    else
        return factorial(n) + sumFactorial(n - 1);
}
```

In the long run, the complicated looking expression becomes relatively simple.

It is known that multiplication is nothing more than repeated addition. Although easily said, it may not be that easy to prove, unless it is by recursion.

Example 5.3. Given two positive integers, **a** and **b**, a recursive definition can be expressed as follows:

$$a * b = \begin{cases} a, \text{if } b = 1 \\ a + a * (b-1), \text{where is an integer, and } b > 1 \end{cases}$$

This definition, like the factorial definition is easily coded in its natural form, as shown below.

```
int multiply(int m, int n)
{
    if (n == 1)
        return m;
    else
        return m + multiply(m, n - 1);
}
```

Listing 5.3 shows the full definition of the class Recursion which implements three recursive methods – factorial, sumFactorial, and multiply.

// Listing 5.3 Recursive definition for factorial, sum factorial, and multiplication
1.
2.   class Recursion
3.   {
4.   int factorial(int n) throws IllegalArgumentException

```
5.      {
6.          if (n < 0)
7.              throw new IllegalArgumentException("Can't find factorial of " + n);
8.
9.          return( n == 0 )? 1: n * factorial(n - 1);
10.     }
11.     int sumFactorial(int n) throws IllegalArgumentException
12.     {
13.         if (n < 0)
14.             throw new IllegalArgumentException("Can't sum factorial for " + n);
15.
16.         return ( n == 0 || n == 1)? 1: factorial(n) + sumFactorial(n - 1);
17.     }
18.     int multiply(int m, int n)
19.     {
20.         if (n == 0)
21.             return n;
22.         if (m == 0)
23.             return m;
24.         if (m == 1)
25.             return n;
26.
27.         if (n < 0)
28.         {
29.             m = - m;
30.             n = -n;
31.         }
32.     return (n == 1)? m: m + multiply(m, n - 1);
33.     }
34. }
```

In analyzing the definition of factorial, we know that there is no definition for finding the factorial of a negative number. Hence, we take exception to such a situation, and treat this an exception. See **Lines 7** and **14**.

Notice that with the multiplication, either one, or both multiplicands can be negative. If the second multiplicand is negative, then we have to change the sign on both values. If we do not, then the process would end in an infinite loop, since it is the second value that would be decreasing. In this case it would be moving further away to the left, from one. When it comes to multiplication by zero, only one of the multiplicand should be zero, not both. Line 20 thru 23 take care of the situation.

Listing 5.4 shows a test class that determines which of the methods is to be called. Notice that neither of the factorial methods handled the exception, both pass the exception on to the test class, where it is handled by main.

// Listing 5.4 Test class

```
1.    class TestRecursion
2.    {
```

```
3.          public static void main(String[] arg)
4.          {
5.               Recursion r = new Recursion();
6.
7.               boolean done = false;
8.               while(!done)
9.               {
10.                   String s = "Find\n1. Factorial\n2. Sum factorial\n3. Multiplication\n4. Quit";
11.                   int i = GetData.getInt(s);
12.                   try
13.                   {
14.                       switch(i)
15.                       {
16.                           case 1:
17.                               int m = GetData.getInt("Enter value for which to find factorial");
18.                               System.out.println(m + "! is " + r.factorial(m));
19.                           break;
20.                           case 2:
21.                               int n = GetData.getInt("Enter value for which to sum the factorial");
22.                               System.out.println("Sum of " + n + "! is " + r.sumFactorial(n));
23.                           break;
24.                           case 3:
25.                               int p = GetData.getInt("Multiply p * q \nEnter the value of p");
26.                               int q = GetData.getInt("Multiply p * q \nEnter the value of q");
27.                               System.out.println( p + " * " + q + " = " + r.multiply(p, q));
28.                           break;
29.                           case 4:
30.                               done = true;
31.                           break;
32.                           default:
33.                           break;
34.                       }
35.                   }
36.                   catch(IllegalArgumentException e)
37.                   {
38.                       System.out.println(e.toString());
39.                   }
40.               }
41.          }
42. }
```

Self-Check

1. Define the terms *recursion* and *iteration*, and differentiate between them.

2. Consider the following paradox attributed to Zeno:
   Suppose that you want to cross a field. Before you reach the other side, you must get halfway across. Before you reach the halfway, you must get a quarter of the way across, and so on.

Hence, to cross the field you must travel an infinite number of shorter distances; and so it is impossible to get across at all. Explain how this paradox can be expressed recursively. What could be a possible base case, and what could possibly be an inductive step?

3. Write the output from the following program:

```java
public class Mystery
{
    public static void main(String[] args)
    {
        System.out.println("Hello Mystery World!");
        display(9);
    }
    public static void display(int n)
    {
        if (n < 1)
            return;
        else
        {
            for (int i = n; i > 0; i--)
                System.out.print("*");
            System.out.println();
            display(n-1);
        }
    }
}
```

4. Given the following method, describe what this method does.

```java
public static String convert(int n)
{
    if (n == 0)
        return "";
    else
        return convert(n / 2) + ""+ (n%2);
}
```

5. Write the output from the following program:

```java
public class Mystery
{
    public static void main(String[] args)
    {
        System.out.println("Hello Mystery World!");
        display(9);
    }
```

```
public static void display(int n)
{
    if (n < 1)
        return;
    else
    {
        System.out.print(n + ": ");
        for (int i = n; i > 0; i--)
            System.out.print(n);
        System.out.println();
        display(n-1);
    }
}
}
```

6. Given the following program describe what the program does before running it.

```
class Mystery
{
    public static void main(String[] arg)
    {
        int m = 123;
        int n = 2;
        String s = "";
        System.out.println(convert(m, n, s) );
    }
    public static String convert(int n, int b, String s)
    {
        if (n == 0 )
            return s;
        else
        {
            s = (n % b) + s;
            return convert (n/b, b, s);
        }
    }
}
```

Searching a Sorted List

In **chapter 9** of Volume I we studied the binary search algorithm using iteration. Recall that the algorithm requires that the list must first be sorted. In conducting the search, the list must be partitioned into three – the midpoint of the list, and the two sublists, one on either side of the midpoint. See **Figure 5.4**. Let's say we are searching for the value 45. The midpoint is:

$$mid = (0 + 9) /2$$
$$= 4$$

In the figure you will see that this value is not at the midpoint. In addition, we see that it lies to the right of the mid-point, at index 6.

Figure 5.4

[0]		[1]	[2]	[3]	[4]	[5]	[6]	[7]	[8]	[9]
5		7	16	24	25	30	45	50	62	65

The second time around the new sublist is right of the midpoint – that is, indices 5 thru 9. Hence, the new mid-point is now at index 7. It is calculated in similar manner to the previous. That is:

mid = (5+ 9) /2 = 7, see **Figure 5.5**.

Figure 5.5

[0]	[1]	[2]	[3]	[4]	[5]	[6]	[7]	[8]	[9]
5	7	16	24	25	30	45	50	62	65

From this analysis, see that the process consists of one of four outcomes – the items is found at the mid-point of a sublist; the item is not found at all; the process of finding the mid-point on the left; or finding the midpoint to the right. As we see in the code below, this algorithm lends itself to recursion. This implies that the algorithm has two base cases, as well as two inductive steps. The inductive steps are similar to the way that the method was called the first time.

```
// The array would have been sorted in order to use binary search algorithm

boolean binarySearch(int arr[], int key, int low, int high)
{
    if (low > high)  // Base case
        return false;

    int mid = (low + high)/2;

    if (arr[mid] == key)  //  Base case
        return true;
    else if (arr[mid] < key)
        return binarySearch(arr, key, mid + 1, high); // Inductive step
    else
        return binarySearch(arr, key, low, mid - 1); // inductive step
    }
}
```

Searching a Non-Sorted List

Just as recursion can be used to search sorted list, it can also be used to search unsorted lists. For instance, if we want to search a piece of text for a given string, we would first tokenize the string using class such as StringTokenizer. Once the text is tokenized, there are three possible outcomes to be expected from the search – the string is located, the string is not located, or call the method again, and again. Each time that the method is called, the remaining portion of the text is searched. The code below shows a recursive method that searches a piece of text for the first occurrence of a given string. In addition to finding the text, it also finds the position in the text where it is found. This value is represented by the variable, index.

```java
// Recursive method to locate a string in a text

boolean findWord(StringTokenizer t, String word, int index)
{
    if (!t.hasMoreTokens())
        return false;
    else if (t.nextToken().equals(word))
        return true;
    else
        return findWord(t, word, ++index);
}
```

Listing 5.5 shows the complete definition of the class Recursion, which includes the recursive methods binarySearch and findWord.

```java
1.   // Listing 5.5 Recursive definitions to include binarySearch and findWord
2.
3.   import java.util.StringTokenizer;
4.
5.   class Recursion
6.   {
7.       int factorial(int n) throws IllegalArgumentException
8.       {
9.           if (n < 0)
10.              throw new IllegalArgumentException("Can't find factorial of " + n);
11.
12.          return( n == 0 )? 1: n * factorial(n - 1);
13.      }
14.      int sumFactorial(int n) throws IllegalArgumentException
15.      {
16.          if (n < 0)
17.              throw new IllegalArgumentException("Can't sum factorial for " + n);
18.
19.          return ( n == 0 || n == 1)? 1: factorial(n) + sumFactorial(n - 1);
20.      }
```

```
21.        int multiply(int m, int n)
22.        {
23.            if (n == 0)
24.                return n;
25.            if (m == 0)
26.                return m;
27.            if (m == 1)
28.                return n;
29.
30.            if (n < 0)
31.            {
32.                m = - m;
33.                n = -n;
34.            }
35.        return (n == 1)? m: m + multiply(m, n - 1);
36.        }
37.        // The array would have been sorted in order to use binary search algorithm
38.        boolean binarySearch(int arr[], int key, int low, int high)
39.        {
40.                if (low > high)  // Base case
41.                        return false;
42.
43.                int mid = (low + high)/2;
44.
45.                if (arr[mid] == key)  //  Base case
46.                        return true;
47.                else if (arr[mid] < key)
48.                        return binarySearch(arr, key, mid + 1, high); // Inductive step
49.                else
50.                        return binarySearch(arr, key, low, mid - 1); // inductive step
51.        }
52.        // Recursive method to locate a string in a text
53.        boolean findWord(StringTokenizer t, String word, int index)
54.        {
55.                if (!t.hasMoreTokens())
56.                        return false;
57.                else if (t.nextToken().equals(word))
58.                        return true;
59.                else
60.                        return findWord(t, word, ++index);
61.        }
62. }
```

Listing 5.6 shows a modified version of the test class to include calling the methods binarySearch and findWord.

1.   **// Listing 5.6 The test class to include calling binary search and searching**

```
2.
3.    import java.util.StringTokenizer;
4.
5.    class TestRecursion
6.    {
7.        public static void main(String[] arg)
8.        {
9.            Recursion r = new Recursion();
10.           int arr[] = {2 , 4, 6, 8, 10, 12, 14, 16, 18, 20};
11.           String str = "The quick brown fox jumped over the lazy dogs";
12.           boolean done = false;
13.
14.           while(!done)
15.           {
16.               String s = "Find\n1. Factorial\n2. Sum factorial\n3. Multiplication\n4. Perform binary
                  search\n5. Search for word\n6. Quit";
17.               int i = GetData.getInt(s);
18.               try
19.               {
20.                   switch(i)
21.                   {
22.                       case 1:
23.                           int m = GetData.getInt("Enter value for which to find factorial");
24.                           System.out.println(m + "! is " + r.factorial(m));
25.                           break;
26.                       case 2:
27.                           int n = GetData.getInt("Enter value for which to sum the factorial");
28.                           System.out.println("Sum of " + n + "! is " + r.sumFactorial(n));
29.                           break;
30.                       case 3:
31.                           int p = GetData.getInt("Multiply p * q \nEnter the value of p");
32.                           int q = GetData.getInt("Multiply p * q \nEnter the value of q");
33.                           System.out.println( p + " * " + q + " = " + r.multiply(p, q));
34.                           break;
35.                       case 4:
36.                           int key = GetData.getInt("Enter integer value you're looking for");
37.                           System.out.println("The value " + key + " is in the array: "
38.                               + r.binarySearch(arr, key, 0, arr.length-1));
39.                           break;
40.                       case 5:
41.                           int ndx = 0;
42.                           StringTokenizer token = new StringTokenizer(str);
43.                           String word = GetData.getString("Enter word you're looking for");
44.                           System.out.println("The value  " + word + " is in the string: "+
                              r.findWord(token, word, ndx));
45.                           break;
46.                       case 6:
47.                           done = true;
48.                           break;
```

```
49.                    default:
50.                       break;
51.                 }
52.           }
53.           catch(IllegalArgumentException e) {
54.                 System.out.println(e.toString());
55.           }
56.      }
57.   }
58. }
```

Recursion vs Iteration – Which Approach Is Better

Recursion and iteration perform the same kinds of tasks - they repeat segments of codes in order to solve a problem. Although there are no clear answers to which is better, there are however, known trade-offs between, the execution times of both approaches; the amount of memory each uses; and in general, the level of difficulty in the programming itself.

Execution Time

Let us use the problem of finding $\Sigma n!$ to help us understand the time difference of both approaches. **Listing 5.7** shows the code for both recursion and iteration. The method sumFactorial (**Lines 9 thru 12**) shows the recursive definition for $\Sigma n!$ The method also calls the recursive definition for **n!**, which is needed in the process. See **Lines 5 thru 8**.

```
1.   // Listing 5.7 Recursive and iterative definitions for finding Σn!
2.
3.   class Recursion
4.   {
5.        long factorial(int n)
6.        {
7.             return ( n == 0 )? 1: n * factorial(n - 1);
8.        }
9.        long sumFactorial(int n)
10.       {
11.            return (n == 0)? 1: factorial(n) + sumFactorial(n-1);
12.       }
13.       long findFactorial(int n)
14.       {
15.            long product = 1;
16.
17.            for (int i = 1; i <= n; i++)
18.                product = product * i;
19.            return product ;
20.       }
21.       long sumTheFactorials(int n)
22.       {
```

```
23.              long sum = 0;
24.
25.              for (int i = 1; i <= n; i++)
26.                  sum = sum + findFactorial(i);
27.              return sum + 1;
28.          }
29. }
```

Similarly, **Lines 21 thru 28** show the iterative method definition for finding $\Sigma n!$ Also, **Lines 13 thru 20** define **n!** This as you know is needed in the process.

The test class shown in **Listing 5.8** calls both the recursive and the iterative procedures. In each case the calls are timed. The for loop in each case produces the value **n**, for which the value of $\Sigma n!$ is calculated.

Listing 5.8 Timing Recursion and Iteration

```
1.  class TestRecursion
2.  {
3.      public static void main(String[] arg)
4.      {
5.          Recursion r = new Recursion();
6.          System.out.println("Recursion");
7.
8.          for (int i = 1; i <= 15; i++)
9.          {
10.             long begin = System.nanoTime();
11.             long x =  r.sumFactorial(i);
12.             long end = System.nanoTime();
13.             long dif = end - begin;
14.             System.out.println( i + "!  = " + x + "\t\t" + (end - begin)/1000);
15.         }
16.
17.         System.out.println("\nIteration");
18.         for (int i = 1; i <= 15; i++)
19.         {
20.             long begin = System.nanoTime();
21.             long x =  r.sumTheFactorials(i);
22.             long end = System.nanoTime();
23.             long dif = end - begin;
24.             System.out.println( i + "!  = " + x + "\t\t" +  (end - begin)/1000);
25.         }
26.     }
27. }
```

Figure 5.6 shows a sample output for Σn! These values may change slightly, each time that the program is executed. Nevertheless, the result will show that the recursive approach will always take more time to process than the iterative approach.

Figure 5.6

Execution Timing (Units of time)

n	Recursion	Iteration	Σn!
1	17	13	2
2	3	3	4
3	7	4	10
4	9	4	34
5	11	5	154
6	14	6	874
7	17	6	5914
8	22	7	46234
9	25	9	409114
10	31	9	4037914
11	37	11	43954714
12	41	12	522956314
13	51	14	6749977114
14	59	18	93928268314
15	63	20	1401602636314

If we pick any pair of points representing recursion, and a corresponding pair of points representing iteration, we find that recursion spends much more time processing the code than iteration. For example, using **Figure 5.6**, let us choose points, $P_1 = (2, 3)$ and $P_2 = (4, 9)$, for recursion.

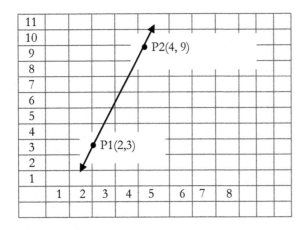

In the graph above, the slope m_1, representing these points is:

$m_1 = (9 - 3)/(4 - 2) = 6/2$

Now choose corresponding iteration points $Q_1(2, 3)$ and $Q_2(4, 4)$, representing iteration.

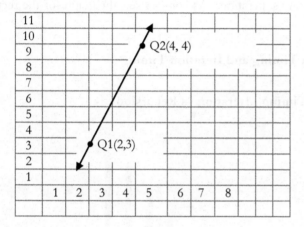

The slope m_2, representing these points is:

$m_2 = (4 - 3)/(4 - 2) = 1/2$

This analysis shows that the rate $m1 : m2 \approx 6:1$.

This means that recursion takes about 6 times the time it takes to loop through the solution than iteration.

If we pick two other pairs of points, let's say:

$P_1 = (7, 17)$, and P2 = 8, 22)

Slope $m_1 = (22 - 17)/ (8 - 7) = 5/1$

Also, $Q_1 = (7, 6)$ and Q2 = (8, 7)

Slope $m_2 = (7 - 6)/ (8 - 7) = 1/1$

Analyzing the outcome of the result of these two sets of points we see that the ration of the slopes $m1 : m2 = 5/1$ is relatively close – 6:1 compared to 5:1. Given the volume of the processing this difference can be disregarded. Thus proving the point that recursion tends to us more time in processing, than is iteration.

In addition, the right column of the table shows the calculation that was performed by both algorithms was the same.

The graph of this table is shown in **Figure 5.7**. The graph shows, apart from the first value, two approximately linear mappings – recursion vs. iteration. As you can see, the graph for the recursion quickly outgrows the graph for iteration.

Figure 5.7 Graph of Recursion Timing and Iteration Timing

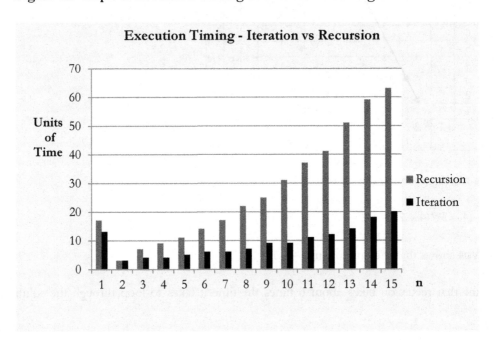

Memory Usage

As you have seen the amount of time spent on a recursive definition, is dependent on the number of times the method calls itself. Much of this time is spent allocating memory to store the partial results after each call. The shaded cells of Figure **5.6** shows that additional memory is needed to store at least the multiplicand of the factorial after each call.

With respect to the iterative approach, only three units of memory are required, as shown by the method findFactorial, below - one unit for each of the variables: **n**, **product**, and **i**. This is true, no matter the number of iterations. That is, memory usage is constant. Using **4!** as an example, the amount of memory required for iteration is three units; this is because the variables are re-used. If we use **20!**, the amount of memory used remains the same.

```
long findFactorial(int n)
{
    long product = 1;
    for (int i = 1; i <= n; i++)
            product = product * i;

    return product ;
}
```

When it comes to recursion, the amount of memory required depends on the number of times that the method calls itself. In the case of 4! at least thirteen units of memory is required – three units for each time that the method calls factorial (shown below) itself, and one for the base case.

```
long  factorial(int n) {
    if ( n == 0)
            return 1;
    else
            return n * factorial(n - 1);

}
```

Analyzing the code, factorial(4) would cause the method to be called four times. **Figure 5.8** illustrates what happens when factorial(4) is called.

Figure 5.8 Additional memory requirement

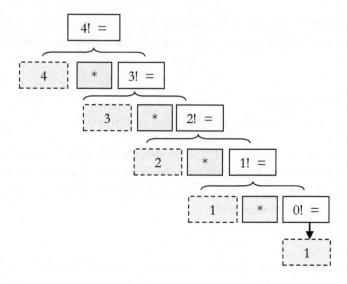

Note, that if **n** grows exceedingly large, the recursive definition may become unusable for the given problem.

Programming Level of Difficulty

When it comes to the program code, very often programmers prefer recursion over iteration. In the case of recursion the solutions are often shorter, and closer to the conceptual abstraction. Although the programs are generally shorter and more incline to resemble the problem, this approach comes with a price. That is, an algorithm that can naturally be expressed iteratively, may not be as easy to understand if expressed recursively. In general, recursion is difficult to understand in some algorithms; also, good recursive solutions may be more difficult to design and test.

Just like recursion, an algorithm that can naturally be expressed recursively may not be as easy to understand if expressed iteratively. It can also be difficult to convert a recursive algorithm into an iterative algorithm, and verifying that the algorithms are equivalent can also be difficult. The listings below compare the recursive definition of factorial of **n!**, with the iterative definition, findFactorial of **n!**.

```
long  factorial(int n)
{
    if ( n == 0)
        return 1;
    else

        return n * factorial(n - 1);
}
```

```
long findFactorial(int n)
{
    long product = 1;
    for (int i = 1; i <= n; i++)
        product = product * i;

    return product ;
}
```

When we analyze the two methods we see that the recursive definition is more readily understood than the iterative definition, as the recursive definition is more aligned to the Mathematical definition:

$$n! = \begin{cases} 1, \text{if } n = 0 \\ n * (n\text{-}1)! \text{, where } \mathbf{n} \text{ is an integer, and } \mathbf{n} > 0 \end{cases}$$

I guess by now you come to realize that one of the reasons why iteration is more readily understood is that recursion predicates itself on the **if/else** construct. The base case will appear first, followed by the inductive step in the else clause. A recursive definition may have multiple base cases, as well as multiple inductive steps. For example:

$1! = 1$

Therefore, if we strictly want to carry out the calculation for n! the algorithm could be defined as:

$$n! = \begin{cases} 1, \text{if } n = 0 \\ 1, \text{if } n = 1 \\ n * (n-1)! , \text{where } \mathbf{n} \text{ is an integer, and } \mathbf{n} > 1 \end{cases}$$

Self-Check

1. Design a recursive algorithm that evaluates x^n, where n is a positive integer.

2. Define an iterative method and a recursive method that take parameters x and n and evaluate x^n. Which of the two approaches was easier to code? Explain.

3. Using the algorithm below, write an iterative definition and a recursive definition that compute the greatest common divisor (gcd) of two integers. The gcd of two integers is the largest integer that divides them both.

$$gcd(m, n) = \begin{cases} n, \text{if } n \text{ divides } m \\ gcd (n, \text{remainder of } m \text{ divide by } n), \text{otherwise} \end{cases}$$

Compare codes and say which definition was easy to write.

Chapter Summary

- Use recursion for clarity, and (sometimes) for a reduction in the time needed to write and debug code, not for space savings or speed of execution.

- Every recursive definition must have a base case; otherwise the recursive process will be an infinite loop.

- Every recursive definition must make progress towards its base case; otherwise this too will be an infinite loop.

- Sometimes a recursive method has more than one base case, and also more than one inductive steps.

- Recursion has large memory usage and time consumption overheads. This takes $O(2n)$ steps in general to solve ! Unusable for large *n*.

Programming Exercises

1. One of the more advanced sorting algorithms is the Quicksort algorithm. This algorithm has a fairly simple concept at the core. The basic concept is to pick one of the elements in the array as a pivot value around which the other elements will be rearranged. Everything less than the pivot is moved left of the pivot (into the left partition). Similarly, everything greater than the pivot goes into the right partition. At this point each partition is recursively quick sorted. The Quicksort algorithm is fastest when the median of the array is chosen as the pivot value. That is because the resulting partitions are of very similar size. Each partition splits itself in two and thus the base case is reached very quickly.

   The algorithm can be stated as follows:

   ```
   quicksort(A, i, k)
     if i < k:
         p := partition(A, i, k)
         quicksort(A, i, p - 1)
         quicksort(A, p + 1, k)
   ```

   Sorting the entire array is accomplished by calling quicksort(A, 1, A.length). The partition operation is step 2 from the description in English, above. It can be defined as:

   ```
   // left - is the index of the leftmost element of the subarray
   // right - is the index of the rightmost element of the subarray
   // number - of elements in subarray = right-left+1

   partition(array, left, right)
       pivotIndex = choose-pivot(array, left, right)
       pivotValue = array[pivotIndex]
       swap array[pivotIndex] and array[right]

       return storeIndex
   ```

   Using this definition, write a Java program that can be used to sort a list of integer values.

2. Write a program that can be used to carry out file activities. Provide methods for each of the following:
   (a) The program opens a text file.
   (b) Provide method to search the file line by line for a given string. If the search is successful, provide information pertaining to the line number, followed by the contents of the line that contains the search argument. For instance given the following the search string: **Java**, the program would search the file line by line generating a result such as the following:

   5: on the island of Java

9: The people of JAVA loves jaVa.

Use the class LineNumberReader for this exercise. Also, search the text recursively.

(c) Write a method that accepts a reference to a file or directory and recursively list all files and directories under that directory.

(d) Write a method that accepts a reference to a file or directory and recursively list all directories under that directory.

(e) Write a method that recursively list all files and directories in the file system.

(f) Write a method that accepts a reference to a file or directory and recursively list all files of a given extension under that directory.

3. Merge sort is a sorting technique that sequences data by continuously merging items in a single sorted list. Every item in the original unordered list is merged with another, creating groups of two. Every two-item group is merged, creating groups of four and so on until there is one ordered list, as shown below.

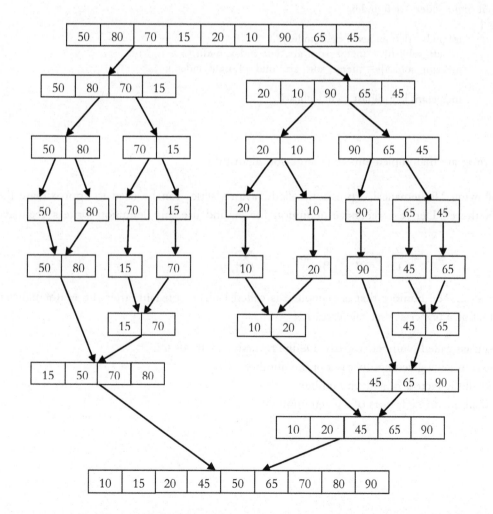

The algorithm is basically as follows:
- (i) Divide the list in halves
- (ii) Merge sort the first half
- (iii) Merge sort the second half
- (iv) Merge both halves back together

This algorithm lends itself well to recursion. The algorithm divides the array to be sorted into halves, sort these two sub-arrays separately, and then combine these sorted sub-arrays to produce solution to the original problem. Once the array is divided, the left sub-array is further divided into sub-arrays until the last sub-array has at most two values. At this point these two values are sorted; likewise, the sub-array to the neighbor (if any) this sorted array, is now sorted and is merged to the already sorted sub-list. Once the left sub-array is sorted and merged, the right sub-array is divided and sorted like the left. When both sub-arrays sorted, they are then merged.

```
merge_sort(int arr[], int left_index, int right_index)
{
    if (right_index > left_index)
    {
        int mid = (left_index + right_index)/2;
        int left_sublist[] = merge_sort( arr, left_index, mid);
        int right_sublist[] = merge_sort( arr, mid+ 1, right_index,);

        merge(arr, left_sublist, right_sublist);
    }
}
```

Write a program that implements the merge-sort algorithm

4. The following Mathematical expression called Taylor's series can be used to approximate the value of the e^x. Derive a recursive definition for e^x, and use this definition write a recursive method.

$$e^x = 1 + \frac{x}{1!} + \frac{x^2}{2!} + \frac{x^3}{3!} + \cdots = \sum_{n=0}^{\infty} \frac{x^n}{n!}$$

When x = 1. The number that is generated is called Euler's constant, after the Mathematician Euler. Define a test class that calculates *e*.

5. Write a class called NumberProperty. Define recursive methods to:
   - (a) Determine if a given number is a prime number.
   - (b) Find all the factors of a given number.
   - (c) Find all the prime factors of a given number.

Chapter 6 An Introduction to Data Structure

Objectives

After reading this chapter you will:

- Have a firm understanding of the Java Collections Framework
- Know the difference between the interfaces – List, Set, Queue and Map
- Know the classes that implement each of the interfaces – List, Set, Queue and Map
- Be better able to decide which class is more appropriate for a given application
- Be able to determine which application would be more suited for the use of Stack, Queue or LinkedList

Introduction

In computer science, the term data structure refers to particular ways of organizing and storing data on a computer so that the data can be manipulated and retrieved with a high degree of efficiency in processing time and hardware resources. There are different ways to arrange data on a computer, which calls for different algorithms to access and manipulate the data. There are algorithms that are described as general purpose data structures, and others that are highly specialized for specific tasks.

Two of the most frequently use general purpose data structures at the introductory stage of programming are array and ArrayList. An array as you know is a fixed size data structure that stores data contiguously in memory. The data must be of the same data type, whether primitive types or reference types. ArrayList on the other hand is a class that implements a variable size array that also stores data contiguously in memory. In addition, all of the data must be objects.

Some highly specialized data structures are Stack, Queue, LinkedList, and HashMap. Stack defines a data structure where only one end of the list can be accessed at all times. Queue on the other hand allows the data to be accessed from either ends of the list. LinkedList makes it easy to access data at any position in the list. In addition, the data is not necessarily stored contiguously as in the above cases. Unlike the other data structures, HashMap requires each unit of information to have two components – one component acts as a key which it uses to locate the data, and the other, the actual data value itself.

In this chapter you will learn about Java's pre-defined interfaces and classes that deal with data structures. First, we will begin with the Java utility interfaces and classes that are referred to as the Collections Framework. This will be followed by a study of some specialized classes where you will learn how to define your own collections.

Collection Framework

The Java platform includes a set of interfaces and classes that are referred to as the collections framework. A collection allows a group of objects to be treated as a single unit. That is, objects can be stored, retrieved and manipulated as elements of collections. Four of the most important interfaces of the Java collection framework are Set, Queue, List and Map. These interfaces present a set of standard utility classes that manage collections. These interfaces and their implementations are found in the **java.util** package. There are two main sets of interfaces within the framework – Collection and Map. The framework that handles singled valued objects is the interface Collection; and the framework that handles (key, value) pair objects is the interface Map.

Figure 6.1 shows the hierarchy of the collections framework that handles single value objects. The entities that are enclosed within broken line rectangles are interfaces, and those within solid line rectangles are classes.

Figure 6.1 The Java Collection Framework

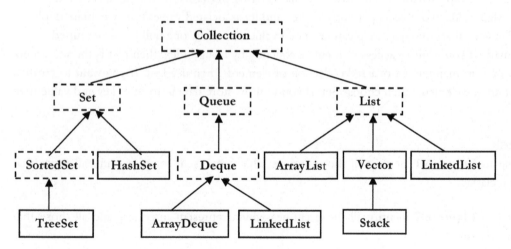

Figure 6.2 shows the hierarchy of the collection framework that handles (key, value) pair of objects. Notice that the only interface in this category is Map.

Figure 6.2 The Java Collection Framework

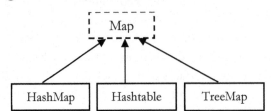

When To Use Set, List, Queue, or Map

In order to decide when to use List, Queue, Set or Map, you need to know what these interfaces are, and what functionality they provide.

The interface **List** provides ordered and indexed collection which may contain duplicates. The position of each object is preserved each time that the program is executed. List can have any number of null elements. A typical application could be storing items. The interface **Set** on the other hand provides an unordered collection of unique objects. That is, duplicates are not allowed. In addition, there is no guarantee which position an object will be stored each time that the program is executed. Set permits only one null element.

The interface **Queue** represents a list of objects that can be accessed from either ends of the collection, with the restriction that the first element to be stored must be the first to be removed from the list. Queue is used by operating systems to sequence jobs such as files that are waiting to be printed. Duplicates are permitted. In addition, the position of each element is guaranteed each time that the program is executed.

The interface **Map** provides a data structure that is based primarily on storing data in a key-value pair format. Map holds two objects per entry - a key and its associated value. It may contain duplicate values, but keys are always unique. Map can have null values, but only one null key is permitted.

In summary, if you want to access elements frequently by using index, then List is the way to go. Also, if you want to maintain an ordered collection of elements then use List. If you want to create a collection of unique elements then choose Set. If you want to store data in form of key and value then use Map.

Self-Check

1. Referring to **Figure 6.1** identify all those entities which represent interfaces and all those that represent classes.

2. Referring to **Figure 6.2** identify all those entities which represent interfaces and all those that represent classes.

3. From the Collections Framework, name two classes that do not preserve the order of elements as they are stored in the collection.

4. From the Collections Framework, name two classes that preserve the order of elements as they are stored in the collection.

5. From the Collections Framework, name all those classes that preserve the order of elements as they are stored in the collection.

6. From the Collections Framework, name those classes that do not accept duplicate elements.

7. From the Collections Framework, name those classes that accept duplicate elements.

8. From the Collections Framework, name the interface which dictates that classes require element pairs when storing data.

9. Which of the following are core interfaces of the collection framework?
    (a) Vector
    (b) Set
    (c) List
    (d) Collection
    (e) Map

The Interface - Collection

The interface, Collection, declares methods that carry out operations on individual elements, as well as groups of elements. The following methods are used to either add individual elements to the collection, to remove individual elements from the collection, or to query the state of the collection.

Method	Meaning
int size()	Determines the number of elements in the collection
boolean isEmpty()	Determines whether or not the list is empty
Object iterator()	Returns an iterator over the elements in this collection which is used to traverse the collection of elements
boolean remove(Object o)	Removes the given object from the collection, if the element was found in the collection
boolean contains(Object o)	Determines if a given object is in the collection
boolean add(Object o)	Adds an element to the collection, if the collection accepts duplicates.

The methods that carry out operations on groups of elements, as if they were a single element are shown below:

Method	Meaning
boolean containsAll(Collection c)	Determines if a given set of elements are in the collection

boolean addAll(Collection c)	Adds all elements of **c** to the collection, if duplicates are permitted.
boolean removeAll(Collection c)	Removes all elements of **c**, from the collection, if all elements are present.
boolean retainAll(Collection c)	Retains all elements of **c**, which are also in the collection.
void clear()	Empties the collection.

The Interface - Set

The interface, Set, which inherits Collection, defines a collection that contains no pair of elements e_1 and e_2 such that e_1**.equals(e_2)**. Also, the order of the elements is not preserved when they are added to the collection.

Set allows group of elements treated as a single unit. For example, let **a** and **b** be two sets, then bulk operations have the meanings as shown below:

Operations	Meaning
a.containsAll(b)	**b** is a subset of **a**
a.addAll(b)	**a** union **b**
a.removeAll(b)	**a** – **b** difference
a.retainAll(b)	**a** intersection b
a.clear()	**a** = empty set

In all of the cases above set **a** is modified, and set **b** remains unchanged.

The Class HashSet

The class HashSet, an implementation of the Set interface, does not support duplicate elements. The method **add** which adds elements to the set returns false when it encounters duplicate elements, to indicate that this new entry was not accepted in the collection. However, if the entry is accepted, it returns true.

Elements are not stored contiguously using HashSet, as a result it is not possible to traverse the collection with the traditional for loop. Instead, you would use the enhanced for loop, or the iterator object. If the enhanced for loop is used, it is not possible to modify the elements in the set while traversing the loop. The class supports four overloaded constructors, as shown below:

Constructor	Meaning
HashSet()	Construct a new empty set
HashSet(Collection c)	A new set with initial collection elements
HashSet(int initialCapacity)	Creates an empty set with an initial capacity
HashSet(int initialCapacity, float loadFactor)	empty set with initial capacity and a specific load factor

The Class TreeSet

The class TreeSet, is an indirect implementation of the Set interface. This class, like the class HashSet does not support duplicate elements. In addition, the elements are not stored contiguously in the collection, hence indices are not applicable. They are sorted in their natural order. Like HashSet, either the enhanced for loop or the iterator must be used to traverse the collection. The class supports four overloaded constructors, as shown below:

Constructor	Meaning
TreeSet()	Constructs a new, empty set, sorted according to the elements' natural order.
TreeSet (Collection <?extends E> c)	Constructs a new set containing the elements in the specified collection, sorted according to the elements' natural order.
TreeSet(Comparator<? super E> comparator)	Constructs a new, empty tree set, sorted according to the specified comparator
TreeSet (SortedSet s)	Constructs a new sorted set containing the same elements as the given sorted set.

Listing 6.1 shows an implementation of the classes HashSet and TreeSet. The class HashSet illustrates the manipulation of the collection of String values individually, as well as in groups. As you can see, **Lines 14, 19,** and **32** call the method add to add elements individually to each set. **Lines 36** and **40** show how elements are manipulated as groups of element through the methods **addAll** and **containsAll. Line 42** also shows how group operations are done via a constructor.

Listing 6.1 Implementing Set – HashSet and TreeSet

```
1.    import java.util.Set;
2.    import java.util.HashSet;
3.    import java.util.TreeSet;
4.    import java.util.Iterator;
5.    import java.util.Collection;
6.
7.    class SetExample {
8.        public static void main(String[] arg) {
9.            String [] group1 = {"Bernadine", "Elizabeth", "Gene", "Elizabeth", "Clara"};
10.           String [] group2 = {"John", "Jerry", "Elizabeth"};
11.           String [] group3 = {"Bill", "Harry", "Elizabeth"};
12.
13.           Set <String>set1 = new HashSet<String>(); // Create first set of elements
14.           add(group1, set1);
15.           Iterator i = set1.iterator();
16.           System.out.println("HashSet set1:\t "+display(i));
17.
18.           Set set2 = new HashSet(); // Create second set and add elements
```

```
19.         add(group2, set2);
20.         i = set2.iterator();
21.         System.out.println("\nHashSet set2:\t"+display(i));
22.
23.         Set set3 = set1; // set3 references the same object that set1 is referring
24.         i = set3.iterator();
25.         System.out.println("\n set3 references set1:\t "+display(i));
26.
27.         set2.retainAll(set3); // Intersection
28.         i = set2.iterator();
29.         System.out.println("\nset2 = set2 intersect set3:\t"+display(i));
30.
31.         Set set4 = new HashSet(); // Create a fourth set
32.         add(group3, set4);
33.         i=set4.iterator();
34.         System.out.println("\nAdd elements to set4:\t"+display(i));
35.
36.         set4.addAll(set3); // Union
37.         i=set4.iterator();
38.         System.out.println("\nset4 union set3: \t"+display(i));
39.
40.         System.out.println(" \nset4.containsAll(set3):\t" + set4.containsAll(set3));
41.
42.         Set sortedSet = new TreeSet(set4); // Create a sorted set and sort set4.
43.         i=sortedSet.iterator();
44.         System.out.println("\nSet 4 Sorted:\t"+display(i));
45.
46.     }
47.     static void add(Sting[] names, Collection s) {
48.         for (int i = 0; i < names.length; i++)
49.             s.add(names[i]);
50.     }
51.     static String display(Iterator i)  {
52.         if (!i.hasNext())
53.             return "";
54.         else
55.             return i.next()+" " + display(i);
56.     }
57. }
```

Before we start the analysis of the code in detail, we will take a look at three things that worth noting. Firstly, you would have noticed that **Lines 9** thru **11** define three arrays of string values. Secondly, **Lines 47** thru **50** define a method called **add** which accepts an array of string values and add them to the respective collection. Lastly, the method called **display** recursively extracts each string from the collection, and return these values.

Single Operations

In the segment of codes below, a HashSet object, set1, has been created, and the add method is called to add the array, group1, to the set. As you can see, the collection has four string values when the display method is called. See **Figure 6.3**.

```
Set <String>set1 = new HashSet<String>(); // Create first set of elements
add(group1, set1);
Iterator i = set1.iterator();
System.out.println("HashSet set1:\t "+display(i));
```

In this listing, notice that the name Elizabeth did not appear a second time in the output. This because the class does not accommodate duplicate elements.

Figure 6.3

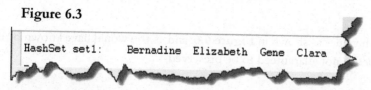

```
HashSet set1:    Bernadine  Elizabeth  Gene  Clara
```

In the listing below a new HashSet, set2, has been created and is populated with the array group2. When the values are displayed, we see that they are not listed in the order that they were added, this is because HashSet does not preserve order. See **Figure 6.4**. You may ask why the order was preserved in set1. This is just by co-incidence. Chances are that if you should run the program again, or run it on a different machine you would get a different arrangement of values.

```
Set set2 = new HashSet(); // Create second set and add elements
add(group2, set2);
i = set2.iterator();
System.out.println("\nHashSet set2:\t"+display(i));
```

Figure 6.4

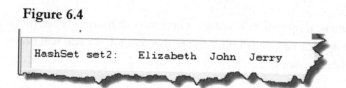

```
HashSet set2:    Elizabeth   John   Jerry
```

Bulk Operations

The following section looks at three group operations – **retainsAll** (the intersection of two sets), **addAll** (the union of two sets), and **containsAll** (sub set). First we examine intersection of two sets. In **Listing 6.1** Line **23**, the reference variable, **set3**, was set to point at **set1** which had values - "Bernadine", "Elizabeth", "Gene", and "Clara". The code below shows the group operation **retainsAll**, the intersection of two sets. Notice that the entire operation occurs within the method itself. The output, **Figure 6.5** shows the single value, Elizabeth that is common to both sets.

```
set2.retainAll(set3); // Intersection
i = set2.iterator();
System.out.println("\nset2 = set2 intersect set3:\t"+display(i));
```

Figure 6.5

```
set2 = set2 intersect set3: Elizabeth
```

The code below creates set4 with values as shown in **Figure 6.6**, and as you would have known by now the order of how they were added is not guaranteed to be preserved.

```
Set set4 = new HashSet(); // Create a fourth set
add(group3, set4);
i=set4.iterator();
System.out.println("\nAdd elements to set4:\t"+display(i));
```

Figure 6.6

```
Add elements to set4:    Elizabeth  Harry  Bill
```

Another well-known Mathematical operation is union, where two or more sets are merged to form a single set. When this operation is carried out duplicates are thrown out. As you will notice in the third group of statements below the statement:

```
set4.addAll(set3);
```

The method **addAll** forms the union of set3 and set4. The complete operation is shown in the segment of code below, and the result is shown in **Figure 6.7**.

```
Set set3 = set1; // set3 references the same object that set1 is referring
i = set3.iterator();
System.out.println("set3 references set1: "+display(i));

Set set4 = new HashSet(); // Create a fourth set
add(group3, set4);
i=set4.iterator();
System.out.println("Add elements to set4: "+display(i));

set4.addAll(set3); // Union
i=set4.iterator();
System.out.println("set4 union set3: "+display(i));
```

The result of using the bulk operation method addAll(..).

Figure 6.7

```
set3 references set1: Bernadine  Elizabeth  Gene  Clara
Add elements to set4: Elizabeth  Harry  Bill
set4 union set3: Bernadine  Elizabeth  Harry  Gene  Clara  Bill
```

The third form of group operations is a query, which determines if all the elements of one group are in another group. In this example the statement is:

set4.containsAll(set3)

This method attempts to determine if all the elements of set3, are members of set4. See the usage below, and the output of **Figure 6.8**.

```
System.out.println(" \nset4.containsAll(set3):\t" + set4.containsAll(set3));
```

Figure 6.8

```
set4.containsAll(set3): true
```

Sorting Bulk Operation

The last operation to be considered in this section is sorting. In this context, the class that is needed for this operation is the class TreeSet. This class sorts the strings in their natural order as they are being added to the set. To have them sorted in descending order would necessitate using the method descendingSet(). **Figure 6.9** shows the sorted result, in its natural order.

Set sortedSet = new TreeSet(set4); // Create a sorted set and sort set4.
i = sortedSet.iterator();
System.out.println("\nSet 4 Sorted:\t"+display(i));

Figure 6.9

Set 4 Sorted: Bernadine Clara Elizabeth Gene

Self-Check

1. Given that the variables **set1** and **set2** are references to two distinct set objects, what is the result of the following operation?

    set1.add(set2)

    Select one the one correct answer.
    (a) set2 contains all elements in set1 and set2 combined.
    (b) set2 remains unchanged
    (c) set1 contains all elements in set1 and set2 combined.
    (d) set1 remains unchanged

2. What is a HashSet?

3. What is a TreeSet?

4. Difference between HashSet and TreeSet?

5. Name the interface that is used to represent collections that maintain unique elements in order.

6. True or False. A HashSet maintains an ordered collection of objects whereas a TreeSet does not.
   Select one:
   (a) True
   (b) False

The interface - List

Unlike the Set interface, the List interface preserves the order of the elements as they are entered. In addition to using the enhanced for loop or the iterator object, the list can be access by index, using the traditional looping structures. List accommodates duplicates also. A summary of the more frequently used methods is shown below:

Methods for Elements Accessed by Index

boolean add(Object o)	Appends the specified element to the end of this list
void add(int index, Object o)	Inserts the specified element at the specified position in this list
Object get(int index)	Returns the element at the specified position in this list
Object set(int index, Object o)	Replaces the element at the specified position in this list with the specified element
Object remove(int index)	Removes the first occurrence of the specified element from this list, if it is present

Methods for Interrogating the List

int indexOf(Object o)	Returns the index of the first occurrence of the specified element in this list, or -1 if this list does not contain the element
int lastIndexOf(Object o)	Returns the index of the last occurrence of the specified element in this list, or -1 if this list does not contain the element.
boolean isEmpty()	Returns true if this list contains no elements.

Classes That Implement List

In this section, we will study two implementations of List – the class ArrayList and the class Vector. The class ArrayList as you may already know from **Volume I Chapter 10**, represents an automatic re-sizeable array. It is used in place of array when the size of the list is not known ahead of time. A summary of its constructors is shown below:

Constructor	Meaning
ArrayList()	Constructs an empty list.
ArrayList(Collection c)	Constructs a list containing the elements of the specified collection, in the order they are returned by the collection's iterator
ArrayList(int initialCapacity)	Constructs an empty list with the specified initial capacity.

The class Vector, like the class ArrayList implements a re-sizable array of objects. Like the ArrayList, it components can be accessed using the iterator as well as either of the **for** loops. Also, the size of a Vector can grow or shrink as needed to accommodate adding or removing items after the Vector has been created. A summary of its constructors is shown below:

Constructor	Meaning
Vector()	Constructs an empty vector so that its internal data array has size 10 and its standard capacity increment is zero.
Vector(Collection c)	Constructs a vector containing the elements of the specified collection, in the order they are returned by the collection's iterator.
Vector(int initialCapacity)	Constructs an empty vector with the specified initial capacity and with its capacity increment equal to zero.
Vector(int initialCapacity, int increment)	Constructs an empty vector with the specified initial capacity, and capacity increment.

When To Use ArrayList over Vector

When it comes to ArrayList and Vector, the two classes are very similar. However, there are some major differences between them. In terms of similarity, both classes are good for retrieving elements from a specific position in the list, or for adding and removing elements from either ends of the list. The remainder of this section outlines the differences between both classes.

All the programs that you have written so far are referred to as sequential programs. With sequential programs, each has a beginning, an execution sequence, and an end. In programming this model is referred to as a single threaded program. In general a thread is similar to a sequential program. That is, a single thread also has a beginning, an end, a sequence, and at any given time during the runtime of the thread there is a single point of execution. However, a thread itself is not a program. It cannot run on its own, but runs within a single program. There are situations also, where a single program may have multiple threads requiring the same resource at the same time for different purposes. When this situation arises, it is a good idea to protect the resources from unintended access. This is where ArrayList and Vector exhibit their major differences.

The foremost difference between Vector and ArrayList is that Vector is synchronized, and ArrayList is not. What this means is that Vector operates safely in a multi-threaded environment. This is not the case of ArrayList, ArrayList was designed for single-threaded environment. For example, whereas Vector safeguards against multiple threads accessing a file; ArrayList does not. Also, Vector defaults to doubling the size of its internal array when the original size is exhausted; while the ArrayList increases its internal array size by 50 percent.

Example 6.1 The following program which features three classes – **Friend**, **MyVector**, and **TestMyVector** - demonstrates the use of the class Vector. The data to be stored is represented by the class **Friend**. See **Listing 6.2**.

// Listing 6.2 – This class stores the data for each person

```
1.    public class Friend
2.    {
3.        String lastname, firstname;
4.
```

```
5.          Friend(String f,  String l){
6.                  this.lastname = l;
7.                  this.firstname = f;
8.          }
9.          public String getFirstname(){
10.                 return firstname;
11.         }
12.         public String getLastname(){
13.                 return lastname;
14.         }
15.  }
```

Listing 6.3 shows the class MyVector which creates a Vector object with an initial capacity, and an incremental factor. It also makes use of several of the methods from the class Vector, either to store, manipulate, and/or to query the objects in the list. First the constructor creates a Vector of a given size with a specified incremental factor. The class demonstrates the use of some of the more used method – adding (appending to the list), inserting an object at a specified position in the list; replacing a given object within the vector, and deleting an element from the vector. These are demonstrated by the methods **add**, **insert**, **replace**, and **delete**, respectively. Other methods for retrieving data are **getIterator**, **size** and **getCapacity**, retrieve the relevant information from the list.

```
// Listing 6.3

1.   import java.util.Vector;
2.   import java.util.Iterator;
3.
4.   public class MyVector
5.   {
6.           private Vector <Friend>v;
7.
8.           public MyVector(int initiaCapacity, int increment){
9.                   v = new Vector<Friend>(initiaCapacity, increment);
10.          }
11.          public void add(Friend f) {
12.                  v.addElement(f);  // Append  data to the list
13.          }
14.          public void insert(int i, Friend f){
15.                  v.add(i, f);
16.          }
17.          public void replace(Friend f, int i){
18.                  v.set(i, f);
19.          }
20.          public Friend delete(int i){
21.                  return (Friend)v.remove(i);
22.          }
23.          public Iterator getIterator() {// Generates and returns iterator for the vector
```

```
24.                    return (Iterator)v.iterator();
25.              }
26.              public int size() {  // Retrieve the size of the list, not the capacity
27.                    return v.size();
28.              }
29.              public int getCapacity(){    // Retrieve the capacity of the vector
30.                    return v.capacity();
31.              }
32.  }
```

The test class TestMyVector shown in **Listing 6.4** indirectly creates a vector of initial capacity of 4, and an incrementing factor of 2. See **Line 5**.   It also supplies the class MyVector with data; and it displays the state of the vector in terms of its size, its capacity and names of each friend object.

Listing 6.4 Test class

```
1.    import java.util.Iterator;
2.
3.    public class TestMyVector {
4.        public static void main(String arg[]) {
5.              MyVector mv = new MyVector(4, 2); // Values with which to create vector
6.
7.              System.out.println("Append Friend to the list");
8.
9.              mv.add(new Friend("John", "Brown"));
10.             mv.add(new Friend("Mary", "Henry"));
11.             mv.add(new Friend("James", "Small"));
12.
13.             System.out.println("Capacity is " + mv.getCapacity() + "\tSize = " + mv.size());
14.             Iterator i = mv.getIterator();
15.             display(i);
16.
17.             System.out.println("-----------------------------");
18.             System.out.println("Insert Friend into the list");
19.             mv.insert(2, new Friend("Carmen", "Goary"));
20.             System.out.println("Add a Friend to the list");
21.             mv.add(new Friend("Joseph", "Morgan"));
22.
23.             System.out.println("\nCapacity is " + mv.getCapacity() + "\tSize = " + mv.size());
24.             i = mv.getIterator();
25.             display(i);
26.
27.             mv.replace(new Friend("Karen", "Smith"), 2);
28.
29.             System.out.println("-----------------------------");
```

```
30.              System.out.println("\nReplace a Friend into the list");
31.              System.out.println("Capacity is " + mv.getCapacity() + "\tSize = " + mv.size());
32.              i = mv.getIterator();
33.              display(i);
34.
35.              System.out.println("-----------------------------");
36.              System.out.println("\nRemove Friend friend the list");
37.              Friend f = mv.delete(2);
38.
39.              System.out.println("Friend deleted is " + f.getFirstname() + " " + f.getLastname());
40.
41.              System.out.println("-----------------------------");
42.              System.out.println("\nCapacity is " + mv.getCapacity() + "\tSize = " + mv.size());
43.              i = mv.getIterator();
44.              display(i);
45.      }
46.      public static void display(Iterator i)
47.      {
48.              while (i.hasNext())
49.              {
50.                  Friend f = (Friend) i.next();
51.                  System.out.println(f.getFirstname() + "\t" + f.getLastname());
52.              }
53.      }
54. }
```

In the Listing you will notice:

(a) **Lines 9 thru 11** add three friends to the list

(b) **Line 19** inserts a friend at location 2 in the list. Recall that Vector, like ArrayList, numbers its index starting from zero. Therefore, inserting an object at location 2, has the effect of displacing the fourth element in the list. In this case, Friend ("James Small") is now at location 3.

(c) **Line 21** adds another friend to the list. This is now the fifth Friend in the list. This adding of this new Friend to the list has the effect of appending to the list.

(d) **Line 27** replaces a friend with another friend. Notice that the size of the list in this case does not change. This action is neither a deletion nor an insertion, but rather it should be interpreted as a replacement of one Friend with another.

(e) **Line 37** deletes a friend from the list. This action has the effect of removing the third Friend from the list, causing the list to be shortened by one. In addition, the method not removes the object from the list, but it also returns a copy of it. Hence the statement:

```
Friend f = mv.delete(2);
```

Notice that for each activity (a) thru (e), the state of the list is displayed.

Figure 6.10 shows the output from the program.

Figure 6.10 Output from program

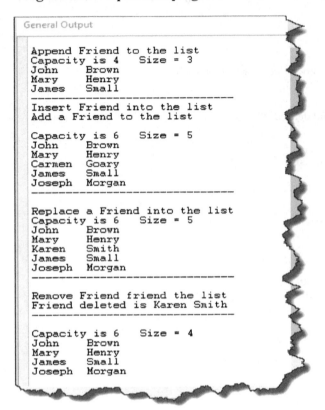

```
General Output

Append Friend to the list
Capacity is 4    Size = 3
John      Brown
Mary      Henry
James     Small
----------------------------------
Insert Friend into the list
Add a Friend to the list

Capacity is 6    Size = 5
John      Brown
Mary      Henry
Carmen    Goary
James     Small
Joseph    Morgan
----------------------------------

Replace a Friend into the list
Capacity is 6    Size = 5
John      Brown
Mary      Henry
Karen     Smith
James     Small
Joseph    Morgan
----------------------------------

Remove Friend friend the list
Friend deleted is Karen Smith
----------------------------------

Capacity is 6    Size = 4
John      Brown
Mary      Henry
James     Small
Joseph    Morgan
```

Self-Check

1. What is the List interface?

2. What are the main implementations of the List interface?

3. Difference between ArrayList and Vector?

4. How to obtain Array from an ArrayList?

5. Differentiate between the interface List and the interface Set.

6. Which of the following are the main collection interfaces?
    (a) HashSet
    (b) Set
    (c) Vector
    (d) Collection

(e) List

(f) ArrayList

7. True or False. Select one.

HashSet has the ability to store objects in specific location in a list. indices are used to access each element in the set.

8. Which of the following classes implements the List interface?
   (a) Vector
   (b) Arrays
   (c) ArrayList
   (d) LinkedList
   (e) HashSet

9. What is difference between List and a Set?

10. What is difference between Arrays and ArrayList?

11. What is the difference among List, Set and Map interfaces?

Classes That Implements Map

The interface Map defines a data structure that requires a pair of information to be stores as a unit. The first component in the pair is referred to as a **key**, and the second, the actual record or data associated with the key, sometimes referred to as the **value**. This interface is a member of the Java Collections Framework; however, it is not a derivative of the interface, Collection. This interface provides three collection views – Hashtable, HashMap, and TreeMap. , which allow a map's contents to be viewed as a set of keys, collection of values, or set of key-value mappings. While TreeMap preserves the order of the data, Hashtable and HashMap do not. The table below shows the methods that are in the interface.

Methods	Meanings
void clear()	Removes all entries from this map
boolean containsKey(Object key)	Returns true if this map contains a value for the specified key
boolean containsValue(Object value)	Returns true if this map contains a value for the specified key.
Set<Map.Entry<K,V>> entrySet()	Returns a Set view of the mappings contained in this map.
boolean equals(Object key)	Compares the specified object with this map if they are identical.

V get(Object key)	Returns the value to which the specified key is mapped, or null if this map contains no mapping for the key
boolean isEmpty()	Returns true if this map contains no key-value mappings.
Set<K> keySet()	Returns a Set view of the keys contained in this map
V put(K key, V value)	Associates the specified value with the specified key in this map
V remove(Object key)	Removes the mapping for a key from this map if it is present or null if there is none.
int size()	Returns the number of key-value mappings in this map.
Collection <K> values()	Returns a Collection view of the values contained in the map

Hashtable

Hashtable is a synchronized (key – value pair) data structure that is used to efficiently lookup values without relying on searching a list linearly. The way that a hash table is set up is that the key is hashed into an index value for an internal array. This means that two keys could be mapped to the same index. When this happens the array that is associated with this index is increased in order to store the value. This array is referred to as a bucket. You can think of a hash map like a filing cabinet as shown in **Figure 6.11,** where each drawer represents a bucket, and each bucket multiple partitions for the documents that fall in that drawer.

Figure 6.11 – Filing cabinet

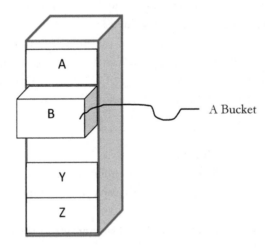

In the case of the electronic version the key is hashed or mapped to an integer value which is used as the entry to the respective bucket. See **Figure 6.12**.

Figure 6.12 Hashtable

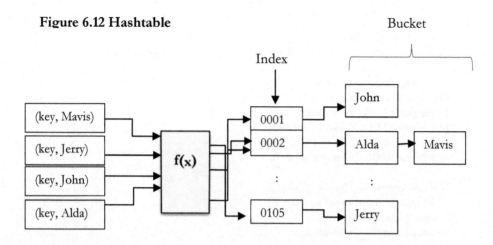

The table below shows the constructors for the class Hashtable.

Constructor	Meaning
Hashtable()	Creates a new Hashtable with default initial capacity of 11 and a default load factor of 0.75
Hashtable(int initialCapacity)	Creates a new Hashtable with a specified initial capacity and a default load factor of 0.75
Hashtable(int initialCapacity, float increment)	Creates a new Hashtable with a specified initial capacity and a specified load factor

When accessing data, if a key is re-mapped to a given index, it is simply a matter of traversing the bucket which contains the data. In this sense Hashtable is more efficient than a linear array. Hashtable does not allow null key nor null value pair. Also, Hashtable does not preserve the order of how the data was stored.

The class ConcurrentHashMap (Java 1.7) can be used instead of the class Hashtable, as ConcurrentHashMap has the same specifications as Hashtable, but we will continue with Hashtable. **Listing 6.5** creates a Hastable with key-value pair integer-string, and loads the table with five pairs of values.

```
// Listing 6.5

1.    import java.util.Hashtable;
2.    import java.util.Map;
3.    import java.util.Set;
4.    import java.util.Iterator;
5.
6.    public class MyHashtable
7.    {
8.         public static void main(String[] args)
```

```
9.          {
10.              // Creating a Hashtable
11.              Hashtable<Integer, String> htable = new Hashtable<Integer, String>();
12.
13.              /*Adding elements to HashMap*/
14.              htable.put(20030, "James Nelson");
15.              htable.put(22030, "Larry Smith");
16.              htable.put(40030, "Deloris Morris");
17.              htable.put(30030, "Carmen Goary");
18.              htable.put(10030, "Carmen Smith");
19.
20.              System.out.println("Key\t\tValue");
21.              /* Display content using Iterator*/
22.              Set set = htable.entrySet();
23.              Iterator iterator = set.iterator();
24.
25.              while(iterator.hasNext())
26.              {
27.                  Map.Entry mentry = (Map.Entry)iterator.next();
28.                  System.out.println( mentry.getKey() + "\t" + mentry.getValue());
29.              }
30.          }
31.  }
```

The output from the program shown in **Figure 6.13** demonstrates that the order of the data is not preserved when they are added to the list.

Figure 6.13

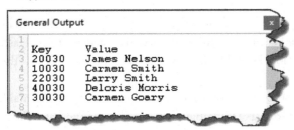

```
General Output                                    x
1
2    Key       Value
3    20030     James Nelson
4    10030     Carmen Smith
5    22030     Larry Smith
6    40030     Deloris Morris
7    30030     Carmen Goary
8
```

HashMap

HashMap like Hashtable is designed to store, retrieve, and manipulate key-value items efficiently. Unlike Hashtable, HashMap does not protect the data when the data is being accessed by multiple threads. Also, HashMap allows one null key and any number of null values to be stored. In addition, HashMap is much faster and uses less memory than Hashtable as HashMap is unsynchronized. The table below shows the constructors for the class HashMap.

Constructor	Meaning
HashMap()	Creates a new HashMap with default initial capacity of 16 and a default load factor of 0.75

HashMap(int initialCapacity)	Creates a new HashMap with a specified initial capacity and a default load factor of 0.75
HashMap(int initialCapacity, float increment)	Creates a new HashMap with a specified initial capacity and a specified load factor
HashMap(Map<? extends K, ? extends V> m)	Constructs a new HashMap with the same mappings as the specified Map.

Listing 6.6 shows the use of the class HashMap. As indicated, the pair-value entries are Integer – String. See creation of HashMap object **Line 9**. As you will notice, on **Lines 12** thru **16**, five entries were added to this list. Unlike array or ArrayList, the use of index is not relevant, Lines 22 and 28 returns the HashMap of objects as a set, thus using the iterator to extract the values. To locate an entry, the key is used. Hence although we know that the entry 10030 is the 5th entry, we cannot use an index of 4, we have to use the key. It follows that in order to remove an entry we must locate the entry by the key. See the method remove – **Lines 37** thru **41**.

```
// Listing 6.6

1.    import java.util.HashMap;
2.    import java.util.Map;
3.    import java.util.Iterator;
4.    import java.util.Set;
5.
6.    public class MyHashMap {
7.        public static void main(String args[]) {
8.            /* This is how to declare HashMap */
9.            HashMap<Integer, String> hmap = new HashMap<Integer, String>();
10.
11.           /*Adding elements to HashMap*/
12.           hmap.put(20030, "James Nelson");
13.           hmap.put(22030, "Larry Smith");
14.           hmap.put(40030, "Deloris Morris");
15.           hmap.put(30030, "Carmen Goary");
16.           hmap.put(10030, "Carmen Smith");
17.
18.           System.out.println("Key\t\tValue");
19.
20.           Set set = hmap.entrySet();
21.           display(set);
22.
23.           remove(hmap, 40030);
24.           System.out.println("\nMap key and values after removal:");
25.
26.           set = hmap.entrySet();
27.           display(set);
28.       }
29.       static void display(Set s) {
```

```
30.              Iterator i = s.iterator();
31.
32.              while(i.hasNext()) {
33.                      Map.Entry hentry = (Map.Entry)i.next();
34.                      System.out.println( hentry.getKey() + "\t" + hentry.getValue());
35.                      }
36.              }
37.              static void remove(HashMap hmap, int key) {
38.                      if(hmap.containsKey(key))
39.                      {
40.                              System.out.println("\nValue of key " + key + " is "+ hmap.get(key) + " remove
                               entry");
41.                              hmap.remove(key);
42.                      }
43.              }
44.      }
```

Figure 6.14 shows the output from the program above.

Figure 6.14

```
Key       Value
20030     James Nelson
22030     Larry Smith
40030     Deloris Morris
30030     Carmen Goary
10030     Carmen Smith

Value of key 10030 is Carmen Smith remove entry

Map key and values after removal:
20030     James Nelson
22030     Larry Smith
40030     Deloris Morris
30030     Carmen Goary
```

The output from the program shown in **Figure 6.14** demonstrates that the order of the data is preserved when they are added to the list. Also, the neat thing about the method containsKey, is that it conducts the search, without the programmer having to write a search algorithm.

TreeMap

The class TreeMap, like the classes Hashtable and HashMap store the data in key-value format. However, unlike them both TreeMap stores their data in the natural ordering of the keys. This means that numeric type keys would sorted in the ascending order, and strings would be stored in lexicographical order. The table below shows the four over loaded constructors of the class.

Constructor	Meaning
TreeMap()	Constructs a new, empty tree map, using the natural ordering of its keys.
TreeMap(Comparator<? super K> comparator)	Constructs a new, empty tree map, ordered according to the given comparator.
TreeMap(Map<? extends K,? extends V> m)	Constructs a new tree map containing the same mappings as the given map, ordered according to the natural ordering of its keys.
TreeMap(SortedMap<K,? extends V> m)	Constructs a new tree map containing the same mappings and using the same ordering as the specified sorted map.

Listing 6.7 shows usage of the class TreeMap. Notice that it is used similar to Listing 6.6. However as you will notice in the output TreeMap sorts and stores the data as they are being entered. That is, there is no need to call any sort method carry out the sorting, it is done automatically.

Listing 6.7

```
1.    .import java.util.TreeMap;
2.    import java.util.Set;
3.    import java.util.Iterator;
4.    import java.util.Map;
5.
6.    public class MyTreeMap {
7.        public static void main(String args[]) {            // This is how to declare
          TreeMap
8.            TreeMap<Integer, String> tmap = new TreeMap<Integer, String>();
9.            // Adding elements to TreeMap
10.           tmap.put(20030, "James Nelson");
11.           tmap.put(22030, "Larry Smith");
12.           tmap.put(40030, "Deloris Morris");
13.           tmap.put(30030, "Carmen Goary");
14.           tmap.put(10030, "Carmen Smith");
15.
16.           System.out.println("Key\t\tValue");
17.           // Display content using Iterator
18.           Set set = tmap.entrySet();
19.           Iterator iterator = set.iterator();
20.           while(iterator.hasNext()) {
21.               Map.Entry mentry = (Map.Entry)iterator.next();
22.               System.out.println(mentry.getKey() +  "\t"+ mentry.getValue());
23.           }
24.      }
25.  }
```

Figure 6.15 shows the sorted output.

Figure 6.15

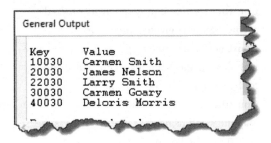

```
General Output

Key      Value
10030    Carmen Smith
20030    James Nelson
22030    Larry Smith
30030    Carmen Goary
40030    Deloris Morris
```

Self-Check

1. What are the differences between a HashMap and a Hashtable in Java?

2. Differentiate between HashMap and Hashtable.

3. (True or False) Hashtable does not allow null keys or values, while HashMap allows one null key and any number of null values.

3. Which of the following classes implements the Set interface?
    (a) HashMap
    (b) TreeSet
    (c) Hashtable
    (d) HashSet
    (e) SortedSet

4. Can duplicate keys be added in a HashMap? What will happen if we attempt to add duplicate values?

Chapter Summary

- Data structure refers to the way that data is organized, accessed, and manipulated so as to bring about efficiency in both processing time and hardware resources.

- The Java collections framework presents a set of interfaces and classes that allow groups of data to be treated as a single unit.

- There are two main interfaces within the framework – Collections and Map.

- The interface Collections has three main sub interfaces for general data structures as well as highly specialized data structures. These interfaces are Set, Queue, and List.

- The interface Collections handles single value items, and the interface Map handles pair value items.

- The classes HashMap and HashTable are similar the way that they store data - in a key-value pair. Both implements the interface Map. However, they differ from each other in the following way - whereas Hashtable is synchronized, HashMap is not.

- HashMap does not accommodate duplicate keys. If we attempt to do so, the previous value for the key is overwritten.

- HashMap and TreeMap are different from each other in the way that they are stored in memory. Whereas TreeMap stores the keys in their natural order, HashMap stores the key value pairs randomly.

Programming Exercises

1. Consider the following - write a program that keeps track of an inventory of motor car. In your solution design a class called MotorCarDatabase that stores motor cars by their names and the quantity of cars associated with each car. Also design a method that determines when to acquire more of a particular car when the inventory is below a given quantity. Once it is determined that the inventory is low, the inventory must be replenish by a certain amount. At the end of each business day print the inventory in alphabetical order by name.

   Solve this problem using the following classes in the solution:
   - HashMap
   - HashTable
   - TreeMap

2. Write a Java program that keeps a database of student records. Each student's record must be stored in the form of a pair of values — (student id number, information), where information consists of the student's id, name, address, and set of courses.

3. Repeat problem 2, but this time sort the records by id number, as they are being added to the list.

Chapter 7 Specialized Lists – Stack ▪ Queue ▪LinkedList▪

Objectives

After reading this chapter you will:

- Know three highly specialized data structures – Stack, Queue and LinkedList
- Be able to determine which of the three structures is more suitable for a given problem.
- Be able to define your own LinkedList data structure

Stack

The concept of stack is one of the most useful data structures in computer science. The first section of this chapter describes the concept, and shows through one example how valuable it is in solving some computer problems.

Stack is a special type of linear data structure in which items are added at one end of the list, and are removed in the reverse order in which they were added. That is, the most recently added item is the first one to be removed. This data structure is sometimes called *last-in, first-out (LIFO)*. You can think of a stack like a stack of cards, or like a stack of trays in a tray holder of a cafeteria.

In terms of application, some calculators use an algorithm called Reverse Polish Notation (RPN) to evaluate arithmetic expressions. Calculators that use RPN, use stack to store their values. All compilers use stack to parse the syntax of expressions, program blocks, and program statements, before translating the code into low level code.

Stack can be implemented in one of three ways – array based, linked list based, and the pre-defined class, Stack, found in the java.util package. We will discuss the Java pre-defined class Stack in this section.

The class Stack has only one constructor, shown below, that creates an empty stack.

Constructor   Description

Stack()   Constructor – when the stack is first created, It has no element

By the strict definition of stack, the methods shown below are all that are necessary. The methods that the class inherits are superfluous.

Methods	Description
boolean empty()	Determines if the stack is empty
Object peek()	Looks at the object at the top of this stack without removing it from the stack.
Object pop()	Removes the object at the top of this stack and returns that object
Object push(Object item)	Pushes an item onto the top of this stack.
int search(Object o)	Returns the position where an object is on this stack.

Example 7.1 The concept of stack as we have mentioned, is extremely important in computer science. For instance, it can be used to evaluate ordinary arithmetic expressions, that may contain arithmetic operators (+, -, *, /). Although there are several ways to carry out this exercise, we will use this three step algorithm to solve this problem. That is, given an arithmetic expression that may contain parentheses:

1. Verify that the expression, called infix expression, is properly formed as far as parentheses are concerned.
2. If the parenthesized expression is properly formed, convert the expression from an infix expression to its equivalent postfix expression, called Reverse Polish Notation (RPN).
3. Evaluate the postfix expression, if possible.

Step 1 - Verify that the expression
Given an arithmetic expression, called infix expression, verify that it is properly formed with respect to the parentheses. To determine this do the following:

1. Create an empty stack to store the left parenthesis only.
2. Scanned the arithmetic expression from left to right, one character at a time.
    While there are more characters in the arithmetic expression
    {

    > If the character is a left parenthesis '(', push it on to the stack. However if the character is a right parenthesis, ')', visit the stack and pop the top element from off the stack. All other characters must be ignored.

    }
3. If the stack contains any element at the end of reading the infix expression, then the conclusion is that the parentheses were not balanced.

Because we may be removing elements from the stack, then there is a possibility of attempting to remove elements from an empty stack. This could give rise to an EmptyStackException being raised, which could cause the program to terminate abnormally if the exception is not taken care of. If the program should throw an exception at this stage then this is another condition telling us that the parentheses were unbalanced initially.

Consider the following infix arithmetic expression: **(50 + 100) / ((15 - 20) * 25)**

Using the algorithm outlined above, the following table shows the state of the stack after each character is scanned.

Input	Analyze input	Action	State of Stack
Read token	(: left parenthesis	push	(
Read token	50 : number	skip	(
Read token	+ : arithmetic operator	skip	(
Read token	100 : number	skip	(
Read token	) : right parenthesis	pop	Stack is empty
Read token	/ : arithmetic operator	skip	Stack is empty
Read token	(: left parenthesis	push	(
Read token	(: left parenthesis	push	((
Read token	15 : number	skip	((
Read token	- : arithmetic operator	skip	((
Read token	20 : number	skip	((
Read token	) : right parenthesis	pop	(
Read token	* : arithmetic operator	skip	(
Read token	25 : number	skip	(
Read token	) : right parenthesis	pop	Stack is empty
Read token	End of input	No action	Stack is empty

Listing 7.1 shows a class called Arithmetic. The method, isBalance, uses the above algorithm to determine if the parentheses, if any, are balanced. If the expression has no parentheses, then the stack will always be empty. Hence the expression is valid with respect to parentheses only.

// Listing 7.1 - Class determines if parentheses are balanced

```
1.   import java.util.Stack;
2.
3.   public class Arithmetic
4.   {
5.        private Stack<Object> stk; // To store left parentheses
```

```
6.          private String expression;
7.          private int length;
8.
9.          public Arithmetic(String expression)
10.         {
11.             stk = new Stack<Object>();
12.             this.expression = expression;
13.             this.length = expression.length();
14.         }
15.         // Determine if parentheses are balanced
16.         boolean isBalance()
17.         {
18.             int index = 0;
19.             boolean fail = false;
20.             try
21.             {
22.                 while (index < length && !fail)
23.                 {       // Read to the end of the list, unless EmptyStackException occured
24.                     char ch = expression.charAt(index);
25.
26.                     switch (ch)
27.                     {
28.                         case Constants.LEFT_NORMAL:
29.                             stk.push(new Character(ch));
30.                             break;
31.                         case Constants.RIGHT_NORMAL:
32.                             stk.pop();
33.                             break;
34.                         default:
35.                             break;
36.                     }//end of switch
37.                     index++;
38.                 }//end of while
39.             }//end of try
40.             catch (EmptyStackException e)
41.             {
42.             System.out.println(e.toString());
43.             fail = true;
44.             }
45.             return (stk.empty() && !fail);
46.     } // end isBalance
47. }
```

Listing 7.2 shows the definition of the interface, Constants, with the definition for the constants left and right parentheses.

Listing 7.2

```
1.    public interface Constants
2.    {
3.         public static final char LEFT_NORMAL = '(',
4.                               RIGHT_NORMAL = ')';
5.    }
```

Listing 7.3 shows the test class. It defines an integer array with five arithmetic expressions, which it tests to determine if the parentheses are balanced. **Line 15** calls the method isBalance for this determination.

```
// Listing 7.3

1.    class Calculator
2.    {
3.         public static void main(String[] arg)
4.         {
5.              String s[] = { "5 + ) * 4 + ( 2",
6.                             "10 + 30 * 5",
7.                             "( 20 + 30 ) * 50 ",
8.                             "( 50 + 100 ) / ( ( 15 - 20 ) + 25 )",
9.                             "( 30 * ( 100 - 4 ) + ( 20 / 20 - 5 ) + 65"
10.                                };

11.
12.             for (int i = 0; i < s.length; i++)
13.             {
14.                  Arithmetic a = new Arithmetic(s[i]);
15.                  if (a.isBalance())
16.                       System.out.println(s[i] + " is valid - with respect to
                         parentheses\n");
17.                  else
18.                       System.out.println(s[i] + " is invalid - with respect to
                         parentheses\n");
19.             }
20.        }
21. }
```

Figure 7.1 shows the output where the first and last expressions have unbalanced parentheses.

Figure 7.1 Output from the program

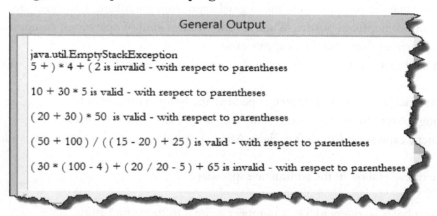

General Output

```
java.util.EmptyStackException
5 + ) * 4 + ( 2 is invalid - with respect to parentheses

10 + 30 * 5 is valid - with respect to parentheses

( 20 + 30 ) * 50  is valid - with respect to parentheses

( 50 + 100 ) / ( ( 15 - 20 ) + 25 ) is valid - with respect to parentheses

( 30 * ( 100 - 4 ) + ( 20 / 20 - 5 ) + 65 is invalid - with respect to parentheses
```

Self-Check

1. Which of the following statements are true about the data structure called **stack**?
    (a) A stack is an ordered collection of elements, where the elements are added to and remove from the collection at the one end called the stack top.
    (b) Elements can be added to and remove from any position in the list as long as long as the index is not out of bounds.
    (c) A stack is characterized as a last-in, first-out (LIFO) list.
    (d) A stack is an ordered collection of elements, where the elements are added to and remove from the collection at either end called the stack top.

2. Consider the following segment of code.

    ```
    Stack s = new Stack();
    s.push("P");
    s.pop();
    s.push("Q");
    s.push("R");
    s.push(s.peek());
    System.out.println(s.toString());
    ```

    When the code gets executed, the output is:
    (a) [P, R, R]
    (b) [Q, R, R]
    (c) [R, R, Q]
    (d) [Q' R]
    (e) [P, Q, R]

Step 2 - Convert From Infix To Postfix

Once we discover that the parentheses in the original expression are balanced, the next step is to convert the expression from infix to postfix. When it comes to this kind of operations, computers do well with postfix expressions than with infix expressions.

Given that an arithmetic expression is properly formed with respect to parentheses, do the following:

1. Create an empty stack to store any arithmetic operator and left parentheses only.
2. Establish a string to store the postfix expression – the output from the conversion.
3. Scan the arithmetic expression from left to right. After a symbol is scanned, there are four rules to observed:

    While there are more symbols in the arithmetic expression:
    {

    i.   If the symbol is an operand (i.e., a number), write it to the output string.
    ii.   If the symbol is a left parenthesis '(', push it onto the stack.
    iii. If the symbol is ')', do the following:
          Pop everything from the operator stack down to the **first** '('. Write each item popped from the stack to the output string, but do not write either of the parentheses on the output string. Discard them.
    iv.   If the symbol scanned is an arithmetic operator, check the following:
          If the operator on the top of the stack has higher or equal precedence, than the one that was currently read, that operator is popped from off the stack, and is written to the output string, and the currently read operator is placed on the stack. If this is not the case, nothing is removed from the stack, but the currently read operator is placed on the stack.

    }
4. After the arithmetic expression is exhausted, any operator remaining on the stack is popped from off the stack, and is written to the output string.

Consider the following infix arithmetic expression: **(50 + 100) / ((15 – 20) * 25)**
Using the algorithm outlined above, the following table shows the state of the stack, and the state of the postfix string as each token (the number, left parenthesis, right parenthesis, and arithmetic operator) is encountered.

Input	Analyze input	Action	State of stack	Output string
Read (	Left parenthesis	push	(	
Read 50	Operand	Write to output string	(	50
Read +	Operator,	Stack top has (, so push	(+	50
Read 100	Operand	Write to output string	(+	50 100

Read)	Right parenthesis	Pop each item down to first left parenthesis. Write each item to the output, except the parenthesis	(	50 100 +
			empty	50 100 +
Read /	Stack is empty	push	/	50 100 +
Read (	Left parenthesis	push	/ (	50 100 +
Read (	Left parenthesis	push	/ ((	50 100 +
Read **15**	Operand	Write to output string	/ ((	50 100 + 15
Read **-**	Operator	Stack top has (, so push	/ ((-	50 100 + 15
Read **20**	Operand	Write to output string	/ ((	50 100 + 15 20
Read)	Right parenthesis	Pop each item down to first left parenthesis. Write each item to the output, except the parenthesis	/ ((	50 100 + 15 20 -
			/(	50 100 + 15 20 -
Read *****	Operator	Stack top has (, so push	/ (*	50 100 + 15 20 -
Read **25**	Operand	Write to output string	/ (*	50 100 + 15 20 - 25
Read)	Right parenthesis	Pop everything down to first left parenthesis. Write each item to the output, except the parenthesis	/ (	50 100 + 15 20 – 25 *
			/	50 100 + 15 20 – 25 *
			empty	50 100 + 15 20 – 25 * /

Listing 7.4 shows the method convert2Postfix that implements the above algorithm of step 2. The three supporting methods – isNumber, isOperator, and hasHigherPrecedence - are defined following this method.

```
// Listing 7. 4

48.   String convert2Postfix()
49.   {
50.       String  postfix = "";
51.       Scanner scan = new Scanner(expression);
52.       char current;
53.       boolean fail = false;
54.
55.       while (scan.hasNext() && !fail)
56.       {
57.           String token = scan.next();
58.
```

```
59.            if (isNumber(token)) // Bullet # 1
60.                postfix = postfix + token + Constants.A_SPACE;
61.            else
62.            {
63.                current = token.charAt(0);
64.                if (current == Constants.LEFT_NORMAL)  // Bullet # 2
65.                    stk.push(new Character(current));
66.                else if (current == Constants.RIGHT_NORMAL) // Bullet # 3
67.                {
68.                    try
69.                    {
70.                        Character topmost = (Character) stk.pop();
71.                        char top = Character.valueOf(topmost);  //Value on stack top
72.
73.                        while (top != Constants.LEFT_NORMAL)
74.                        {
75.                            postfix = postfix + top + Constants.A_SPACE;
76.                            top = (Character) stk.pop();
77.                        }
78.                    }
79.                    catch (EmptyStackException e)
80.                    {
81.                        fail = true;
82.                    }
83.                } // End bullet # 2 and 3
84.                else if (isOperator(current)) // Bullet # 4
85.                {
86.                    try
87.                    {
88.                        char top = (Character) stk.peek();
89.                        boolean higher = hasHigherPrecedence(top, current);
90.
91.                        while (top != Constants.LEFT_NORMAL && higher)
92.                        {
93.                            postfix = postfix + stk.pop() + Constants.A_SPACE;
94.                            top = (Character) stk.peek();
95.                        }
96.                        stk.push(new Character(current));
97.                    }
98.                    catch (EmptyStackException e)
99.                    {
100.                        stk.push(new Character(current));
101.                    }
102.                }
103.            }
104.            }
105.    try
106.    {
107.      while (!stk.empty()) // Bullet # 5
108.        postfix = postfix + stk.pop() + Constants.A_SPACE;
109.    }
```

```
110.    catch (EmptyStackException e)
111.    {
112.        e.printStackTrace();
113.    }
114.    return postfix;
115.}// End convert 2 postfix
```

In **Listing 7.4, Line 65** shows where we are re-using the stack without clearing it. There is no need to clear it, because this method, convert2Postfix can only be called if the stack is empty from the previous step – checking for balanced parentheses.

The following are the supportive methods named in the method convert2Postfix. **Listing 7.5** shows the definition of the method isNumber.

The method accepts a String value and attempts to parse it to integer. If the value is parsed then it is considered an integer, and the methods returns true; otherwise, it returns false, which is an indication that the string was written incorrectly. For example, if one types **6P88**, with the embedded letter **P**, this would cause a problem; it cannot be parsed into an integer. Hence the method returns false, that the cluster of characters cannot form a number.

```
//Listing 7.5  Determine if the token is an integer

116.    boolean isNumber(String s)
117.    {
118.        boolean number = true;
119.
120.        try
121.        {
122.            Integer.parseInt(s);
123.        }
124.        catch(NumberFormatException e)
125.        {
126.            number = false;
127.        }
128.        return number;
129.    }
```

Listing 7.6 determines whether or not a given character, (+, - , * and /) is one of the four arithmetic operators.

Referring to **Listing 7.5**, as you known, if a string value cannot be parsed into a number, using one of the parse method in any of the wrapper classes, then NumberFormatException will be raised. Hence, there is no better way to handle this kind of situation than with exception handling technique.

//Listing 7.6 Determine if the token is one of the four arithmetic operators

```
130.    boolean isOperator(char ch) {
131.        boolean operator;
132.        switch(ch) {
133.            case Constants.MULTIPLICATION:
134.            case Constants.DIVISION:
135.            case Constants.ADDITION:
136.            case Constants.SUBTRACTION:
137.                operator = true;
138.            break;
139.            default:
140.                operator = false;
141.            break;
142.        }
143.        return operator;
144.    }
```

In the listing, notice that we are using the switch statement for a logical or statement.

Listing 7.7 determines if the character on the top of the stack has higher or equal precedence than the one that was currently read, as shown by the nested switch. That is, multiplication and division have higher precedence over addition and subtraction.

// Listing 7.7 Determine which token has higher precedence

```
149.    boolean hasHigherPrecedence(char top, char current) {
150.        boolean higher;
151.
152.        switch(top) {
153.            case Constants.MULTIPLICATION:
154.            case Constants.DIVISION:
155.                switch(current) {
156.                    case Constants.ADDITION:
157.                    case Constants.SUBTRACTION:
158.                        higher = true;
159.                    break;
160.                    default:
161.                        higher = false;
162.                    break;
163.                }
164.            break;
165.            default:
166.                higher = false;
167.            break;
168.        }
169.        return higher;
170.    }
```

Referring to **Listing 7.7**, we are using the switch statement both as a logical-OR, and a logical-AND in order to determine level of precedence.

Listing 7.8 shows the test class called Calculator, that in addition to determine if the infix expression is has balanced parentheses, it also converts those expressions that are valid to their postfix form.

// Listing 7.8 The test class

```
1.      class Calculator {
2.          public static void main(String[] arg) {
3.              String s[] = { "5 + ) * 4 + ( 2",
4.                              "10 + 30 * 5",
5.                              "( 20 + 30 ) * 50 ",
6.                              "( 50 + 100 ) / ( ( 15 - 20 ) * 25 )",
7.                              "( 30 * ( 100 - 4 ) + ( 20 / 20 - 5 ) + 65"
8.                          };
9.
10.             for (int i = 0; i < s.length; i++) {
11.                 Arithmetic a = new Arithmetic(s[i]);
12.                 if (a.isBalance())
13.                 {
14.                     System.out.println(s[i] + " is valid - with respect to parentheses");
15.                     System.out.println("The postfix string is " + a.convert2Postfix() + "\n");
16.                 }
17.                 else
18.                     System.out.println(s[i] + " is invalid - with respect to parentheses\n");
19.             }
20.         }
21.     }
```

Figure 7.2 shows the output generated from the expressions given. Here we see that first and the last expressions are invalid.

Figure 7.2

```
java.util.EmptyStackException
5 + ) * 4 + ( 2 is invalid - with respect to parentheses

10 + 30 * 5 is valid - with respect to parentheses
The postfix string is 10 30 5 * +

( 20 + 30 ) * 50  is valid - with respect to parentheses
The postfix string is 20 30 + 50 *

( 50 + 100 ) / ( ( 15 - 20 ) * 25 ) is valid - with respect to parentheses
The postfix string is 50 100 + 15 20 - 25 * /

( 30 * ( 100 - 4 ) + ( 20 / 20 - 5 ) + 65 is invalid - with respect to parentheses
```

In Figure 7.2, notice that for each valid expression, when converted to postfix, the parentheses disappear, which is what we want.

Step 3 - Evaluate the post fixed expression

This step also requires a stack. This time it is used for storing operands only. In reading the postfix expression, each time that an operator is encountered from the input string (the postfix expression), the stack is re-visited and the two topmost operands are removed from the stack for calculation. The algorithm is as follows:

1. Initialize an empty stack to store operands only.
2. Read the input string (the postfix expression)
    While there are more symbols in the postfix string, consider the following;
    {
        i. If the token is an operand, push it onto the stack.
        ii. If the token is an operator
          {
            a) Pop the two topmost values from the stack, and store them in the variables **t1**, the topmost, and **t2** the second value.
            b) Calculate the partial result in the following order **t2 operator t1**
            c) Push the result of this calculation onto the stack.
               NOTE: If the stack does not have two operands, a malformed postfix expression has occurred, and evaluation should be terminated.
          }
    }
3. When the end of the input string is encountered, the result of the expression is popped from the stack.
    NOTE: If the stack is empty, or if it has more than one operand remaining, the result is unreliable.

Step 3 – Evaluate the postfix expression will be left as an exercise.

Self-Check
1. Given the following postfix expressions:
    (a) 30 50 + 60 *
    (b) 30 50 60 * +
    (c) 30 50 60 + *
    Use the algorithm of step 3, make tables, similar to step to evaluate each of the expressions.

2. If you were to remove an element from a stack, what runtime abnormality could you expect, and state how you would prevent the program from terminating abnormally? Support your explanation with an example.

3. List two applications where the concept of stack would be appropriate. Give brief reason for each application stated.

4. Given that the identifiers A, B, C, and D are operands; and the symbols *, +, and - are operators. Used Step 3 of the Reverse Polish Notation algorithm, to convert the following postfix expression to infix expression.

    A B + C D - *

    Show your working.

5. When the infix expression 2 + 3 * 5 is converted to postfix, the result is:
    (a) * 3 5 + 2
    (b) 2 3 + 5 *
    (c) 3 5 * 2 +
    (d) 2 3 * 5 +
    (e) 2 3 5 * +

6. Given the following arithmetic expression:

    20 + 50 / (40 - 15 * 2) * 5

    Which of the following represents the postfix form of the original expression?
    (a) 20 50 40 15 2 * / - * 5 +
    (b) 20 50 + 40 15 * / 2 * 5 –
    (c) 20 50 40 (15 2 *) / 5 * +
    (d) 20 50 40 15 2 * - / 5 * +

7. Consider the following post fixed expression:

    3 5 * 7 2 - +

    When the expression is evaluated, using Step 3 of the Reverse Polish Notation, the result is:
    (a) 20
    (b) 0
    (c) 10
    (d) 31
    (e) 28

Queue

Queue simply defines a sequence or list of items that are waiting to be processed. For instance, when you wait your turn in a bank to be attended to by the bank teller, you are in a queue; and when you call a customer service hotline, you may hear a message such as this:

"Thank you for calling ABC Bank. Your call will be answered by the next available operator. Please wait."

What happens in this situation is that your call has been placed in a queuing system, and it has to wait its turn for it to be answered.

In computing activities, one of the functions of an operating system is scheduling; and scheduling algorithms almost always involve a queue. For instance, if you are in an environment where there are multiple users on a network of computers, you probably share a printer with other users. When you request to print a document, your request is added to the print queue, and will have to wait its turn to be printed. When your request reaches the front of the print queue, it is then that your file is printed.

As you will notice, a queue exhibits the behavior of *first-come-first-serve*. The traditional way of expressing the phrase is, *First-In-First-Out* (FIFO). Queue has one basic rule – operate from either end of the list. For instance, when an element is to be added to the list, it must be added to the rear of the list as the last element to be added (appended). When an element is to be removed from the list, it can only be the element at the extreme opposite of the rear, the front.

As you have seen in **Figure 7.1** the interface Queue extends the interface Deque, which stands for "double ended queue". Queue and Deque have different names for appending elements in the queue and for removing elements from the queue, as shown below.

Queue	Deque	Operation
boolean add(E e)	void addLast(**E** e)	Appends the specified element at the end of the deque
E remove()	E removeFirst()	Retrieves and removes the first element of this deque.

Two implementations of Deque are the classes ArrayDeque and LinkedList. We will study ArrayDeque in this section. ArrayDeque is a resizable-array that has no capacity restrictions.

Example 7.3 Suppose that there is an unknown number of programmers who make frequent request for using the single printer that is available. Assume that at any moment between one and three requests are made. Write a program that mimics this situation.

The solution to this problem requires implementing a queue that stores and releases each print job as depicted in **Figure 7.3**.

Figure 7.3 Jobs in a queue

Figure 7.3 is showing that currently there are three jobs awaiting to be processed. They are waiting because job 6 is being processed in the QueueProcessor module – the printer. Any job to the right of the QueueProcessor module are finished jobs. From the Figure we see that **Job5** has just been printed, and **Job 6** is now being processed by the Queue Processor.

Let us define a print job as a class with the following characteristics:
- name – representing the name of the file to be printed, and
- size – the size of the file in kilobytes.

Listing 7.9 shows the definition of the class – PrintJob.

```
// Listing 7.9

1.    class PrintJob // The job object that is to be created
2.    {
3.          String name;
4.          int size;
5.
6.          PrintJob(String s, int t)
7.          {
8.                name = s;
9.                size = t;
10.         }
11.         String getName()
12.         {
13.               return name;
14.         }
15.
16.         int getSize()
17.         {
18.               return size;
19.         }
20.   }
```

Let us define the entity QueueProcessor the task of creating a queue, adding print jobs to the queue, processing and removing each job within a certain time, and displaying the state of the queue continuously.

Listing 7.10 shows the class QueueProcessor. **Line 16** of the constructor creates the queue. **Line 19** of the method adds - appends a new job to the queue. The method called processingTime, **Lines 22 thru 32** processes each job according to its size. See the while loop of **Line 27** and **28**. The method remove – **Line 33 thru 41** - remove each processed job from the queue. It shoud be noted that the queue could be empty at any point. It is against this background that we catch NoSuchElementException. In addition, the method called **display** shows the state of the queue continuously.

Listing 7.10

```
1.   /**
2.   Queue operations - add, remove, peek, iterate
3.   Implementation ArrayQue
4.   */
5.
6.   import java.util.Deque;
7.   import java.util.ArrayDeque;
8.   import java.util.Iterator;
9.   import java.util.NoSuchElementException;
10.
11.  public class  QueueProcessor {
12.        Deque dq;
13.        PrintJob o;
14.
15.        public QueueProcessor() {
16.            dq = new ArrayDeque();
17.        }
18.
19.        void add(PrintJob o){
20.            dq.add(o);
21.        }
22.        int processingTime(){
23.            o = (PrintJob)dq.peek();
24.            int size = o.getSize();
25.            long begin = System.nanoTime();
26.
27.            while(size > 0)
28.                size--;
29.            long end = System.nanoTime();
30.
31.            return (int)(end - begin);
32.        }
33.        String remove(){
34.            try{
35.                PrintJob jb = (PrintJob)dq.remove();
36.                return jb.getName();
37.            }
38.            catch(NoSuchElementException e){
39.                return e.getMessage();
40.            }
41.        }
42.        void display(){
43.            Iterator i = dq.iterator();
44.
45.            while (i.hasNext()) {
46.                PrintJob j = (PrintJob)i.next();
47.                System.out.print(j.getName() + " | ");
48.            }
```

```
49.            System.out.println();
50.        }
51.  }
```

Listing 7.11 shows the test class - TestMyQueue – which creates a QueueProcessor that runs forever, as shown in the **for** loop – **Line 7**. Using the Random number generator class, **Line 9** generates the number of jobs to be created. The **for** loop that spans Line 12 thru 17 generates the number of print jobs to be processed. The print statements that follow display the state of the queue before a job is processed, the time that it takes to process a job, and the state of the queue after a job has been processed.

Listing 7.11

```
1.    import java.util.Random;
2.
3.    class TestMyQueue{
4.        public static void main(String[] arg){
5.            QueueProcessor qp = new QueueProcessor ();
6.
7.            for ( ; ; ) {
8.                Random rand = new Random();
9.                int jobs = rand.nextInt(3) + 1; // Generating the number of jobs to join the queue
10.               System.out.println("\nNumber of jobs joining the queue: " + jobs);
11.
12.               for (int i = jobs; i > 0; i--) {// Get the jobs one by one and add them to the queue
13.                   String s = GetData.getString("Enter the name of file to be printed");
14.                   int size = GetData.getInt("Enter approx. size of file (KB)");
15.                   PrintJob jb = new PrintJob(s, size);
16.                   qp.add(jb);
17.               }
18.
19.               System.out.println("State of the print queue before  job is removed from queue");
20.               qp.display();
21.
22.               int time = qp.processingTime();
23.               System.out.println("Processing time for:   " + qp.remove() + " " + time );
24.
25.               System.out.println("State of the queue after removing job in front position");
26.               qp.display();
27.           }
28.       }
29.  }
```

Figure 7.4 shows the dialog boxes for inputting the name of each job and the assume size of each job.

Figure 7.4

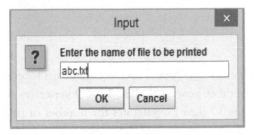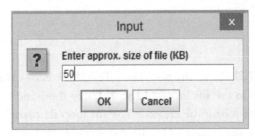

Figure 7.5 shows an output from the program. In the first instance there is one job – xyz.txt of size 50BK. In the second instance there are three jobs – abc.java, u.txt, and abc.doc of sizes 100KB, 500KB and 150KB, respectively. In the third instance there are also three jobs; during this time job abc.txt that was at the front of the queue is being processed, leaving five jobs remaining in the queue.

Figure 7.5

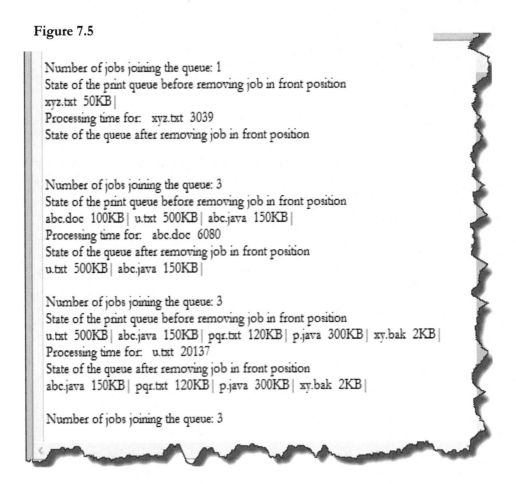

Self-Check

1. The term FIFO refers to the data structure called:
   (a) Stack
   (b) Linked list
   (c) Queue
   (d) Null
   (e) Vector
   Select ONE

2. What is meant by the term FIFO?

3. Differentiate between the terms, LIFO and FIFO.

4. If you were asked to write a program to parse your Java program to determine balance curly braces and parentheses, what data structure would you use, LIFO or FIFO? Explain.

LinkedList

The data structure called LinkedList is a finite sequence of elements called nodes, where insertion of nodes occurs at any point in the list, and at any time in the list. Also, deletion of nodes can take place from any point in the list, and at any time. Whether it is inserting, deleting, or simply traversing the list, you can do so without ever having to mention about indexing of the list.

Java defines a LinkedList class, but we will not be using that class. We will be designing our own, because we need the concept in subsequent courses to create more complex data structures.

Structure of a LinkedList

As mentioned, a linked list is a set of nodes. A node is comprised of two components. One of the components stores the data, and the other stores the address of the node that succeeds it, if any. The component that stores an address is referred to as the link field of the node. See **Figure 7.6**.

Figure 7.6 - A node

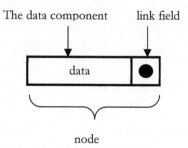

node

Figure 7.7 shows a LinkedList of four nodes (I, II, III, and IV). Each node is stored at memory address (512, 1024, 768, and 4096), respectively. The first node is stored at address 512; the second at address 1024; the third at address 768; and the fourth at address 4097. Can you see how the nodes are linked?

Figure 7.7 A Linked List of Nodes

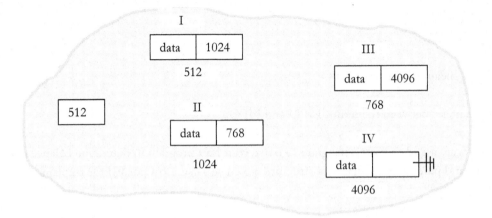

In **Figure 7.8** we reproduce Figure 7.7, except that this time we connect each node by the address value that is stored in the address part of the node with an arrow.

Figure 7.8 LinkedList of nodes

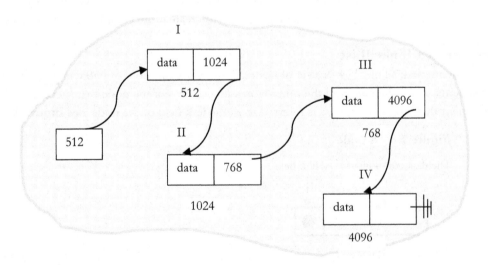

On closer examination, you will notice that the nodes are not stored contiguously as in the case of array and ArrayList. Each node is connected to the next by address rather than by index. The first node in a list is referenced by a variable described as the header address. The last node connects to no succeeding node, so it is assigned the null address, indicating the end of the list.

Usually LinkedLists are represented as a chain of connected nodes as shown in **Figure 7.9**, and not as shown in **Figures 7.7** and **7.8**.

Figure 7.9 - A Linked List of four nodes.

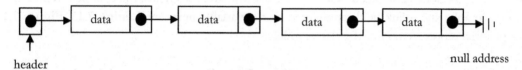

header   null address

When coding it is not practical to know the address of each node. This is left up to the compiler and the operating system to resolve all addresses, your responsible is to write the necessary code to direct the program how to connect the nodes.

Figure 7.10 shows a list consisting of a single node. This node is referenced by the variable called **list**. The part that stores the data we will call **data** for now. Later we will add meaning to it. The address part we will call **next**, any other variable name is just as good. At this point the link field **next** contains the null address, signifying the end of the list. To refer to the data component of the node we say list dot data, written as **list•data**; and to refer to the link field, **next**, we say list dot next, written as **list•next**. The statement **list•next = null** assigns the null address to the link field variable.

Figure 7.10 - A Linear Linked List containing one node.

list
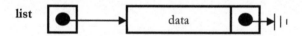

The statement **list = null** abandons the list, by disconnecting the header reference from the list. See **Figure 7.11**. In this context there is no way of re-connecting the list with the header reference.

Figure 7.11 An abandoned list

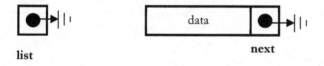

list   next

In a linked list data structure, the header reference and the link reference are of the same type. Hence, linked lists are referred to as self-referencing data structure. This kind of data structure can be used to design more complex data structures such as stacks, queues, and binary trees.

Representing LinkedList in Java

The Java Collection Framework defines a class called **LinkedList**, as you saw in **Figure 7.1**. As we said earlier, we will not use this class; instead we will design and construct a linked list, in order to have a better understanding of it.

Let us design a node class called **Node**. This class will have two fields: the data field represented by a string variable; and a link field represented by the variable **next**. See **Listing 7.12**. **Figure 7.12** shows a pictorial representation of the class, Node.

Listing 7.12 - The class

```
1.   class Node
2.   {
3.       String data;
4.       Node next;
5.   }
```

Figure 7.12 – Representation of the class

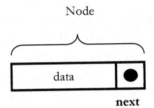

Listing **7.13** shows the initialization each of the fields. Notice that the linked field, **next**, points to no node; instead it is assigned the null address, as shown by **Line 9**. **Figure 7.13** shows a pictorial representation of the class.

Listing 7.13 – Fields are initialized

```
1.   class Node
2.   {
3.       String data;
4.       Node next;
5.
6.       Node(String s)
7.       {
8.           data = s;
9.           next = null;
10.      }
11.  }
```

Figure 7.13 - Representation of the initialized fields

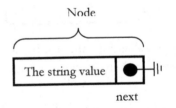

Self-Check

1. You are asked to design a program that will maintain a linked lis of telephone customer records sorted by last name. As part of the design process write a class called TelephoneNode; where a telephone node is comprised of the following data fields – the customer's name, address and telephone number.

Creating a LinkedList in Java

As we mentioned earlier, you can create and maintain a linked list in one of three ways – adding nodes to the front of the list (pre-pending); adding nodes to the rear of the list (appending), and adding nodes at any position in the list (inserting). The following section will show how to pre-pend nodes.

To create a linked list it is necessary to implement a class that will be used to create and maintain the list. In order to create any linked list you must first need to create an empty list which will grow once we start to add nodes. Let us call this class **LinkedNode**. **Listing 7.14** shows a partial definition of the class.

Listing 7.14 Creating an empty linked list

```
1.   class LinkNode
2.   {
3.        Node list;
4.
5.        LinkNode()
6.        {
7.            list = null;
8.        }
9.   }
```

In **Listing 7.15, Line 3** declares an instance variable, called list that will be used as the principal variable for maintaining the linked list. **Line 7** creates an empty list.

Prepending nodes to a LinkedList

We will now define a method called prepend, that adds a node at the beginning of the list. In order to do this you must first create the new node and set this new node to the front of the list. **Listing 7.15** shows the definition of the method, prepend.

Listing 7.15 Prepending a node

```
10.  void prepend(String s)
11.  {
12.        Node temp = new Node(s);
13.        temp.next = list;
14.        list = temp;
15.  }
```

In Listing 7.14 the method accepts the string value (Line 10), and uses that value to create the node. See **Line 12**. A pictorial representation is shown in **Figure 7.14**.

Figure 7.14

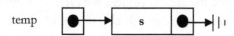

Let us assume that the list has two nodes as shown in **Figure 7.15**. Then we must place this new node as the first node from the left, in the list.

Figure 7.15 - A LinkedList of two nodes.

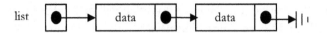

Prepending to a list requires two steps. First, set the reference of **temp.next** point to the head of the list, as shown in **Figure 7.16.** The statement on Line13 shows the code:

temp.next = list;

Figure 7.16 – Prepending a node – step 1.

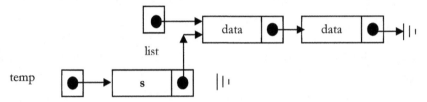

Secondly, make the reference, list, point to the new node, temp – as shown in **Figure 7.17.**

Figure 7.17 – Prepending a node – step 2.

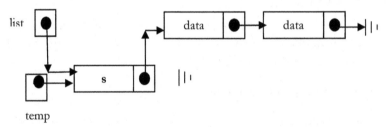

The actual statement that causes this re-arrangement of reference is shown on **Line 13**. That is:

list = temp;

Hence, **Listing 7.17** shows the complete list of now three nodes. Note that if the list is empty, this algorithm still works.

Appending nodes to a LinkedList

Appending a node to a list requires traversing the list, visiting every node, starting from the first to the last. That is, loop through the list and update the reference field for each node visited. When traversing a linked list you should never use the original reference variable that points to the beginning of list; rather, get an auxiliary reference variable to do that task. In this example we declare and initialize an auxiliary reference variable called current, as follows:

ListNode current = list;

Figure 7.18 shows the effect of this statement. That is, the variable current, points to the first node of the list.

Figure 7.18 - Reference variable current points to the head of list.

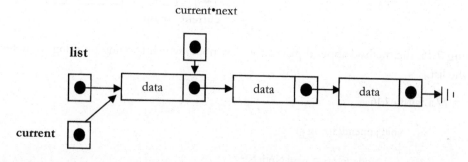

In **Figure 7.18**, the address component of the first node (**current.next**) points to the second node in the list. In order for the reference, current to visit the second node, it must point to the node to which **current.next** is pointing. The required code for this statement is:

current = current.next;

Figure 7.19 shows the effect of the above statement.

Figure 7.19 - current = current.next;

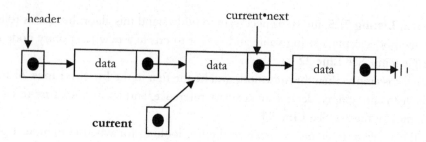

Now while the variable current is pointing to the second node in the list, **current.next** is pointing to the third node.

If we repeat the statement a second time, then the reference variable **current** will now be pointing to the third node. In addition to traversing the list, you must determine when **current.next** is pointing to null. When it is determined, divert **current.next** from pointing to null, and let it point to the new node that **temp** is pointing to. At this point **current.next** is pointing to null, the end of the list. Let us now point to the new node that is referenced by the variable, **temp**. See **Figure 7.20**.

Figure 7.20 - New node temp is appended to the list

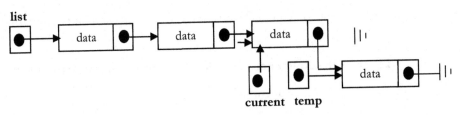

current   temp

In **Listing 7.16**, the method append places the new node, which is being pointing to by temp, at the end of the list.

```
// Lisitng 7.16

22.  void append(String s)
23.  {
24.       Node temp = new Node(s);
25.
26.       if (isEmpty())
27.            list = temp;
28.       else
29.       {
30.            Node current = list;
31.            while (current.next != null)
32.                 current = current.next;
33.            current.next = temp;
34.       }
35. }
```

As shown in **Listing 7.15**, the steps necessary to understand this algorithm are as follows:

a) The method accepts a string value and uses it to create a new temporary node reference by the variable temp. See **Line 22**.

b) If the list is empty, then this new node will be the first in the list. See **Lines 26** and **27**.

c) If the list is not empty, declare an auxiliary reference, and let this auxillary reference point to the beginning of the list. See **Line 30**.

d) Use the auxiliary reference to traverse the list, looking for when **current.next** points to the null address. See **Lines 31** and **32**.

e) As soon as we know when **current.next** is pointing to the null address, change its direction, and let it point to the new node instead. See **Line 33**.

This way of appending nodes to a list has a flaw. It works fine if the list is short. If the list is very long, then the program will spend most of its time traversing the list. The alternate to this is establish a second auxiliary reference variable right for the start. This variable must be set to trail the variable current, which is doing the traversing. When a new node is to be appended, the sequence of actions is as follows:

- First the trailing node is set to the current node
- Next, let the reference field of the current node point to the new node, and
- Thirdly, point the current reference to the new node.

This approach never require an explicit traversal of the list, because the current reference always point at the last node. **Listing 7.17** shows the modified class LinkedNode.

Listing 7.17

```
1.   class LinkNode {
2.       private .Node list, current;
3.
4.       LinkNode () {
5.           list = null;
6.       }
7.
8.       void append(String s) {
9.           Node temp = new Node(s);
10.
11.          if (list == null)
12.          {
13.              list = temp;
14.              current = list;
15.          }
16.          else
17.          {
18.              Node back = current;
19.              current.next = temp;
20.              current = temp;
21.          }
22.      }
23. }
```

According to the listing, the program starts with two reference variables – list, the principal reference variable, and current, the secondary which references a current node. See **Line 2**. Initially the list is empty. See **Line 5**. The method append, creates anew node each time that it is called. See Line 9. When appending nodes to the list, the first time that the method is called, the list would have been empty, and so both the principal reference, list; and the secondary reference, current point to the this node.

Subsequent to placing the first node, every time that a new node is to be appended, a railing reference variable called. **back**, is set to the last node, being pointed to by current. See Line 18.

Following this action, the reference **current.next** points to the new node, making it the last node in the list. The principal reference is then pointed to this last node. With this approach you will never have to use a loop, as the code shows.

Listing 7.18

```
1.   class MakeList
2.   {
3.       public static void main(String[] arg)
4.       {
5.           LinkNode list = new LinkNode();
6.
7.           long begin = System.nanoTime();
8.           for (int i = 0; i <= 10000; i++)
9.               list.append_iterate( "Danger on the Waters");
10.          long end = System.nanoTime();
11.
12.          System.out.println("Iterative time:     " + (end - begin)/1000000 + " msec");
13.
14.          begin = System.nanoTime();
15.          for (int j = 0; j <= 10000; j++)
16.              list.append_no_iterate("Danger on the Waters");
17.          end = System.nanoTime();
18.          System.out.println("None iterative time:   " + (end - begin)/1000000 + " msec");
19.      }
20.  }
```

Listing 7.18 creates 10,000 nodes for each method – iterate versus non-iterate[1], and made remarkable discovery about the time difference between the two methods. See **Figure 7.21**.

Figure 7.21

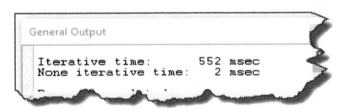

```
General Output

Iterative time:        552 msec
None iterative time:     2 msec
```

Inserting Nodes Into a LinkedList

You can insert a node anywhere in the list. Usually we use this method to maintain an ordered list. This property requires traversing the list, looking for the position where to insert the node. When the

---

[1] The methods names have been changes in order to differentiate each call.

position is found, re-arrange the reference fields so as to accommodate the new node. **Figure 7.22** shows finding the position where to insert the new node.

Figure 7.22 – Finding where to insert new node into the list

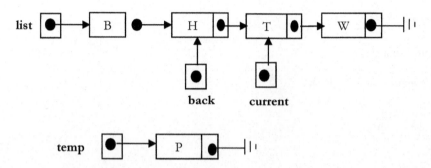

According to **Figure 7.22**, the new node pointed to by temp must be inserted between the second and the third node, referenced by variables **back** and **current**, respectively. Once the location has been found, it is just a matter of re-arranging **temp.next** and **back.next** to accommodate the new node. See **Figure 7.23**.

Figure 7.23 –Insert new node into the list

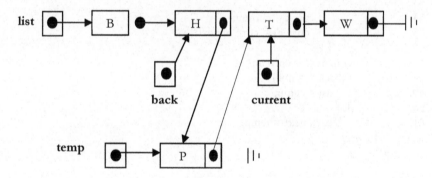

According to **Figure 7.23**, in preparing to traverse the list we introduce the two auxiliary reference variables, one that will traverse the list, and the other that will trail this current reference that is traversing the list. Here we establish the variable current which is used to traverse the list, and back which trails current. This means that we can pinpoint between what two nodes the new node must be inserted. The order in which the variables are re-assigned is of utmost important. If we move **back.next** first, then we would lose the remainder of the list. The order must be:

```
temp.next = current
back.next = temp
```

This leaves us with two problems though – what happens when current is pointing to the end of the list? This would suggests that the new node must be at the end of the list. And, if back has not started to trail current, then it means that the new node must be at the front of the list. **Listing 7.19** shows the code for this algorithm.

```
// Listing 7.19

37.   void insert(String s)
38.   {
39.        Node temp = new Node(s);
40.
41.        if (isEmpty())
42.             list = temp;
43.        else
44.        {
45.             Node back = null;
46.             Node current = list;
47.             boolean found = false;
48.
49.             while (current != null && !found)
50.                  if( temp.getData().compareTo(current.getData()) < 0)
51.                       found = true;
52.                  else
53.                  {
54.                       back = current;
55.                       current = current.next;
56.                  }
57.             temp.next = current;
58.             if (back == null)
59.                  list = temp;
60.             else
61.                  back.next = temp;
62.        }
}
```

In **Listing 7.18** See **Lines 39** creates the node that must be inserted in the list. The heart of this method is the while loop which spans Lines 49 thru 56. This segment of codes determine the position where the new node must be placed. When the loop is exited re-organize the references are re-organized. In all cases let the **temp•next** point to where **current** is pointing. See **Line 57**. Now, depending on the state of back, we will know how to position the node. That is, if **back** is still null, then it means that the new node must be at the front of list. If back is not null, then the new node must fall between the two nodes – back and current. Hence, we let **back•next** point to **temp**. See **Lines 58** thru **61**.

Deleting Nodes From a LinkedList

To remove a node, requires knowing something about the node, in particular what information is contained within the data component of the node. This necessitates traversing the list, and examine each node you encounter. Once the node is located, re-arrange the references so that the particular node is excluded. This part of the algorithm runs parallel to inserting anywhere in the list.

Extracting Values from a LinkedList

To extract values from a linked list we must visit each node in the list. For each node use the expression **current.data**. **Listing 7.20** which re-defines the toString method shows how this is done.

```
// Listing 7.20

65.  public String toString()
66.  {
67.       String result = "";
68.       Node current = list;
69.
70.       while (current != null)
71.       {
72.            result += current.data + "\n";
73.            current = current.next;
74.       }
75.       return result;
76.  }
```

Advantages and Disadvantages of LinkedList

The principal benefit of a linked list over a conventional array is that the list elements can easily be inserted or removed without reorganization of the entire list. Because Linked lists are a dynamic data structures, memory is allocated and de-allocated as needed. In addition, insertion and deletion of nodes are easily implemented.

Linked list has the tendency of using extra memory due to references are required per node. Nodes in a linked list must be read in order from the beginning, as linked lists are inherently sequential access. If the data that is required is near, or at the end of a long list, then accessing the data could be very time consuming. This happens in part that the nodes are not stored contiguously, hence this greatly increase the time required to access individual elements within the list. Another major difficulty arises in linked lists when it comes to traversing the list in reverse manner. Linear linked lists are extremely difficult to navigate backwards.

Self-Check

1. (True or False). Inserting nodes at the end of a LinkedList is more time-efficient than inserting them at the front of the list.

2. (True or False). When inserting nodes in a linked list the best method of keeping a sorted list is the method of inserting at the back and the front.

3. Using the codes for the method prepend, make requisite diagrams to show the code is valid if the list is empty.

4. The following class LinkedNode represents a node.

```
1.   class LinkedNode
2.   {
3.        int data;
4.        LinkedNode next;
5.        LinkedNode(int i)
6.        {
7.            data = i;
8.            next = null;
9.        }
10.  }
```

(a) If the variable **list** represents a linked list of these nodes, define a method that traverses the **list,** and print the data in the list.

(b) A node called **temp** must be inserted at the front of the list. (where temp is defined as:

LinkedNode temp = new LinkedNode(200));

Define a method that inserts this node at the front of the list.

(c) Given that the variable **list** represents a reference to the above linked list of nodes. Define a method called countNodes that counts and returns the number of nodes in the list.

5. Given that the variable **list** represents a reference to a linked list of nodes, where a node is defined as follows:

```
class Node
{
    String data;
    Node next;

    Node(String d)
    {
        data = d;
        next = null; // The link field
    }
}
```

Define a method called delete, which removes the last node in the list.

6. Which data structures is applied when dealing with a recursive function? Stack, Queue, or LinkedList. Explain.

7. You are asked to design a program that will maintain a linked list of telephone customer records sorted by last name. As part of the design process you are to develop a class called TelephoneNode; where a telephone node comprises of the customer's name, address and telephone number. From this description design the class TelephoneNode. Define any other class(es) that you think can support the definition of the class TelephoneNode.

Chapter Summary

- Linked list is one of the simplest but most commonly used data structures in programming.

- Linear linked list is fundamental to other complex abstract data structures such as stacks, queues, circular list, and binary trees.

- Linked lists allow insertion and removal of nodes at any point in the list without disturbing the data from its position, which proves to be of major advantage over arrays and ArrayList.

- Linear linked list has the tendency of using extra memory than other linear list because it requires extra memory to reference each node.

Programming Exercises

1. Complete the RPN program by supplying the code for evaluating the postfix expression.

2. Extend the RPN program to include square brackets and curly braces. For example, expressions of the following kind should be considered:

- 2 + { 2 * (10 − 4) / [{ 4 * 2 / (3 + 4) } + 2] − 9 }
- 2 + } 2 * (10 − 4) / [{ 4 * 2 / (3 + 4) } + 2] − 9 {

Only the following are considered valid nesting:

    ()
    { }
    [ ]
    { ( ) }
    [( )]
    [{ }]
    [{ ( ) }]

Implement the above two algorithms for the following binary operators: addition +, subtraction -, multiplication *, division /, and modulus operation %. All operations are integer operations. To keep things simple, place at least one blank space between each token in the input string.

3. Write a menu driven program that either accepts words and their meanings, or displays the list of words in lexicographical order (i.e. as in a dictionary). When an entry is to be added to the dictionary you must first enter the word as one string, and then enter the meaning as separate string. A word may have more than one meaning, and may be entered at separate times. When this occurs, place each successive meaning on a separate line. This new meaning must be preceded by a dash. For example, if you enter the following words and with their meanings in the following order: **Library**, **School**, **Cup**, and **School**, then your output should be a display as shown below.

```
Cup – a container from which we drink.
Library – a collection of books
School – a place of learning
        - any group of fish
```

Another requirement - from time to time words become obsolete. When this happens, such word must be removed from the dictionary.

Use the concept of linked list to carry out this exercise. You will need at minimum the following classes:
*   A WordMeaning class that hold the name of a word and its meaning.
*   A WordMeaningNode class that creates the node of information and its link field.
*   A WordList class that creates and maintain a linked list of words and their meanings.
*   A Dictionary class that test your classes.

For the output, the program should produce two scrollable lists:
*   The current list of words and their meanings, and
*   The list of the deleted words. Do not list the meanings.

4. Librarians get books from time to time. Formally, when a librarian gets a book, the title would be recorded manually in alphabetical order. This means frequent re-writing of the list. Write a program such that as a book is received, it is automatically placed in the right sequence. From time to time books become obsolete. When a book becomes obsolete it is removed the collection. The program must take this into consideration also.

Use the concept of linked list to implement this idea, by designing the following classes:
*   Book - this class the holds the title of book.
*   BookNode – this class creates the node of information and its link field.
*   BookList – this class creates and maintains the linked list of book titles in alphabetically order, and.
*   Library – this is the test class that co-ordinate the activities of the other classes.

5. In most programming languages, the compiler carries a preprocessing step to determine if certain statements will compile. For instance it may check to see if parentheses match.

Write a Java program that simulates the actions of a preprocessor, to detect if certain Java constructs are syntactically correct. **Table 1** shows the types of Java statement formats under consideration, and also example of each statement.

Table 1

Format		Example
Statement	data_type = expression	int x = 3 + (10 – 4) * (10 + 4)

Method	<attrib> rt name(<parameter>)
	{
	    <statement>
	}
		public void display(int n)
		{
		    int arr[ ] = new int[n];
		    System.out.println(x[2]);
		}

class	<attrib> class Name
	{
	  dt fields;
	  <attrib> Name(<parameter>)
	    {
	      method (<parameter>);
	    }
	  <attrib> rt method(<parameter>)
	    {
	
	    }
	}
		public class MyParser
		{
		  public static void main(String [ ] arg
		)
		  {
		    display (10);
		  }
		  static void display(int x)
		  {
		    /*
		      My pre-processor
		    */
		  }
		}

Table 2 shows the delimiters under consideration.

Table 2

Delimiters	Symbol
Left parenthesis	(
Right parenthesis	)
Left curly braces	{
Right curly braces	}
Left square brackets	[
Right square brackets	]
Forward slash	/
Star (multiplication symbol)	*

Note: In your implementation, design a class called Preprocessor that accepts a file that represents the program to be analyzed. The class will contain, among other possible methods, a method that determines whether or not the statement in the file are valid, with respect to the delimiters of **Table 2**. Do not be concerned with other symbols.

1. You will need a test class. You may want to name it MyPreprocessor.
2. You may have to enter all statements on a single line, unless you will be reading the input from a file, in which case the file would be read using presumable the class BufferedReader or LineNumberReader.
3. Your output would echo the input, and say whether or not the input passed the preprocessing stage.
4. You are to use the concept of **stack** to determine if the constructs are syntactically correct.

Chapter 8 Graphical User Interface Programming

Objectives

After reading this chapter you will learn how to:

- Create frame with title, using the Java pre-defined container class called JFrame
- Change the frame's default icon.
- Change background and foreground color of a frame.
- Change the default cursor of a frame.
- Add components such as menus, menu items, and buttons to a frame.
- Add JPanel container to JFrame container objects.
- Use layout managers to position and align components within the container.

Introduction

Graphical User Interface (GUI) programming is that type of program that allows the user to interact with the computer via graphical icons such as menus, menu items, buttons, scrollbars, , and text fields. The programs that we have written so far, to a large extent, were text based, except for when the JOptionPane class was used. However, GUI lends itself from simple command line interaction to point-and-click iteration with graphical icons.

Java has a large collection of classes that enables us to write GUI programs. Java GUI programming involves two main packages - the abstract windows toolkit (**awt**) package, and the Swing package. The awt package is a subset of the original java classes, referred to as the Java Foundation Clases (JFC). The awt was designed so that programmers do not have worry about the details of tracking the mouse or reading the keyboard, nor attend to the details of writing to the screen. These detail activities are taken care of by the operating system. The programmer's responsibility at this stage is to choose the appropriate classes, and statement from these classes to build meaningful GUI programs.

The user interfaces provided by the awt are plat-form dependent, because they use each platform's native GUI toolkit. In this regard, using the same code on different machine, the look-and-feel of the user interface that is generated may differ from one type of machine to another.

Swing on the other hand provides classes that have the ability to create graphical user interface (GUI) components, such as described above, that are independent of the plat-form on which the program runs. In this context the interface is uniform across multiple plat-forms. **Figure 8.1** shows the inheritance chain of awt and swing packages.

Figure 8.1 The inheritance hierarchy of awt **and** swing

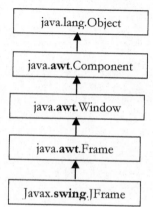

Components and Containers

Before we begin to design GUIs, it is important to know what components are, and what containers are. Items such as menus, menu items, buttons, scrollbars, and text fields, are components. They are the smallest individual object of the interface. They are what allow the user to interact with the program. Components cannot stand alone on a widow, they have to be placed within a unit that can accommodate multiple components. These units are called containers. Two typical containers are frame and panels. Whereas components cannot be nested, containers can.

In this chapter you will learn how to create a frame and attach menus, menu items, and buttons to the frame. We will learn how to position the frame on the screen and set the size of the frame. Also, we will learn how to change the background color of the frame, change the cursor while the programming is running.

Creating Frames

We begin the discussion with the creating of frames using the class, JFrame. We will create a customized frame that is independent of an application, and then launch it from a test class. Let us call this class MyJFrame, which will inherit the class JFrame for much of its functionalities. Examining the class JFrame, we note two of the more frequently used overloaded constructors shown below.

- **JFrame()**   Constructs a new frame that is initially invisible
- **JFrame(String** title)   Creates a new, initially invisible Frame with the specified title.

In designing the class we will use the second constructor for setting the title of the frame. **Listing 8.1** shows the code for the class MyJFrame. As you will notice, the class JFrame has to be imported, since it will be used to create a specialized frame, as indicated on **Line 3**. In addition, the constructor of our class MyJFrame is requesting the superclass JFrame to set the title of the frame in place. See **Line 7**. If the parameterless constructor were to be used, and a title were to be required, then this could be done at a later time, using the method **setTitle()**.

// Listing 8.1 Build a frame with title only

```
1.    import javax.swing.JFrame;
2.
3.    public class MyJFrame extends JFrame
4.    {
5.        public MyJFrame(String title)
6.        {
7.            super(title);
8.        }
9.    }
```

Listing 8.2 shows the test class, MyWindow, that launches a MyJFrame object, and sets the object visible on the screen. See **Lines 5** and **6**, respectively. Without **Line 6** the frame would not show up on the computer screen, because the default state of the method setVisible is **false**.

// Listing 8.2 This program an introduction to GUI programming.

```
1.    public class MyWindow
2.    {
3.        public static void main(String[] arg)
4.        {
5.            MyJFrame f = new MyJFrame(Constants.TITLE);
6.            f.setVisible(true); // Show the frame
7.        }
8.    }
```

The value for **Constants.TITLE** shown on Line 5 of the test class is defined in an interface called Constants. See **Listing 8.3**. The idea is to separate the entities, in keeping with the concept of cohesion.

// Listing 8.3 Interface Constants

```
1.   public interface Constants
2.   {
3.          String  TITLE  = "My First Java Graphical User Interface (GUI) Program";
4.   }
```

The output from the program can be seen in **Figure 8.2**. It is that small rectangle seen in the extreme upper left corner of the display screen. Look carefully and you will see that it has the characteristics of a frame – with a frame icon, the minimize button, the maximize button, and the close button.

Figure 8.2

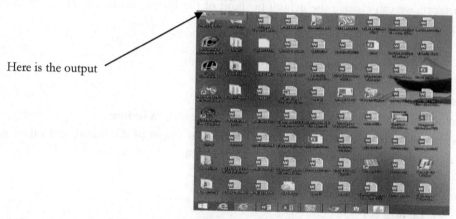

Here is the output

In the Figure, there are a few things worth noting. Firstly, the position where the frame is located is the default location of the (x, y) coordinate system, whose value is (0, 0). Secondly, without specifying a size for the frame the default size is governed by the default image icon, and the three default buttons - the minimize button, the maximize button, and the close button. Thirdly, note that the x-axis grows positively to the right, and the y-axis grows positively vertically.

Changing Properties of a Frame

You can change some of the default values of a frame. For instance, you can change the image icon, the position of the frame, the size of the frame, the background, and foreground color of the frame. You can also change the style cursor when the frame comes into focus. Before we do any of the above let us first understand the inheritance hierarchy of the JFrame class. As seen in **Figure 8.3,** the class JFrame is coming from a long lineage of classes. This means that instead of looking in the immediate JFrame class for a particular method, we may have to look along the inheritance chain.

Figure 8.3 Inheritance hierarchy of the JFrame class

java.lang.Object
    └ java.awt.Component
        └ java.awt.Container
            add
        └ java.awt.Window
                setBounds, setVisible
            └ java.awt.Frame
                    setBackground, setCursor
                └ javax.swing.JFrame
                    getContentPane, setJMenuBar, setDefaultCloseOption, setIconImage, setLayout

For instance, we can change the default position of the frame and also resize it, by using one of the following overloaded methods:

> void   setBounds(intx, int y, int width, int height)
> void   setBounds(Rectangle r)

These methods are not in the class JFrame; they are in the class **Window**.

Let us choose an arbitrary point (x, y), to represent the origin of the frame, and values width and height, to represent the new size the frame. See **Listing 8.4**.

// Listing 8.4

```
1.   public interface Constants
2.   {
3.        int X_POS    = 250,
4.            Y_POS    = 200,
5.            WIDTH    = 500,
6.            HEIGHT   = 350;
7.
8.            String TITLE  = "My First Java Graphical User Interface";
9.   }
```

Listing 8.5 shows the modification to the test class. **Line 10** shows the creating of a specified rectangle with coordinate (Constants.X_POS, Constants.Y_POS), and also a user defined size, Constants.WIDTH andConstants.HEIGHT. **Line 11** sets the frame according to the specified rectangle.

```
// Listing 8.5

1.   import java.awt.Rectangle;
2.
3.   public class MyWindow
4.   {
5.       public static void main(String[] arg)
6.       {
7.           MyJFrame f = new MyJFrame(Constants.TITLE);
8.
9.           // Change the location and size of the frame
10.          Rectangle r = new Rectangle(Constants.X_POS, Constants.Y_POS,
                                   Constants.WIDTH,Constants.HEIGHT);
11.          f.setBounds(r);
12.
13.          f.setVisible(true);
14.      }
15.  }
```

Figure 8.4 shows the new frame which is located away from the default origin, and has a longer length and width, than those of the default frame. Notice that the title of the frame can be seen, likewise the frame image, and the three buttons – minimize, maximize, and closed buttons.

Figure 8.4

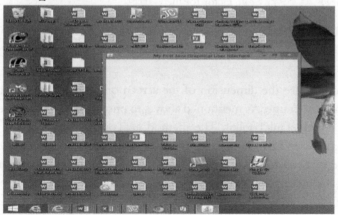

Although to change the origin of the frame, or changing the frame size is as easy as we discussed above, changing the background color for example for every possible platform is not that easy. What

Java does however to make this possible, is to provide a class called Toolkit that provides an interface to platform-specific details like window size, available fonts, and screen resolution. When you want a Toolkit object, you ask for it by using the class method **Toolkit.getDefaultToolkit()** or the **f.getToolkit()** method, where **f** represents a frame object.

For example, the following methods provide the requisite information that you might need in an application:

Return type	Method name
Image	getImage()
String[]	getFontList()
int	getScreenResolution()
Dimension	getScreenSize()
Toolkit	getDefaultToolkit()

In the following example, we will use the frame size to determine how big we should design the frame. That is, we find the dimension of the screen on which the application is running, and use some scale factor values to design the frame. **Listing 8.6** uses scale factors **WIDTH** and **HEIGHT**, to represent the width and height of the frame, respectively. See Lines **5** and **6**.

// Listing 8.6

```
1.   public interface Constants
2.   {
3.       int X_POS      = 250,
4.           Y_POS      = 200,
5.           WIDTH      = 3,  // Scale factor for the x-axis
6.           HEIGHT     = 5;  // Scale factor for the y-axis
7.
8.       String TITLE   = "My First Java Graphical User Interface";
9.   }
```

Listing 8.7 shows how to use the dimension of the screen on which the program is running to determine how big we make the frame. As mentioned above, to know the size of a screen we use either the method getToolkit or getDefaultToolkit. The method getToolkit speaks to the toolkit for the current frame (f.getToolkit()). See **Line 12**. Having the toolkit, we can now get the size of the screen (Dimension getScreenSize()). See **Line 13**. The class Dimension contains instance variables **width** and **height**, which are used to extract the width and height, respectively. See **Line 16**. Also, **Lines 1** and **2** shows the importation of the classes Toolkit and Dimension.

```
// Listing 8.7

1.    //Adding features that will enhance the frame
2.    import java.awt.Toolkit;
3.    import java.awt.Dimension;
4.    import java.awt.Rectangle;
5.
6.    public class MyWindow
7.    {
8.        public static void main(String[] arg)
9.        {
10.            MyJFrame f = new MyJFrame(Constants.TITLE);
11.
12.            Toolkit t = f.getToolkit(); // Get features of this frame
13.            Dimension size = t.getScreenSize(); //Get dimension of screen
14.
15.            // Set properties for my frame
16.            Rectangle r = new Rectangle(Constants.X_POS, Constants.Y_POS,
                        size.width/Constants.WIDTH, 2 * size.height/Constants.HEIGHT);
17.            f.setBounds(r);
18.            f.setVisible(true);
19.        }
20. }
```

Figure 8.5 shows the output of the new frame, with its dimensions width and height determined by the size of the screen, on which the program is running.

Figure 8.5

Other frame operations could involve changing the frame icon, or determine what must be done with the frame once the program is terminated. The frame image is in the upper left corner of the frame. Below are two methods that are used to change the frame image and disposes of the frame object, respectively.

```
void        setIconImage(Image)
void        setDefaultCloseOperation(int)
```

In its usage, let's say that the string "coffee.jpg" is an image file, the statement:

```
setIconImage( new ImageIcon ("coffee.jpg").getImage())
```

creates the image icon, and uses that object to replace the current frame image.

When an application such as a JFrame application is running, if we simply click the close button, the frame is discarded, but the program is still running. However, the method:

```
setDefaultCloseOperation(int)
```

does not only discards the frame object, but also terminates the program. The requisite int value is determined by the constant:

```
JFrame.EXIT_ON_CLOSE
```

Listing 8.8 shows how these two operations are implemented.

```
// Listing 8.8 Listing Changing frame icon and setting default close operation

1.   import java.awt.Rectangle;
2.   import java.awt.Toolkit;
3.   import java.awt.Dimension;
4.   import javax.swing.ImageIcon;
5.   import javax.swing.JFrame;
6.
7.   public class MyWindow {
8.        public static void main(String[] arg)  {
9.             MyJFrame f = new MyJFrame(Constants.TITLE);
10.            // Get features of this frame
11.            Toolkit t = f.getToolkit();
12.            //Get dimension of screen
13.            Dimension size = t.getScreenSize();
14.            // Set new properties for my frame
```

```
15.                    Rectangle r = new Rectangle(Constants.X_POS,
                            Constants.Y_POS, size.width/Constants.WIDTH, 2 *
                            size.height/Constants.HEIGHT);
16.                    f.setBounds(r);
17.
18.                    // Other frame operations
19.                    f.setIconImage(new ImageIcon("coffee.jpg").getImage()); //
                                            //Change frame icon
20.                    f.setDefaultCloseOperation(JFrame.EXIT_ON_CLOSE); //
                                            //Close frame and terminate the program
21.                    f.setVisible(true);
22.            }
23. }
```

Figure 8.6 shows the changed frame image icon. The close operation cannot be shown. However when you run the program you will observe it.

Figure 8.6

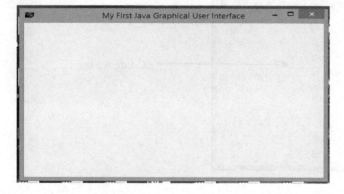

AWT versus Swing

As was mentioned briefly in the introduction, when developing a GUI program in Java, there are two packages with components such as buttons, icons, and menu items, that you will most likely use to build your programs. These packages are the Abstract Window Toolkit (**awt**) and Swing.

The **awt** provides the connection between your application and the native system on which your program runs. This is because awt components depend on native code counterparts (called peers) to handle their functionality. Thus, these components are often referred to as heavyweight components. Hence, GUI programs written purely with the awt, more closely reflect the look and feel of the operating system on which they run.

Swing on the other hand does not have this close relationship with the native platform. As a result, the look-and-feel is the same from one native platform to the next. That is, swing components do not depend on peers to handle their functionality. Thus, these components are often called lightweight components. In addition swing has wider set of components that are used to build GUI programs.

Both packages complement one another when building GUI programs, in that swing builds and attaches the components to the frame, and awt embellishes the components by rendering color, fonts, etc.

The ContentPane

Because swing does not work directly with the native platform, it uses what is called the content pane of the frame on which to hang components. In other words, if components are placed directly onto the frame, they will not be seen in the GUI. Consider for a moment a frame with a thin film as shown in **Figure 8.7**, and that this film can be peeled off. Well the content pane of a frame could be likened to this illustration. So to add components such as buttons onto the frame, or even to change the background color of the frame, would necessitate obtaining the content pane first, then render it, and then re-place it (except that we do not actually write code to replace it).

Figure 8.7 content pane

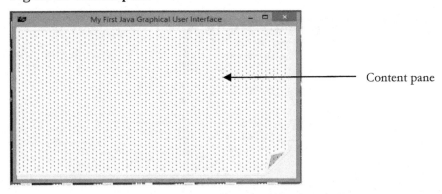

With this knowledge, let us do two things to the frame. Let us change the background color of the frame, and change the style cursor when the mouse enters the frame. **See Listing 8.9, Lines 28** thru **30**.

//Listing 8.9 Change background color and cursor

```
1.    import java.awt.Rectangle;
2.    import java.awt.Toolkit;
3.    import java.awt.Dimension;
4.
5.    import java.awt.Container;
6.    import java.awt.Color;
```

```
7.   import java.awt.Cursor;
8.
9.   import javax.swing.ImageIcon;
10.  import javax.swing.JFrame;
11.
12.  public class MyWindow
13.  {
14.      public static void main(String[] arg)
15.      {
16.          MyJFrame f = new MyJFrame(Constants.TITLE);
17.          // Get features of this frame
18.          Toolkit t = f.getToolkit();
19.          //Get dimension of screen
20.          Dimension size = t.getScreenSize();
21.          // Set new properties for my frame
22.          Rectangle r = new Rectangle(Constants.X_POS, Constants.Y_POS,
                 size.width/Constants.WIDTH, 2 * size.height/Constants.HEIGHT);
23.          f.setBounds(r);
24.          // Other frame operations
25.          f.setIconImage(new ImageIcon("coffee.jpg").getImage()); // Change frame icon
26.          f.setDefaultCloseOperation(JFrame.EXIT_ON_CLOSE); // Close frame and
                 terminate the program
27.
28.          Container c = f.getContentPane(); // Get the contentPane
29.          c.setBackground(Color.YELLOW);  // Change background color
30.          c.setCursor( Cursor.getPredefinedCursor(Cursor.WAIT_CURSOR ));//
                 Change cursor
31.
32.          f.setVisible(true);
33.      }
34.  }
```

Figure 8.8 shows the output of the program. The change in the background color, and the change of cursor were done by the following three statements. Notice that first we must obtain the content pane of the frame before doing any rendering – see **Line 28**. Next, change the background color – **Line 29**. Finally, change the cursor – **Line 30**. These three lines of codes depended on the awt package for the classes Container, Color, and Cursor. See **Lines 5 thru 7**.

```
28. Container c = f.getContentPane(); // Get the contentPane
29. c.setBackground(Color.YELLOW); // Change background color
30. c.setCursor( Cursor.getPredefinedCursor(Cursor.WAIT_CURSOR ));//Change cursor
```

Figure 8.8

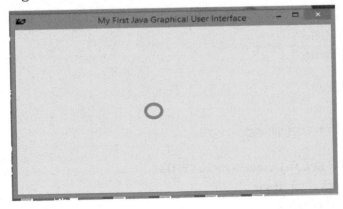

Self-Check

1. Name three classes that we have used in this section that are found in the **awt** package.

2. Name four styles of cursors found in the class cursor.

3. Name five colors (constants) found in the class Color.

4. What happens when you add a component directly to a JFrame and not to the content pane?

5. Differentiate between a **Container** object and a **Component** object. Support your answer with one example of each.

6. In what class is method **getContentPane()** found?

7. In what class is the method **setBackground()** found?

8. In what is the method **setCursor()** found?

9. In what is the method **getPredefinedCursor()** found?

Setting up Menus

As you know, a menu is a set of options from which one can make choices. In terms of programming however, a menu choice represents a category of options called menu items. A menu item can either be a string, a radio button, or a check box. Before you can establish a menu onto a frame, however, you must first prepare the space by creating what is called a menu bar.

Setting the Menu bar

In terms of Java, menu bar is a horizontal bar that is located immediately below the title bar of the frame. On the menu bar, you will hang the menu choices. **Figure 8.9** is an illustration where the menu bar goes. We say that it is an illustration because menu bars are not visible, until it has at least one menu choice attached to it.

Figure 8.9 Menu bar

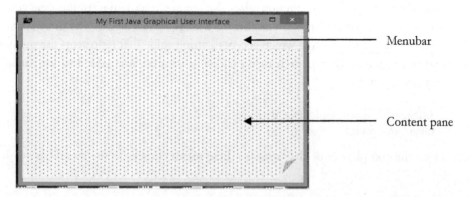

Once the menu bar has been set up, the content pane is reduced as shown if **Figure 8.9.**

In order to establish the menu bar onto the frame, we have to create a JMenubar object, as shown in **Listing 8.10**. Notice that you first must create the JMenubar object as shown in **Line 14**, and then make the reservation in **Line 15**. Notice also that the class JMenuBar is a swing entity, hence it has to be imported. See **Line 4**.

Listing 8.10

```
1.   // Reserving/setting up the menubar.
2.
3.   import javax.swing.JFrame;
4.   import javax.swing.JMenuBar;
5.
6.   public class MyJFrame extends JFrame
7.   {
8.       JMenuBar menubar;
9.
10.      public MyJFrame(String title)
11.      {
12.          super(title);
13.          // Set up the menubar.
14.          menubar = new JMenuBar();
15.          setJMenuBar(menubar);
16.      }
17.  }
```

Adding Menu Choices to the Menubar

Once the menu bar is in place, you can now place the menu choices on it. In this case you will use a JMenu object, in which case you will have to import the class JMenu. The class has three constructors, however the preferred constructor is that which accepts a string value that represents the menu choice.

The way that this works, is that as each menu choice is created, it is added to the menu bar, as shown the pair of codes below.

```
JMenu mi = new JMenu("File");
menubar.add(mi);
```

Listing 8.11 shows the complete code that attaches three menu choices to the menu bar – File, Tool, and Help.

```
1.  // Listing 8.11 Adding menu choices to the menubar.
2.
3.  import javax.swing.JFrame;
4.  import javax.swing.JMenuBar;
5.  import javax.swing.JMenu;
6.
7.  public class MyJFrame extends JFrame {
8.      JMenuBar menubar;
9.      JMenu mi; // for menu choices
10.
11.     public MyJFrame(String title) {
12.         super(title);
13.
14.         menubar = new JMenuBar();
15.         setJMenuBar(menubar);
16.
17.         buildMenu();
18.     }
19.     void buildMenu() {
20.         mi = new JMenu("File"); // Adding the first menu choice
21.         menubar.add(mi);
22.         mi = new JMenu("Tool"); // Add a second menu choice
23.         menubar.add(mi);
24.         mi = new JMenu("Help"); // Add a third menu choice
25.
26.         menubar.add(mi); // Add menu choices to the menubar
27.     }
28. }
```

Figure 8.10 shows the output from the program. In the code, **Lines 20** thru **26** are responsible for creating and attaching the menu choices to the menu bar.

Figure 8.10 Three menu choices are attached to the menu bar

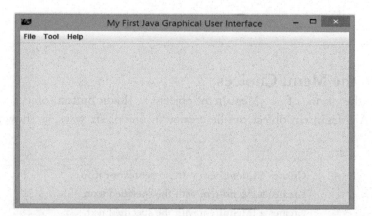

Although the code in the method above works, it is tedious and error prone. A better approach of expressing the code is to place the string representing each menu choice in an array, as shown in **Listing 8.12, Line 9**.

```
// Listing 8.12

1.   public interface Constants
2.   {
3.       int X_POS = 500,
4.           Y_POS = 300,
5.           WIDTH = 3,
6.           HEIGHT = 5;
7.
8.       String TITLE  = "My First Java Graphical User Interface",
9.           MENU[] = {"File", "Tool", "Help"};
10. }
```

Once the array of choices has been established, it is simply a matter of looping through the array, reading the values and attaching them to the menu choices, and the menu choices to the menu bar. See the **for** loop of **Listing 8.13**. When the program is executed, the result is the same as Figure 8.10.

Listing 8.13

```
1.   void buildMenu() {
2.       for (int i = 0; i < Constants.MENU.length; i++) {
3.           f = new JMenu( Constants.MENU[i] );
4.           menubar.add(f);
5.       }
6.   }
```

Adding Menu Items to the Menu Choices

A menu item can take the form of a JMenuItem object, a JRadioButton object, or a JCheckBoxMenuItem object. A JMenuItem object can be created in one of six ways, as shown the following set of constructors.

JMenuItem()	Creates a JMenuItem with no set text or icon.
JMenuItem(Icon icon)	Creates a JMenuItem with the specified icon.
JMenuItem(String text)	Creates a JMenuItem with the specified text.
JMenuItem(String text, Icon icon)	Creates a JMenuItem with the specified text and icon.
JMenuItem(String text, int mnemonic)	Creates a JMenuItem with the specified text and keyboard mnemonic.
JMenuItem(Action a)	Creates a menu item whose properties are taken from the specified Action.

Listing 8.14 shows the creation of three JMenuItem objects – Open, Save, and Close – that are added to the menu choice **f**, File menu choice. Groups of menu items can be separated from other groups by using the method **addSeparator()** from the class JFrame. See **Line 7.**

Listing 8.14

```
1.   void buildMenu() {
2.       f = new JMenu( "File");
3.       mi = new JMenuItem("Open"); // First menu item for menu choice File
4.       f.add(mi); // Add this first menu item to the menu choice
5.       mi = new JMenuItem("Save");  // Second menu item for menu choice File
6.       f.add(mi);
7.       f.addSeparator();
8.       mi = new JMenuItem("Close");  // Third menu item for menu choice File
9.       f.add(mi);
10.      menubar.add(f);
11.  }
```

Figure 8.11 shows the output from the program. This time the menu choice File has three menu items. The first two are separated from the third, using the separator method.

Figure 8.11

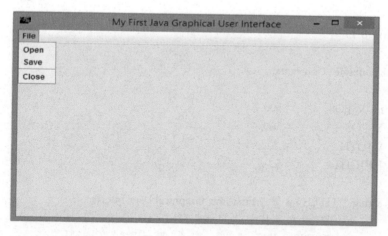

Figure 8.12 shows a continuation of the GUI program. Notice the following – the menu choice Tool has a drop down menu with two menu items – Search and Sort. In order to get the option "Edit" as a menu choice, it must be considered a menu choice, and not a menu item, thus forming what is called cascading menu. The option Edit contains a drop down menu of three radio buttons as you can see.

Figure 8.12

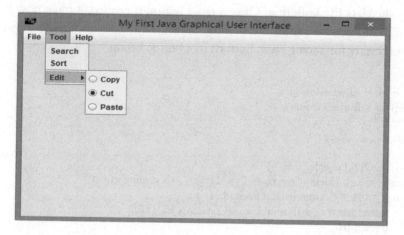

In constructing the program we define a few arrays as the input for configuring the menu. See **Listing 8.15**. In Listing 8.10, we make the array MENU, the menu choices. See **Line 9**. Next, we make the array FILES, the menu items corresponding to MENU[0] (File). That is, each string in the array FILES represents a file menu item. Where there is a dash, we treat it as a separator, by calling the method addSeparator(). Next, we make MENU[1] (Tool) correspond to the array TOOL. The first two entries will be treated as menu items, but option TOOL[2], (Edit) will be treated as a menu choice, that will take on the array EDIT.

```
// Listing 8.15

1.   public interface Constants
2.   {
3.        int X_POS       = 500,
4.            Y_POS       = 300,
5.            WIDTH       = 3,
6.            HEIGHT      = 5;
7.
8.        String   TITLE  = "My First Java Graphical User Interface",
9.                 MENU[] = {"File", "Tool", "Help"},
10.               FILES[] = {"New", "Open", "-", "Save", "-","Close"},
11.               TOOL[] = {"Search", "Sort", "Edit"},
12.               EDIT[] = {"Copy", "Cut", "Paste"};
13.  }
```

The menu items for the Edit option as you see must be treated as clusters of options, where only one option can be selected at a time. These buttons are called radio buttons – the class that creates radio button objects is the class JRadioButton. Once a radio button is created, it must now be added to a particular group of buttons, by using a ButtonGroup object. The segment of code shown below is the minimum code necessary for adding radio buttons to a button group.

```
JRadioButton jrb =  JRadioButton();
ButtonGroup bg = ButtonGroup();
        ........................
        ........................

if (Constants.TOOL[k].equals("Edit"))
        JMenu m = new JMenu(Constants.TOOL[k]); // Cascading menu
        for (int l = 0; l < Constants.EDIT.length; l++) {
                m.add(jrb = new JRadioButton(Constants.EDIT[l]));
                bg.add(jrb);
        }

f.add(m);
```

Listing 8.16 shows the complete code for the choices MENU[0] and MENU[1]. The remaining options follow similar pattern.

Listing 8.16

```
1.   /*
2.   This section actually builds the menuitem onto each menu choice.
3.   */
4.
5.   import javax.swing.JFrame;
6.   import javax.swing.JMenuBar;
7.   import javax.swing.JMenu;
8.   import javax.swing.JCheckBoxMenuItem;
9.   import javax.swing.JMenuItem;
10.  import javax.swing.JRadioButton;
11.  import javax.swing.ButtonGroup;
12.
13.  public class MyJFrame extends JFrame
14.  {
15.      JMenuBar menubar;
16.      JMenu f;
17.      JMenuItem mi;
18.      JRadioButton jrb;
19.      ButtonGroup bg;
20.
21.      public MyJFrame(String title)
22.      {
23.          super(title);
24.          // The menubar is invisible
25.          menubar = new JMenuBar();
26.          setJMenuBar(menubar);
27.          bg = new ButtonGroup();
28.          buildMenu();
29.      }
30.      void buildMenu()
31.      {
32.          for (int i = 0; i < Constants.MENU.length; i++)
33.          {       //Build and add each menu choice onto the menubar
34.              f = new JMenu(Constants.MENU[i]);
35.
36.              switch(i)
```

```
37.                 {
38.                     case 0: // Add menu items
39.                         for (int j = 0; j < Constants.FILES.length; j++)
40.                             if (Constants.FILES[j].equals("-"))
41.                                 f.addSeparator();
42.                             else
43.                                 f.add(mi = new JMenuItem(Constants.FILES[j]));
44.                     break;
45.                     case 1:
46.                     for (int k = 0; k < Constants.TOOL.length; k++)
47.                         if (Constants.TOOL[k].equals("Edit"))
48.                         {
49.                             f.addSeparator();
50.                             JMenu m = new JMenu(Constants.TOOL[k]); // Cascading
                                menu
51.                             for (int l = 0; l < Constants.EDIT.length; l++)
52.                             {
53.                                 m.add(jrb = new JRadioButton(Constants.EDIT[l]));
54.                                 bg.add(jrb);
55.                             }
56.                             f.add(m);
57.                         }
58.                         else
59.                             f.add(mi = new JMenuItem(Constants.TOOL[k]));
60.                     break;
61.                     /*      case 2:
62.                     Pattern is the same
63.                     break;
64.                     */
65.                 }
66.                 menubar.add(f);
67.         }
68.     }
69. }
```

Self-Check

1. Name three kinds of menu item we can place on a menu choice.

2. Name the three classes that we have used to place menu items onto menu choices in this section.

3. What is the purpose of the class ButtonGroup?

4. In what class is the method **addSeparator()** found?

5. Consider the following Java codes.

```java
import javax.swing.JFrame;
import javax.swing.JMenuBar;

public class MyJFrame extends JFrame {
    JMenuBar bar;
    MyJFrame(String s) {
        super(s);
        JMenuBar bar = new JMenuBar();
        setJMenuBar(bar);
    }
}
```

What statement(s) best describe what the code does when it is compiled and executed?
   (a) The inherited class JFrame sets the title for MyJFrame.
   (b) The code sets up the menu items onto the menu bar.
   (c) The sets in place the menu bar. Without an attached menu choice it is not visible
   (d) The codes sets up the menu choices.

6. (True or False). Any class that inherits JFrame is making a customized frame by adding any features it sees fit.

7. The following segment of code has errors. Find and correct these errors.

```java
import java.swing.JFrame;

public MyFrame extend JFrame
{
    super("My First GUI");  // Let JFrame set the title
}
```

Buttons

Push button, simply referred to as button, is another type of component object that you will frequently find on a GUI. A button can be created in several ways as shown by the following set of constructors.

JButton ()	Creates a button with no set text or icon.
JButton (Icon icon)	Creates a button with the specified icon.
JButton (String text)	Creates a button with the specified text.
JButton (String text, Icon icon)	Creates a button with the specified text and icon.
JButton (String text, int mnemonic)	Creates a button with the specified text and keyboard mnemonic.
JButton (Action a)	Creates a button item whose properties are taken from the specified Action.

Layout Managers

Once a button has been created, the next step is to place it in a container object such as the content pane of a frame. This requires what is referred to as a layout manager. A layout manager as the term suggests, is an object that controls the size and the position of components, such as buttons, in a container. Java defines eight layout managers - FlowLayout, GridLayout, BorderLayout, GridBagLayout, CardLayout, GroupLayout, BoxLayout, and SpringLayout. We will study the first four in this book. The general pattern of specifying a particular layout manager is as follows:

LayoutManager lm = new LayoutManager (<parameter>)
c.setLayout(lm);

or simply

c.setLayout(new LayoutManager (<parameter>));

Where **LayoutManager** is any of the layout manager classes stated above, and **c** is the reference to a container object.

FlowLayout Manager

FlowLayout manager is the simplest of the layout managers. It simply lays out components in a single row, starting a new row if its container is not sufficiently wide. The constructors below show the three different ways of constructing a FlowLayout object.

FlowLayout()	Creates a FlowLayout object with a centered alignment, and horizontal and vertical gaps of 5 pixels between components.
FlowLayout(int align)	Creates a FlowLayout object with the indicated alignment and horizontal and vertical gaps of 5 pixels between components. Alignment constants are – CENTER, LEFT, RIGHT, LEADING or TRAILING.

FlowLayout (int align, int hgap, int vgap)	Creates a FlowLayout object with the indicated alignment, and the indicated horizontal and vertical gaps. The hgap and vgap arguments specify the number of pixels to put between components.

Figure 8.13 demonstrates the meaning of vgap and hgap.

Figure 8.13

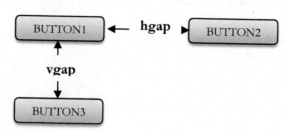

Listing 8.17 creates and lays out five buttons in the content pane of the frame, using FlowLayout manager. See **Line 19**. The buttons are laid out from left to right; and each is placed at a distance of 70 pixels apart horizontally from each other, and 10 pixels vertically. See **Line 20**. It is expected that there could be image file(s). Hence, the code checks for this possibility. See **Line 24**.

```
// Listing 8.17

1.    import javax.swing.JFrame;
2.    import javax.swing.JButton;
3.    import java.awt.Container;
4.    import java.awt.FlowLayout;
5.    import javax.swing.ImageIcon;
6.
7.    public class MyJButton extends JButton
8.    {
9.         MyJFrame f;
10.
11.        MyJButton(MyJFrame f)
12.        {
13.            this.f = f;
14.        }
15.        public void addFlowLayout()
16.        {
17.            JButton b;
```

```
18.
19.            Container c = f.getContentPane();
20.            f.setLayout(new FlowLayout( FlowLayout.LEFT, 70, 10 ));
21.
22.            for (int i = 0; i < Constants.BUTTON.length; i++)
23.            {
24.                if (Constants.BUTTON[i].endsWith("jpg"))
25.                    b = new JButton(new ImageIcon(Constants.BUTTON[i]));
26.                else
27.                    b = new JButton(Constants.BUTTON[i]);
28.                f.add(b);
29.            }
30.        }
31. }
```

Figure 8.14 shows the output from the program. Notice that, in addition to the menu choices, there are now five buttons added to the frame. These buttons are sized by default according the length of the string, and the size of the image.

Figure 8.14

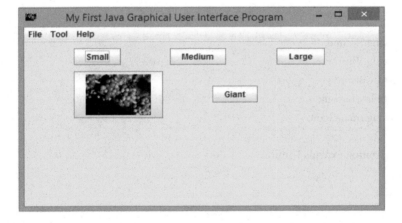

This layout manager is not frequently used to build GUIs, since the buttons tend to be unstable in a given position when the container is resized. For example, when placed in a frame, if the frame is resized down to its minimum, the button formation is in a single column. When resized to its maximum, the buttons tend to form a single row.

GridLayout Manager

GridLayout manager lays out components in a rectangular grid of **m** rows by **n** columns. The container is divided into equal-sized rectangles, and one component is placed in each rectangle. The constructors shown below are the three ways that this class can layout components in a container.

GridLayout()	Creates a grid layout with a default of one column per component, in a single row.
GridLayout(int rows, int columns)	Creates a grid layout with a specified number of rows and columns.
GridLayout (int rows, int column, int hgap, int vgap)	Creates a GridLayout object with the indicated number of rows and columns, and the indicated horizontal and vertical gaps.

Diagrammatically, this is what 2 rows by 3 columns frame of five buttons looks like, using GridLayout manager, instead of FlowLayout.

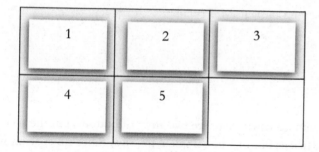

Listing 8.18 lays out the five buttons as in the previous listing, but this time using GridLayout manager. In this case an imaginary grid of two rows and three columns have been reserved. See **Line 19**.

```
// Listing 8.18

1.   import javax.swing.JFrame;
2.   import javax.swing.JButton;
3.   import java.awt.Container;
4.   import java.awt.FlowLayout;
5.   import javax.swing.ImageIcon;
6.
7.   public class MyJButton extends JButton
8.   {
```

```
9.        MyJFrame f;
10.
11.       MyJButton(MyJFrame f)
12.       {
13.           this.f = f;
14.       }
15.       public void addGridLayout()
16.       {
17.           JButton b;
18.           Container c = f.getContentPane();
19.           f.setLayout(new GridLayout(2, 3));
20.
21.           for (int i = 0; i < Constants.BUTTON.length; i++)
22.           {
23.               if (Constants.BUTTON[i].endsWith(".jpg"))
24.                   b = new JButton( new ImageIcon( Constants.BUTTON[i]));
25.               else
26.                   b = new JButton(Constants.BUTTON[i]);
27.               c.add(b);
28.           }
29.       }
30. }
```

Figure 8.15 shows the output of the program in which there are two rows of buttons, but the second row is partially filled, since there aren't sufficient buttons to complete the row. Since no spacing was provided, then the buttons fit closely to each other.

Figure 8.15

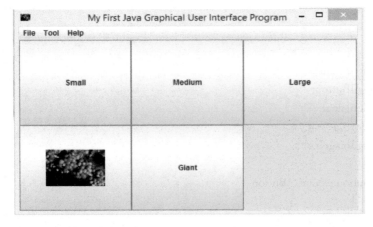

Self-Check

1. Differentiate between the layout managers, FlowLayout and GridLayout.

2. When using the GridLayout manager, if we want space around the components in a container, what constructor should be used to guarantee this?

3. Referring to Listing 8.18, replace Line 19 with the following code:

    ```
    f.setLayout( new GridLayout(2, 3, 20, 10));
    ```

    Explain to someone the difference between this new output, and that of Figure 8.14.

BorderLayout Manager

The BorderLayout manager lays out the buttons following the position of the cardinal points of a rectangle – EAST, WEST, NORTH, SOUTH, and CENTER. The diagram below shows these five cardinal positions occupied by a BorderLayout manager.

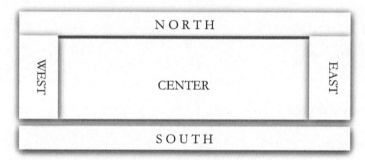

The class has two constructors as shown below:

BorderLayout()	Constructs a new border layout with no gaps between components.
BorderLayout(int hgap, vgap)	Constructs a new border layout with specified gaps between components.

Listing 8.19 lays out five buttons, one in each of the cardinal points of the frame. If the parameterless constructor is used, then there will be no space between any of the components, as you will see in the output of **Listing 8.19**. In the listing, Line 19 creates a BorderLayout object; and **Lines 21** thru **34** create each button, and add them to the container.

// Listing 8.19

```java
1.    import javax.swing.JFrame;
2.    import javax.swing.JButton;
3.    import java.awt.BorderLayout;
4.    import javax.swing.ImageIcon;
5.
6.    public class MyJButton extends JButton
7.    {
8.        MyJFrame f;
9.
10.       MyJButton(MyJFrame f)
11.       {
12.           this.f = f;
13.       }
14.
15.       public void addBorderLayout()
16.       {
17.           JButton b;
18.
19.           f.setLayout(new BorderLayout());
20.
21.           b = new JButton("North");
22.           f.add(b, BorderLayout.NORTH);
23.
24.           b = new JButton("WEST");
25.           f.add(b, BorderLayout.WEST);
26.
27.           b = new JButton("Center");
28.           f.add(b, BorderLayout.CENTER);
29.
30.           b = new JButton("EAST", new ImageIcon(Constants.BUTTON[3]));
31.           f.add(b, BorderLayout.EAST);
32.
33.           b = new JButton("SOUTH");
34.           f.add(b, BorderLayout.SOUTH);
35.       }
36. }
```

Figure 8.16 shows the five buttons, one at each of the five cardinal points on the frame. Because the patameterless constructor is used, then there are no gaps between the buttons.

Figure 8.16 using BorderLayout

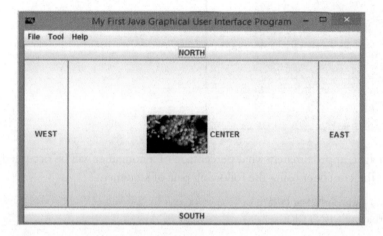

When multiple related components are to be placed in a container, it is best to place them on a panel, and then place the panel at one these positions on the content pane of the frame, as we will see later in this Chapter.

Self-Check

1. Modify Listing 8.xxx so that it produces an output similar to the following.

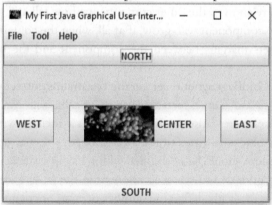

2. Modify Listing 8.xxx so that it produces an output similar to the following.

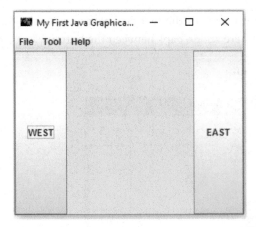

3. Using BorderLayout manager, approximately what percentage of a container will be occupied, if a single button is placed in the container using the following pair of statement?

> JButton b = new JButton("CENTER");
> f.add(b, BorderLayout.CENTER);

Where **f** is a reference to a JFrame container.

GridBagLayout Manager

GridBagLayout offers the most flexibility in positioning components vertically and horizontally within a container, than the other layout managers. This flexibility comes with a price of having to deal with two other classes - GridbagConstraints and Insets. In positioning a component the programmer has to set values in the GridBagConstraints object that will specify things such as, where in the container the component will appear in relation to the other components; how tall and how wide the component is going to be; also, how the component will grow, if at all, when the container is resized. Then there is the class Insets which sets margins between the component and the border of the container – top, left, bottom, right.

Most of the work involved in using GridBagLayout is setting the constraints correctly. As you will see, each GridBagLayout object maintains a dynamic, rectangular grid of cells, with each component occupying one or more cells, called its display area. Also, each component is associated with an instance of GridBagConstraints. The constraints object specifies where a component's display area should be located on the grid, and how the component should be positioned within its display area. For instance, the pair of instance variables (gridx and gridy), positions a component in the (x, y) coordinate of the display area. The class has no methods to explicitly define the number of rows or columns in the grid; nor does it has methods to define the size of each cell in the grid. The programmer will have to use imagination to position and size the components.

Depending on the number of components, and the (x, y) coordinate provided, GridBagLayout calculates the number of rows and columns in a grid, by the number of components placed on the screen. If a container has five components lined up horizontally, then the grid consists of five columns and one row. If the container has five components lined up vertically, then the grid consists of one column and five rows.

Positioning out Components

The GridBagConstraints class specifies two instance variables constraints (gridx, gridy), that are used to position each component in the frame. Their descriptions are explained below. The instance variable **fill** is sometimes used to fill out the display area, if the display area is larger than the size of the actual component.

int gridx	Specifies the cell containing the leading edge of the component's display area, where the first cell in a row has gridx = 0
int gridy	Specifies the cell at the top of the component's display area, where the topmost cell has gridy = 0
int fill	This field is used when the component's display area is larger than the component's requested size.

Consider the following set of co-ordinates (0, 0), (1, 0), and (0, 2). Using our knowledge of the Cartesian plain one would believe that the buttons are positioned with two occupied rows, and a blank row, as shown below.

(0, 0)	(1, 0)
(0, 2)	

That is, our intuition leads us to believe that there is a second row, and that this row is empty of components. By definition the constraints specified by (gridx, gridy) merely position the components relative to one another. Therefore, we should expect the components be placed as shown below:

(0, 0)	(1, 0)
(0, 2)	

In this illustration, the buttons are positioned relative to their one another, and not by the way that we have been accustomed to viewing the x-y coordinate system. **Listing 8.20** shows the class MyJButton that positions three buttons using the above coordinates.

Listing 8.20

```
//       This class lays out buttons using x-y coordinate format
1.   import javax.swing.JFrame;
2.   import javax.swing.JButton;
3.   import java.awt.GridBagLayout;
4.   import java.awt.GridBagConstraints;
5.
6.   public class MyJButton extends JButton {
7.        MyJFrame f;
8.
9.        MyJButton(MyJFrame f){
10.           this.f = f;
11.       }
12.       public void addGridBagLayout(){
13.           JButton b;
14.           // Places components in a grid of rows & columns
15.           GridBagLayout gbag = new GridBagLayout();
16.           // Specify the constraints for each component
17.           GridBagConstraints constraints = new GridBagConstraints();
18.           f.setLayout(gbag); // Layout each component
19.
20.           for (int i = 0; i < Constants.BUTTON.length; i++) {
21.               b = new JButton(Constants.BUTTON[i]);
22.               switch(i)
23.               {
24.                   case 0: // Specify the (x,y) coordinate for this component
25.                       constraints.gridx = 0;
26.                       constraints.gridy = 0; // (0, 0)
27.                   break;
28.                   case 1:
29.                       constraints.gridx = 1;
30.                       constraints.gridy = 0; // (1, 0)
31.                   break;
32.                   case 2:
33.                       constraints.gridx = 0;
```

```
34.                     constraints.gridy = 2;
35.                 break;
36.                 default:
37.                 break;
38.             }
39.             gbag.setConstraints(b, constraints);
40.             f.add(b);
41.         }
42.     }
43. }
```

Figure 8.17 shows the actual output from the program. Notice that the buttons are in position relative to one another, and not by what our intuition tells us.

Figure 8.17

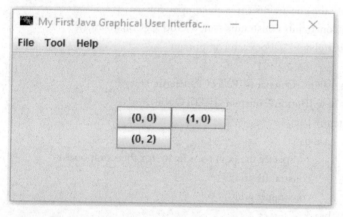

As was mentioned earlier, each GridBagLayout object maintains a dynamic, rectangular grid of cells. This means that components are created, and are placed without regards to the order in which they are added, but rather by the coordinates. **Listing 8.20** creates, and positions four buttons (3 rows by 2 columns) on the frame at the following coordinates (0, 0), (1, 0), (0, 1), and (0, 2). Let us store these pairs of values in an array as shown below.

BUTTON[]= {"(0, 0)", "(1, 0)", "(0, 2)", "(0, 1)"};

Listing 8.20

```
1.  import javax.swing.JFrame;
2.  import javax.swing.JButton;
```

```
3.     import javax.swing.ImageIcon;
4.     import java.awt.Container;
5.     import java.awt.GridBagLayout;
6.     import java.awt.GridBagConstraints;
7.
8.     public class MyJButton extends JButton {
9.         MyJFrame f;
10.
11.        MyJButton(MyJFrame f) {
12.            this.f = f;
13.        }
14.        public void addGridBagLayout() {
15.            JButton b;
16.            // Places components in a grid of rows & columns
17.            GridBagLayout gbag = new GridBagLayout();
18.            // Specify the constraints for each component
19.            GridBagConstraints constraints = new GridBagConstraints();
20.            f.setLayout(gbag); // For each component
21.
22.            for (int i = 0; i < Constants.BUTTON.length; i++) {
23.                b = new JButton(Constants.BUTTON[i]);
24.                switch(i) {
25.                    case 0:
26.                        // Specify the (x,y) coordinate for this component
27.                        constraints.gridx = 0;
28.                        constraints.gridy = 0;
29.                        break;
30.                    case 1:
31.                        constraints.gridx = 1;
32.                        constraints.gridy = 0;
33.                    break;
34.                    case 2:
35.                        constraints.gridx = 0;
36.                        constraints.gridy = 2;
37.                    break;
38.                    case 3: // Image button
39.                        b = new JButton(new ImageIcon(Constants.BUTTON[i]));
40.                        constraints.gridx = 0;
41.                        constraints.gridy = 1;
42.                    break;
```

```
43.                        }
44.                gbag.setConstraints(b, constraints);
45.                f.add(b);
46.          }
47.     }
48. }
```

When the program is executed the buttons are placed relative to each other as shown in **Figure 8.18**. Notice also the order or sequence in which they were added. According to the code (Listing 8.xx), the third button (0, 2) was added, so it seems, to the container, before the fourth. Because of the dynamic nature of the class, the buttons are repositioned, in order to maintain the relative position of each component. **Figure 8.18** shows the relative position of each button in the container.

Figure 8.18

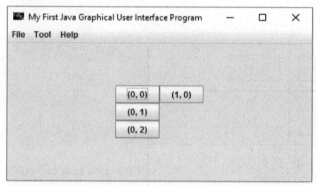

When replaced with the original array of values, the output is shown in **Figure 8.19**. Notice that buttons occupy their relative position, but the size of each component is determined by the length of the string, and the size of the image.

Figure 8.19

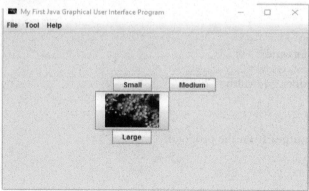

Resizing Components

In Figure 8.xx, notice in that the buttons are placed without any appealing arrangement. This is because the buttons were only positioned by their (x, y) co-ordinates. That is, the constraints on the (x, y) co-ordinate called for three rows and two columns which it did. To resize the buttons would require more constraints on each component. The class GridbagConstraints has instance variables gridwidth, and gridheight, described below, that allows a component to span **n** number of cells horizontally and **m** number of columns vertically, respectively.

int gridwidth	Specifies the number of cells in a column for the component's display area.
int gridheight	Specifies the number of cells in a row for the component's display area.

With these variables we can change the look of a user interface of buttons, by applying one or both constraints on these buttons. For example, let us set the fourth button (3rd row) to span two cells horizontally. That is, the button at location (0, 2) must span two cells horizontally, as shown below.

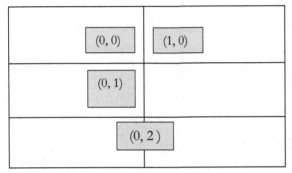

Let button span two cells horizontally

You may be wondering why the entire two cells were not occupied. The command promises that the component will occupy two cells horizontally, which it did. It did not promise to cover the cells from wall to wall. There are other constrains such as the class Insets, that can be used for that purpose later in the chapter. The code necessary to span two cells horizontally, the third statement shown in **case 2** below.

```
case 2:
    constraints.gridx = 0;
    constraints.gridy = 2;
    constraints.gridwidth = 2;
break;
```

Figure 8.20 shows the actual output from the program.

Figure 8.20

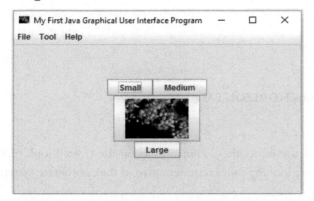

If we were to look at this output carefully, you would see, in comparison with the first row, that this button spans, or at least, is sitting on two cells horizontally.

The class also defines constants that can be used to position components. The table below describes some constants that can be used to reposition components in their respective display area.

CENTER	Put the component in the center of its display area.
HORIZONTAL	Resizes the component horizontally in its display area.
VERTICAL	Resizes the component vertically
REMAINDER	Specifies that this component is the last component in its column or row.
RELATIVE	Specifies that this component is the next-to-last component in its column or row (gridwidth, gridheight), or that this component be placed next to the previously added component (gridx, gridy).
BOTH	Resizes the component both horizontally and vertically.

Focusing on the component at (0, 2), let us set it so that it fills its display are horizontally, as shown in the diagram below. Notice that the other buttons maintain their relative positions and sizes.

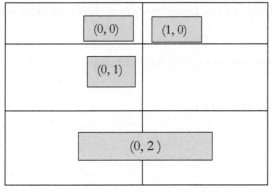

This button was smaller than the display area, so it needs to be filled it out. This where the constant HORIZONTAL comes into effect.

The code necessary for this to happen is the fourth statement of the case statement.

```
case 2:
    constraints.gridx = 0;
    constraints.gridy = 2;
    constraints.gridwidth = 2;
    constraints.fill = GridBagConstraints.HORIZONTAL;
break;
```

When we run the code, **Figure 8.21** shows the effect the command has on the overall look of the interface. In the interim, the other buttons are looking more representative of the coordinate systems.

Figure 8.21

Lastly, setting constraints on the image button so that it is centered in the container at all times. As shown above this button appears to be at the center of the interface, but is not guaranteed if any of the components are to be re-positioned. The way to guarantee this position, is to set the constraint to be centered, as shown in the code below. The effect of this new statement is shown in **Figure 8.22**

```
case 3:
    b = new JButton(new ImageIcon(Constants.BUTTON[i]));// Add image
    constraints.gridx = 0;
    constraints.gridy = 1;
    constraints.fill = GridBagConstraints.CENTER;
break;
```

Figure 8.22

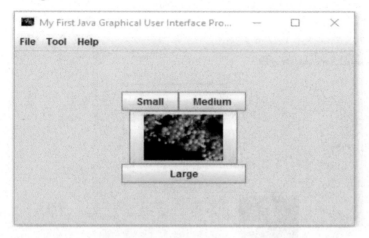

Adjust Components using Insets

Apart from the class GridbagConstraints, the class **Insets** is frequently used to adjust the position of a component in a GridbagLayout object. You may ask what an Insets is. An Insets object is a representation of the borders of a container. It specifies the space that a container must leave at each of its edges. The space can be a border, a blank space (in pixels), or a title.

Figure 8.17 shows that the buttons are positioned more pleasing than Figure 8.16. However, they are hugging each other too closely. This is where the class Insets comes in, to provide space around each component. The format to create an Insets object is as follows:

```
constraints.insets = new Insets(top, left, bottom, right );
```

Where top, left, bottom, and right are integer values in pixels from each border of a container. For instance, let us set inserts for the first button with values as shown below:

```
constraints.insets = new Insets( 50, 75, 0, 75);
```

See case statement below:

```
case 0:  // Specify the (x,y) coordinate for this component
     constraints.gridx = 0;
     constraints.gridy = 0; // (x,y) = (0,0)
     constraints.insets = new Insets(50,75,0,75);
break;
```

Figure 8.23 shows the change in the top, left and right margins of the frame. Also, the change value for top affects the top margin of all three components.

Figure 8.23

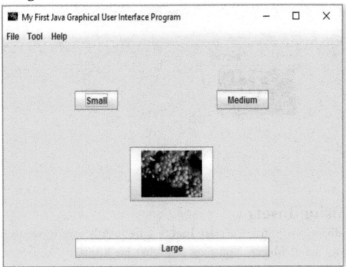

Looking at **Figure 8.23**, with the top alignment set at 50, causes each row to be re-positioned 50 pixels from the top, away from each other. The bottom margin remains unchanged, but the left and right borders are at equal distance from the edge of the frame, by 75 pixels.

Because the last button is so close to the edge of the frame, our intuition tells us to move it up from the edge of the frame. Applying Insets again, this time focusing on the bottom edge.

```
case 2:
        constraints.gridx = 0;
        constraints.gridy = 2;
        constraints.gridwidth = 2;
        constraints.fill = GridBagConstraints.HORIZONTAL;
        constraints.insets = new Insets(0, 75, 50, 75);
break;
```

As shown in the specification, there should be no shift from the top edge; maintain the left and right edges at 75 pixels each; and re-align 50 pixels from the bottom edge of the frame. **Figure 8.24** shows the effect with this change.

Figure 8.24

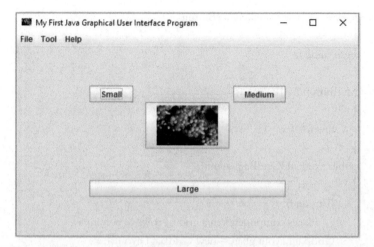

The new Insets, as you see has changed the top border of the image button. Therefore we must reset it at least 50 pixels from the top row of two buttons. We may have to, by trial find values that will make the interface balance. I have chosen an Insets of values as shown below:

```
case 3:
    b = new JButton(new ImageIcon(Constants.BUTTON[i]));// Add image
    constraints.gridx = 0;
    constraints.gridy = 1;
    constraints.fill = GridBagConstraints.CENTER;
    constraints.insets = new Insets(50, 50,50,50);
break;
```

When applied, the output is as shown in **Figure 8.25**.

Listing 8.21 shows a modified version of Listing 8.20, where Insets are placed around buttons to give a more balanced effect. See **Lines 35**, **46**, and **53**.

// Listing 8.21

```
1.   import javax.swing.JFrame;
2.   import javax.swing.JButton;
3.   import javax.swing.ImageIcon;
4.   import java.awt.Container;
5.   import java.awt.GridBagLayout;
6.   import java.awt.GridBagConstraints;
```

```
7.    import java.awt.Insets;
8.
9.    public class MyJButton extends JButton
10.   {
11.       MyJFrame f;
12.
13.       MyJButton(MyJFrame f)
14.       {
15.           this.f = f;
16.       }
17.       public void addGridBagLayout()
18.       {
19.           JButton b;
20.           // Places components in a grid of rows & columns
21.           GridBagLayout gbag = new GridBagLayout();
22.           // Specify the constraints for each component
23.           GridBagConstraints constraints = new GridBagConstraints();
24.           f.setLayout(gbag); // Layout each component
25.
26.           for (int i = 0; i < Constants.BUTTON.length; i++)
27.           {
28.               b = new JButton(Constants.BUTTON[i]);
29.               switch(i)
30.               {
31.                   case 0:
32.                       // Specify the (x,y) coordinate for this component
33.                       constraints.gridx = 0;
34.                       constraints.gridy = 0; // (x,y) = (0,0)
35.                       constraints.insets = new Insets(50,75,0,75);
36.                       break;
37.                   case 1:
38.                       constraints.gridx = 1;
39.                       constraints.gridy = 0;
40.                       break;
41.                   case 2:
42.                       constraints.gridx = 0;
43.                       constraints.gridy = 2;
44.                       constraints.gridwidth = 2;
45.                       constraints.fill = GridBagConstraints.HORIZONTAL;
46.                       constraints.insets = new Insets(0, 75, 50, 75);
```

```
47.                    break;
48.                case 3:
49.                    b = new JButton(new ImageIcon(Constants.BUTTON[i]));
50.                    constraints.gridx = 0;
51.                    constraints.gridy = 1;
52.                    constraints.fill = GridBagConstraints.CENTER;
53.                    constraints.insets = new Insets(50, 50,50,50);
54.                    break;
55.                }
56.                gbag.setConstraints(b, constraints);
57.                f.add(b);
58.            }
59.        }
60. }
```

The effects of these changes are shown in **Figure 8.25.**

Figure 8.25

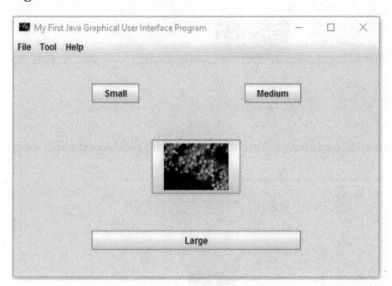

Self-Check

1. Modify Listing 8.20 so that the button containing the image occupies its entire display area as shown below.

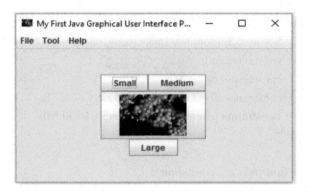

2. Modify Listing 8.20 so that the button containing the image occupies its entire display area as shown below.

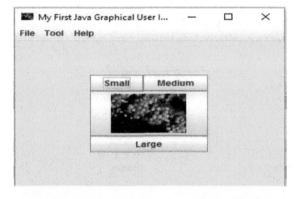

3. Modify the code for Listing 8.20 so that the program produces the following result.

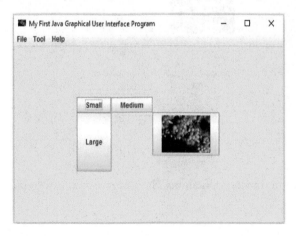

Hint: Notice that there are three rows and three columns; and that the button "Large" is hung vertically.
4.   Modify the code for Listing 820 so that the program produces the following result.

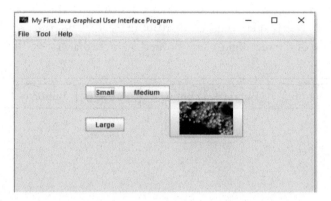

Hint: Notice that there are three rows and three columns, where the second row is the image button.

JPanel

JPanel is a lightweight container that is generally used to group components into a single unit of components. JFrame and JPanel are both containers, however there are differences between them. The size of a JFrame can be set, but that of a JPanel cannot. The size of a JPanel depends on the container in which it is embedded. JFrame has a defined border, but JPanel does not. JFrame can contain JPanel object, but JPanel cannot contain JFrame objects. JPanel comes with a default layout manager, FlowLayout, JFrame does not a specified layout manager, nor is it possible to specify one.

The following are the constructors of JPanel. Notice that in their definitions, the default layout manager, FlowLayout manager is embedded, for the third and fourth JPanel objects.

Constructor	Meaning
JPanel()	Creates a new JPanel with a double buffer and a flow layout, the default layout manager
JPanel(boolean isDoubleBuffered)	Creates a new JPanel with FlowLayout and the specified buffering strategy, the default layout manager.
JPanel(LayoutManager layout)	Create a new buffered JPanel with the specified layout manager
JPanel(LayoutManager layout, boolean isDoubleBuffered)	Creates a new JPanel with the specified layout manager and buffering strategy.

In addition, if there were multiple related images, you could set these in a JPanel, then position the JPanel object in the frame. Also, you could superimpose one image on top of another.

The diagram below shows a rectangle with two sets of buttons – one set (six buttons) laid out in the north of the rectangle, and the other (with sixteen buttons) to the south of the rectangle. From the diagram, the six buttons can be placed on a JPanel with a FlowLayout manager. This panel of buttons is then placed in the north of the rectangle, using BorderLayout manager. The second set of buttons can also be laid out on one another JPanel, using GridLayout manager. The panel of sixteen buttons can now be placed at the south of the rectangle, using BorderLayout manager.

Button 1	Button 2	Button 3	Button 4	Button 5	Button 6

Button			

Listing 8.22 shows two clusters of buttons, one is placed north of the content pane, the other south of the content pane of the frame.

// Listing 8.22

```
1.   import javax.swing.JFrame;
2.   import javax.swing.JButton;
3.   import java.awt.Container;
4.   import java.awt.FlowLayout;
5.   import java.awt.GridLayout;
6.   import javax.swing.ImageIcon;
7.   import java.awt.BorderLayout;
8.   import javax.swing.JPanel;
9.
10.  public class MyJPanel
11.  {
12.      MyJFrame f;
13.
```

```
14.        MyJPanel(MyJFrame f)
15.        {
16.            this.f = f;
17.        }
18.        public void addPanel()
19.        {
20.            JButton b;
21.            // Create panel, p1 and set it as a grid 4 rows and 4 columns of buttons
22.            JPanel jp1 = new JPanel(new GridLayout( 4, 4, 5, 5 ));
23.
24.            for (int i = 0; i < Constants.SYMBOLS.length; i++)
25.            {
26.                // Create each button, and add them to panel, p1
27.                b = new JButton(Constants.SYMBOLS[i]);
28.                jp1.add(b);
29.            }
30.            f.add(jp1, BorderLayout.SOUTH); // Add panel, p1 to the SOUTH of the frame
31.
32.            // Create panel, p2 as a FlowLayout
33.            JPanel jp2 = new JPanel(new FlowLayout( FlowLayout.CENTER, 5, 10));
34.
35.            for (int i = 0; i < Constants.BUTTON.length; i++)
36.            {
37.                // Create each button, and add them to panel, p2
38.                if (Constants.BUTTON[i].endsWith("jpg"))
39.                    b = new JButton(new ImageIcon(Constants.BUTTON[i]));
40.                else
41.                    b = new JButton(Constants.BUTTON[i]);
42.                jp2.add(b);
43.            }
44.            f.add(jp2, BorderLayout.NORTH);  // Add panel, p2 to the SOUTH of the frame
45.        }
46. }
```

The result of this class ia a frame with two panels of buttons – one panel is positioned north of the content pane, and the other to the south. See **Figure 8.26**

Figure 8.26

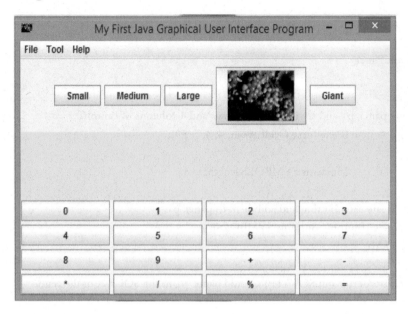

Self-Check

1. Name three kinds of buttons discussed in this section.

2. Assume that the string "vacation.jpg" represents the name of an image file. What is the effect of the following statement?
   new JButton("vacation.jpg", "Vacation Button");

3. In what package is the class GridBagConstraints found?

4. What is the purpose of the class Insets?

5. How many positions does the Insets specifies?

6. What is the purpose of the class GridBagConstraints?

7. What are the similarities and differences between the GridBagLayout manager and the FlowLayout manager?

8. What are the similarities and differences between the GridBagLayout manager and the GridLayout manager?

9. Write a Java statement that would create a button that would have an icon as well as a text label on it.

10. Given the following program, draw a diagram showing the output from it.

```java
import javax.swing.JFrame;
import javax.swing.JButton;
import java.awt.Container;

public class Flow extends JFrame
{
        static String[] arr = {"First", "Second", "Third", " Fourth"};

        public static void main(String[] arg)
        {
                Flow flow = new Flow("Review");
                Container c = flow.getContentPane();
                c.setLayout(new FlowLayout(3));

                for (int i = arr.length - 1; i >= 0; i--)
                        c.add(new JButton(arr[i]) );
                flow.setSize(500, 100);
                flow.setVisible(true);
        }
        Flow(String str)
        {
                super(str);
        }
}
```

Chapter Summary
- Graphical User Interface (GUI) programming is that type of program that allows the user to interact with the computer via graphical icons such as buttons, menus, menu items, checkbox menu items, and radio buttons.

- The class JFrame found in the swing package is used to build frames.
- You can change some of the default values of a frame. For instance, you can change the image icon, the position of the frame, the size of the frame, the background, and foreground color of the frame. You can also change the style cursor when the frame comes into focus.

- When developing a GUI program in Java, there are two packages with components such as buttons, icons, and menu items, that you will most likely use to build your programs. These packages are the Abstract Window Toolkit (**awt**) and Swing.

- Swing does not work directly with the native platform, it uses what is called the content pane of the frame on which to hang components. In other words, if components are placed directly onto the frame, they will not be seen in the GUI.

- Menus can be hung from a frame using the class JMenu, however, you must first prepare the space by creating what is called a menu bar. The menu bar is invisible until you place the first menu choice.

- The class ButtonGroup is used to group menu items such as radio buttons as units.

- Push button, simply referred to as button, is another type of object that you will frequently find on a GUI.

- Once a button has been created, the next step is to place it in a container object such as the content pane of a frame. This requires what is referred to as a layout manager. There are several layout manager classes, four of which are FlowLayout, GridLayout, BorderLayout and GridbagLayout.

- The layout manager GridbagLayout is assisted by two classes - GridbagConstraints and Insets.

- JPanel is a lightweight container which is used to group a set of components together for a better organized look of the components.

Programming Exercises

1. Design a class called MyJFrame to produce output as shown in **Figures 1 – 7.** This frame must be inherited from the class IFrame. The frame must contain only a title as shown in **Figure 1.**

Figure 1

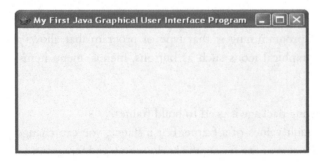

Create a menu bar of choices as shown in **Figure 2.**

Figure 2

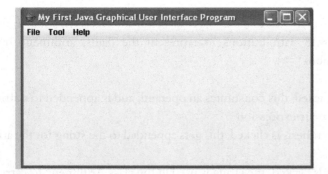

Add menu items to each menu choice as shown in **Figure 3** and **Figure 4**.

Figure 3

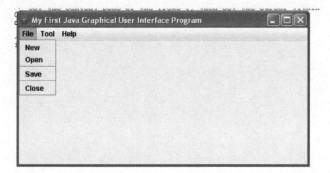

For the menu choice **Tools**, create a cascading menu for the menu choice Edit.

Figure 4

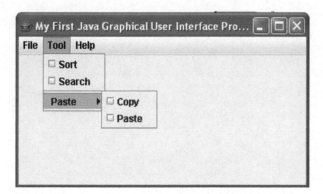

NB. Do not add functionality to the menu.

2. Use the RPN algorithm of Chapter 7 to make a GUI calculator interface. You may refer to the code that produces **Figure 8.18** with buttons to represent the digits, arithmetic operators, parentheses, and the equal symbol (=).
    Operations:
    (a) When a series of digits is clicked, this constitutes an operand, and is appended to a string. This string represents the arithmetic expression.
    (b) When an operator or a parenthesis is clicked, this gets appended to the string for the arithmetic expression.
    (c) When the equal (=) sign it is clicked, the string is used in the class Arithmetic to carry out the calculations where possible, and display the answer.
    Note: Decompose the solution into three classes - Arithmetic.java, CalculatorFrame.java and TestCalculator.java, and an interface Constants.java to store the constants. (Do not add functionality to the calculator).

Chapter 9 Event and Event Handling

Objectives

After reading this chapter you will know:

- The difference between the operations of a console base application program and a Graphical User Interface (GUI) window base program.
- What an event is.
- How events are handled in Java.
- The difference between listener interface and adapter class.
- How to construct code to activate components such as buttons and menu items.

Introduction

All of the programs that we have written so far are called console base application programs. These programs were designed to run statement by statement in sequence, as coded. This means that the next statement to be executed is predictable either by sequence, selection, iteration, recursion, or exception. When it comes to window base Graphical User Interface programs, their operations are not predictable. Recall in Chapter 8 we said that GUI programs allow the user to interact with the computer, using gadget such as buttons and menu items. In this context the next action that the computer will make is not predictable. With a GUI program, it is an action, or stimulus that causes the operating system to react to the component. We refer to such stimulus as an event.

Let us divert for a moment from programming, and let us focus on the cat (we will call Asha) seen in **Figure 9.1**. Asha is resting on a book, presumably quite content, listening for something that may happen to it, it seems.

Figure 9.1

In like manner a component or a container may be attached to some event source, listening for something to happen to it.

The cat at no time knows if it will be disturbed, but if it does, it will know precisely how to re-act. In term of a GUI, a button for example does not know if it is going to be clicked by the mouse, but if it gets clicked, it will know precisely how to respond.

Java provides several interfaces, called listener interfaces that listen to different kinds of component and container objects. It also provides adapter classes for most of these interfaces, where the programmer can tailor the response of a component when it is clicked.

Event and Event Listener Listener

To give you an idea about event and event listeners, a JButton object for instance listens for the mouse to click it. Hence a button would listen for a MouseEvent object. Similarly, a JMenuItem object will listen to some event, but unlike JButton, it does not listen for mouse event, but listens for what is called an ActionEvent, even though the action depends on the mouse clicking it. The way that events are handled follows this pattern.

1. Just like Asha lying on the book listening for some event, so is a JMenuItem registered onto ActionEvent object, listening for some event. Whereas the cat can listen to multiple event type, the menu item can only listener to one kind of event type.
2. When the cat learns of an even happening to it, it re-acts to the event. Similarly, when a menu item learns of the action of a click, it responds definitively.

For instance, when the menu item File -> **New**, is clicked, one would expect a new blank window to open. This means that the string representing the name of the file must be recognized, as we will see shortly. As an example, let the variable **mi** be a reference to a JMenuItem object. This reference variable listens to some kind of event listener. The event listener type is the interface called ActionListener. This interface has one mutator method, called actionPerformed. This method takes one parameter called, ActionEvent, which contains among other methods, a method called getActionCommand. When a menu item is clicked, this is the method that captures the click, and returns the string value representing the menu item. The general format is:

```
mi.addActionListener( /*.... Some action listener object */);
```

Note that **mi** is like the cat, and the method addActionListener is like the support on which the cat is lying. The parenthesized commented statement means that you must create the action listener object that will tell precisely how the object will behave. The generic code is as follows:

```
mi.addActionListener( new ActionListener() {
            public void actionPerformed(ActionEvent e)
            {
                    /* Code the response to the click e.getActionCommand() */
            }
        }
    );
```

In analyzing the code, the variable **mi**, (the menu item) is attached to the ActionListener object by this segment of the statement:

```
mi.addActionListener ( … );
```

This method call is behaving like the cat lying on the book anticipating some activities. Let us apply this concept to our class MyJFrame from Chapter 8, by trying to identify the menu items **File -> New** and **File -> Open**. That is, when the mouse clicks either of the two options, there must be a response corresponding to each of them. A simple message directed to the command prompt is good enough for the moment. To help understand this principle, let us first consider **Listing 9.1**, and then we will explain it.

Listing 9.1
```
1.   case 0: // Add menu items
2.     for (int j = 0; j < Constants.FILES.length; j++)
3.        if (Constants.FILES[j].equals("-"))
4.            f.addSeparator();
5.        else{
6.            f.add(mi = new JMenuItem(Constants.FILES[j]));
7.            mi.addActionListener(new ActionListener()
8.            {
9.                public void actionPerformed(ActionEvent e)
10.               {
11.                   if (e.getActionCommand().equals("New"))
12.                       System.out.println("New");
13.                   else if (e.getActionCommand().equals("Open"))
14.                       System.out.println("Open");
15.               }
16.           }
17.        );
19.    }
20.  break;
```

In the code above, the reference variable **mi**, of type JMenuItem, is attached to the action listener object. This thought is represented by the expression:

mi.addActionListener(…);

The segment:

new ActionListener()

is creating the object of type ActionListener. This object is called an anonymous object, since the object has no reference (no name) attached to it; hence the term anonymous.

Recall the interface ActionListener has only one method – actionPerformed, which in turn has only one parameter – ActionEvent; and the class ActionEvent has the method called getActionCommand, which returns the string representing the name of the menu item that was clicked. The if/else statement simply seeks to identify which menu item was clicked. Once we can identify the menu item that was clicked, this opens up a new world of possibilities in applications. To see how all this fits into context with the class MyJFrame we look at **Listing 9.2**

```
        // Listing 9.2

1.      import javax.swing.JFrame;
2.      import javax.swing.JMenuBar;
3.      import javax.swing.JMenu;
4.      import javax.swing.JCheckBoxMenuItem;
5.      import javax.swing.JMenuItem;
6.      import javax.swing.JRadioButton;
7.      import javax.swing.ButtonGroup;
8.
9.      import java.awt.event.ActionEvent;
10.     import java.awt.event.ActionListener;
11.
12.     public class MyJFrame extends JFrame
13.     {
14.         JMenuBar menubar;
15.         JMenu f;
16.         JMenuItem mi;
17.         JRadioButton jrb;
18.         ButtonGroup bg;
19.
20.         public MyJFrame(String title){
21.             super(title);
22.             menubar = new JMenuBar();// The menubar is invisible
23.             setJMenuBar(menubar);
24.             bg = new ButtonGroup();
25.             buildMenu();
26.         }
27.         void buildMenu(){
28.             for (int i = 0; i < Constants.MENU.length; i++)
29.             { //Build and add each menu choice onto the menubar
```

```
30.                    f = new JMenu(Constants.MENU[i]);
31.                    switch(i){
32.                        case 0: // Add menu items
33.                        for (int j = 0; j < Constants.FILES.length; j++)
34.                            if (Constants.FILES[j].equals("-"))
35.                                f.addSeparator();
36.                            else
37.                            {
38.                                f.add(mi = new JMenuItem(Constants.FILES[j]));
39.                                mi.addActionListener(new ActionListener()
40.                                {
41.                                    public void actionPerformed(ActionEvent e)
42.                                    {
43.                                        if (e.getActionCommand().equals("New"))
44.                                            System.out.println("New");
45.                                        else if (e.getActionCommand().equals("Open"))
46.                                            System.out.println("Open");
47.                                    }
48.                                }
49.                                );
50.                            }
51.                        break;
52.                        case 1:
53.                        for (int k = 0; k < Constants.TOOL.length; k++)
54.                            if (Constants.TOOL[k].equals("Edit")) {
55.                                f.addSeparator();
56.                                JMenu m = new JMenu(Constants.TOOL[k]); // Cascading menu
57.                                for (int l = 0; l < Constants.EDIT.length; l++) {
58.                                    m.add(jrb = new JRadioButton(Constants.EDIT[l]));
59.                                    bg.add(jrb);
60.                                }
61.                                f.add(m);
62.                            }
63.                            else
64.                                f.add(mi = new JMenuItem(Constants.TOOL[k]));
65.                        break;
66.                        /*case 2:
67.                                // Pattern is the same
68.                        break;
69.                        */
70.                    }
71.                    menubar.add(f);
72.            }
73.        }
74. }
```

As you would have noticed, this code is the same code as in Listing 8.15. The only difference is the action listener code shown on **Lines 39** thru **49**; and of course the import statements, **Lines 9** and **10**. **Figure 9.2** shows the output produced by **Lines 39** thru **49**. That is, when the menu item **File ->Open** and **File->New** menu items were clicked, they were recognized. Since those menu items were the only two options that the **if/else** statement was concerned about, then you would see no other menu items being recognized.

Figure 9.2

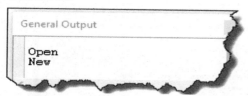

As we have seen in **Listing 9.1**, the code works; it recognizes menu items. A closer look at the code will reveal that if we use the same strategy of defining anonymous object, then very soon the class MyJFrame can become cluttered. This would ruin the concept of cohesion, because for every menu choice there would have to be an anonymous class. This would be evident when the number of menu choices grow. Another problem of clutter would occur when there are many menu items. The if/else statement would be lengthy.

A better approach would be to define an action listener class that implements the interface ActionListener. Inside this class you would define the method actionPerformed, which would specify the action or actions a menu item would make when one is clicked. This would be more cohesive since the various actions would be localized to this class. The general format of this class would be as follows:

```
public class Actions implements ActionListener
{
        public void actionPerformed(ActionEvent e)
        {
            /* Identify menu items and define the necessary action to be taken */
        }
}
```

The class Actions would be a user defined class that implements the interface ActionListener, as indicated by the first line of the code. The effect that this version would have on the class MyJFrame is that wherever the anonymous class would have been defined for a menu item, this would be replaced with the creation of the object for the class Actions. That is:

```
mi.addActionListener(new Actions( ) );
```

Example 9.1
Recall we said earlier that once we can identify a menu item that was clicked, this opens up a new world of possibilities in applications. Let us make ourselves a text editor that operates the following way:

1. When we click the menu item **New**, a new blank text editor window appears, and will have as title the following: "Untitled ......", and the area designated for text is empty of text.
2. When the option **Open** is clicked, the file dialog box, similar to **Figure 9.3** appears.

Figure 9.3

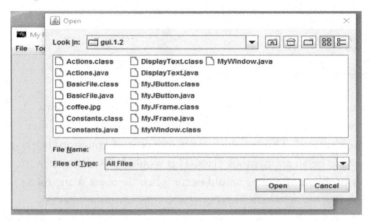

In designing this text editor, when a file is selected, the name of the file will appear in the title bar of the frame, and the contents appear in the contents appear in the new text area of the frame, as shown in **Figure 9.4**.

Figure 9.4

First we will design the class for the text editor. We will re-use the class MyJFrame to display the text, along with its title. We will call this class DisplayText. It will accept two string parameters, the first representing the title, and the second, the contents. The contents will be displayed in a scrollable JTextArea object in the content pane of the frame. See **Listing 9.3**

// Listing 9.3

```
1.   import javax.swing.JTextArea;
2.   import javax.swing.JScrollPane;
3.   import java.awt.Container;
4.
5.   public class DisplayText {
6.       private static JTextArea text;
7.
8.       public DisplayText( String title, String info) {
9.           MyJFrame f = new MyJFrame(title);
10.          Container c = f.getContentPane();
11.          text = new JTextArea(info);
12.          JScrollPane sp = new JScrollPane(text);
13.          c.add( sp );
14.          f.setBounds(100,200, 500, 400 );
15.          f.setVisible(true);
16.      }
17.  }
```

As you will notice, this is a simple class. It accepts two strings – the first representing a title and contents that are to be displayed in their respective area of a new MyJFrame object. Notice also, this class re-uses the class MyJFrame to set up a scrollable pane of size 50 x 400.

Listing 9.4 shows a modified version of the class BasicFile, which reads the contents of the file and returns it. See method getContents, **Lines 37** thru **48**. The class also returns the name of the selected file. See **Line 34** thru **36**.

// Listing 9.4

```
1.   import javax.swing.JFileChooser;
2.   import javax.swing.JOptionPane;
3.   import java.io.File;
4.   import java.io.FileNotFoundException;
5.   import java.io.IOException;
6.   import java.io.LineNumberReader;
7.   import java.io.FileReader;
8.   public class BasicFile {
9.       File f;
```

```
10.
11.      public BasicFile(){
12.          JFileChooser choose = new JFileChooser(".");
13.          int status = choose.showOpenDialog(null);
14.
15.          try{
16.              if (status != JFileChooser.APPROVE_OPTION) throw new IOException();
17.              f = choose.getSelectedFile();
18.              if (!f.exists()) throw new FileNotFoundException();
19.          }
20.          catch(FileNotFoundException e){
21.              display("File not found ....", e.toString(), JOptionPane.WARNING_MESSAGE);
22.          }
23.          catch(IOException e){
24.              display("Approve option was not selected", e.toString(),
                     JOptionPane.ERROR_MESSAGE);
25.          }
26.      }
27.      void display(String msg, String s, int t){
28.          JOptionPane.showMessageDialog(null, msg, s, t);
29.      }
30.      String getFileName(){
31.          return f.getName();
32.      }
33.      String getContents(){
34.          String s, str = "";
35.
36.          try{
37.              LineNumberReader lnr = new LineNumberReader(new FileReader(f));
38.              while( (s = lnr.readLine()) != null)
39.              str = str + s + "\n";
40.          }
41.          catch(IOException e)  {
42.          }
43.          return str;
44.      }
45. }
```

Listing 9.5 shows the class Actions which implements the ActionListener interface. The method actionPerformed identifies the menu item that was clicked. Notice that when **File->New** is clicked, a text editor frame is created with title **"Untitled .... "**, and the contents set as the empty string. Likewise when **File->Open** is clicked, it creates an object of the class BasicFile, **Line 16. Line 17** gets the name of the file and the contents of the file, and pass these two values to the class **DisplayText**. The result of which is Figure 9.4.

// Listing 9.5

```
1.   import java.awt.event.ActionListener;
2.   import java.awt.event.ActionEvent;
3.
4.   class Actions implements ActionListener
5.   {
6.       DisplayText dt;
7.
8.       public void actionPerformed(ActionEvent e)
9.       {
10.          if (e.getActionCommand().equalsIgnoreCase("New"))
11.          {
12.              dt = new DisplayText("Untitled..... ", "");
13.          }
14.          else if(e.getActionCommand().equalsIgnoreCase("Open"))
15.          {
16.              BasicFile f = new BasicFile();
17.              dt = new DisplayText(f.getFileName(), f.getContents());
18.          }
19.          else
20.          ; /* ::::::The pattern is the same :::::::::::::::: */
21.      }
22. }
```

Listener Interfaces and Adapter classes

Now that we have an idea of the concept of event and event handling, and the kinds of things that we can do when we capture an event, let us look at some more event listener interfaces and how they are implemented. In general all event listeners originate from some listener interfaces. These interfaces specify abstract method(s) for handling a particular event. The table below shows:

1. The kinds of listener interfaces.
2. The purpose of the type of event, and the event method(s) for each of these interfaces.
3. The adapter class associated with the interface, if any.

Interface	Meaning and Methods	Adapter class
WindowListener	Listens for window activities such as: • windowOpened(WindowEvent e) • windowClosing(WindowEvent e) • windowClosed(WindowEvent e) • windowIconified(WindowEvent e) • windowDeiconified(WindowEvent e) • windowActivated(WindowEvent e) • windowDeactivated(WindowEvent e)	WindowAdapter
HyperlinkListener	Listens for web addresses • hyperlinkUpdate(HyperlinkEvent e)	None
MouseListener	Listens for mouse activities such as: • mouseEntered(MouseEvent e) • mouseExited(MouseEvent e) • mousePressed(MouseEvent e) • mouseClicked(MouseEvent e) • mouseReleased(MouseEvent e)	MouseAdapter
MouseMotionListener	Listens for when the mouse moves, as in being dragged or being repositioned: • mouseDragged(MouseEvent e) • mouseMoved(MouseEvent e)	MouseMotionAdapter
MouseInputListener	Listens for both MouseListener activities and MouseMotionListener activities	MouseInputAdapter
KeyListener	Listens for keyboard (key strokes) as they are being typed, as in: • keyPressed(KeyEvent e) • keyReleased(KeyEvent e) • keyTyped(KeyEvent e)	KeyAdapter
TextListener	This listener receives text events, when the value of the text has changed: • textValueChanged(TextEvent e)	None

Every object that wants to listen to some events must get registered to the particular event source that it is interested in listening to. For example, let **b** be a reference to a button object, and the object would like to listen to a mouse event, the registration would go something like this:

b.addMouseListener(/* Mouse Event object to be defined here */);

The key concept that you are to understand is the role of the registration method. The name of the method that is responsible for registering the object to a type of event source is made up of three words, taken in order:

add . xxxx **Listener**

That is, the method begins with the word **add**, and ends with the word **Listener**, between both words you specify the name of the event source – as in the case of addMouseListener. The following are the registration method for each of the above listener.

Interface	Registration Methods
WindowListener	addWindowListener
HyperlinkListener	add HyperlinkListener
MouseListener	add MouseListener
MouseMotionListener	add MouseMotionListener
MouseInputListener	add MouseInputListener
KeyListener	add KeyListener
TextListener	add TextListener

Window Events

A window event is an indication that a window has changed status, as a result the event is represented by one of the seven methods declared in the interface WindowListener, shown below.

WindowListener Method	Purpose
windowOpened(WindowEvent e)	Invoked the first time that a window is being made visible.
windowClosing(WindowEvent e)	Invoked when the user clicks the close the closed button (X) from the window's system menu.
windowClosed(WindowEvent e)	Invoked when a window has been closed as the result of calling dispose on the window.
windowDeiconified(WindowEvent e)	Invoked when a window is changed from a normal to a minimized state, the (-) button on the window's menu.
windowIconified(WindowEvent e)	Invoked when a window is changed from a minimized to a normal state.
windowActivated(WindowEvent e)	Invoked when the window is set to be the active window (the current window in use).
windowDeactivated(WindowEvent e)	Invoked when a window is no longer the active window (window is replaced by another window). This new window is now the active window).

The class WindowAdapter implements the WindowListener interface, and defines these abstract methods, therefore in most cases the WindowAdapter class is used in preference to the interface. In Chapter 8 we used the method – setDefaultCloseOperation(…) to terminate a frame by application when the close (X) button is clicked. This method gives you no option to do anything prior to terminating the program. If our desire is to do other things prior to closing the application, then window closing event is what we should target. That is re-define the method:

windowClosing(WindowEvent e).

So for instance, to use the windowClosing method for closing down and terminating the application, one write structure the code necessary for doing so as follows:

```
f.addWindowListener(new WindowAdapter()
{
    public void windowClosing(WindowEvent e)
    {
        JOptionPane.showMessageDialog(null, "Window closing", "Window is closing !!! ",
        JOptionPane.INFORMATION_MESSAGE);
        System.exit(0);
    }
}
);
```

Listing 9.6 shows how this code can be applied using the class MyWindow that we developed in Chapter 8.

Listing 9.6 - Featuring Window Event - windowClosing

```
1.    import java.awt.Toolkit;
2.    import java.awt.Dimension;
3.    import javax.swing.ImageIcon;
4.    import java.awt.Rectangle;
5.    import java.awt.Cursor;
6.    import java.awt.Container;
7.    import java.awt.Color;
8.    import java.awt.event.WindowAdapter;
9.    import java.awt.event.WindowEvent;
10.   import javax.swing.JOptionPane;
11.
12.   public class MyWindow {
13.       public static void main(String[] arg) {
14.       MyJFrame f = new MyJFrame(Constants.TITLE);
15.       f.setIconImage(new ImageIcon("coffee.jpg").getImage());
```

```
16.        Toolkit toolkit = f.getToolkit(); // Get features of this frame
17.        Dimension size = toolkit.getScreenSize(); //Get dimension of screen
18.        // Set properties for my frame
19.        Rectangle r = new Rectangle(Constants.X_POS, Constants.Y_POS,
           size.width/Constants.X_WIDTH, 2* size.height/Constants.Y_HEIGHT);
20.        f.setBounds(r);
21.        Container c = f.getContentPane();
22.        c.setBackground(Color.YELLOW);
23.        c.setCursor( Cursor.getPredefinedCursor(Cursor.WAIT_CURSOR ));
24.
25.        f.addWindowListener(new WindowAdapter()
26.                           {
27.                               public void windowClosing(WindowEvent e)
28.                               {
29.                                   JOptionPane.showMessageDialog(null, "Click the OK
                                       button to terminate program","WindowEvent",
                                       JOptionPane.INFORMATION_MESSAGE);
30.                                   System.exit(0);
31.                               }
32.                           }
33.                           );
34.        MyJButton mb = new MyJButton(f);
35.        mb.addGridBagLayout();
36.        f.setVisible(true);
37.    }
38. }
```

That is, this code is a customization of the window system's default closed button found on the upper right corner of the window. The output is show in **Figure 9.5**.

Figure 9.5

Kinds of Mouse Listeners

A mouse event indicates that a mouse action has occurred on a component such as a button. Basically there are two types of mouse events that are listened for – mouse event and mouse motion event that are represented by the interfaces MouseListener, and MouseMotionListener. The registration for each is as follows:

addMouseListener(MouseEvent e)

and

addMouseMotionListener(MouseEvent e)

respectively

A mouse event is an indication that the mouse has changed status, as a result the event is represented by one of the five mutator methods declared in the interface MouseListener, shown below.

MouseListener Method	Purpose
mouseClicked(MouseEvent e)	Invoked when the mouse button has been clicked on a component such as a JButton object. A click is a quick press and release of the mouse button.
mouseEntered(MouseEvent e)	Invoked when the mouse enters onto a component.
mouseExited(MouseEvent e)	Invoked when the mouse leaves from off a component.
mousePressed (MouseEvent e)	Invoked when the mouse button has been pressed on a component such as a JButton object, but is not released immediately.
mouseReleased (MouseEvent e)	Invoked when the mouse button has been let go (released) from off a component such as a JButton object.

Five of the more frequently used MouseEvent are represented by the following methods:

Return Type	Accessor Method	Description
Point	getPoint()	Return the object Point, containing the (x, y) position of the event relative to the source component.
int	getX()	Returns the horizontal (x) position of the event relative to the source component.
int	getY()	Returns the vertical (y) position of the event relative to the source component.
int	getXOnScreen()	Returns the absolute horizontal (x) position of the event.
int	getYOnScreen()	Returns the absolute vertical (y) position of the event.

A mouse motion event is an indication that the mouse has changed status of a drag or a move, as a result the event is represented by one of the two mutator methods declared in the interface MouseMotionListener, shown below.

MouseMotionListener Method	Purpose
mouseDragged(MouseEvent e)	Invoked when the mouse cursor has been moved onto a component but no button is pressed on a component and then dragged.
mouseMoved(MouseEvent e)	Invoked when the mouse cursor has been moved onto a component but no button has been pressed or clicked.

Listing 9.7 shows a customized version of the state of the mouse, by stating what event has occurred, and the coordinates of the mouse, as it moves from one button to another.

Listing 9.7

```
1.    import java.awt.event.MouseEvent;
2.    import javax.swing.event.MouseAdapter;
3.
4.    class MyMouseEvents extends MouseAdapter
5.    {
6.        public void mouseClicked(MouseEvent e) {
7.            System.out.println("Mouse clicked @ (" + e.getX() + "," + e.getY() + ")");
8.        }
9.        public void mousePressed(MouseEvent e) {
10.            System.out.println("Mouse pressed @ (" + e.getX() + "," + e.getY() + ")");
11.        }
12.        public void mouseReleased(MouseEvent e){
13.            System.out.println("Mouse released @ (" +e.getX() + ","+ e.getY() + ")");
14.        }
15.        public void mouseEntered(MouseEvent e){
16.            System.out.println("Mouse entered @ (" +e.getX() + ","+ e.getY() + ")");
17.        }
18.        public void mouseExited(MouseEvent e){
19.            System.out.println("Mouse exited @ (" +e.getX() + ","+ e.getY() + ")");
20.        }
21.    }
```

It should be evedent at this point that the event object of the class MyMouseEvents has been registered onto a button object as the source of the events. This would take us back to the class MyJButton, Listing 8.

Listing 9. 8

```
1.    import javax.swing.JButton;
2.    import javax.swing.ImageIcon;
3.    import java.awt.GridBagLayout;
```

```
4.    import java.awt.GridBagConstraints;
5.    import java.awt.Insets;
6.    public class MyJButton extends JButton {
7.        MyJFrame f;
8.        MyJButton(MyJFrame f) { this.f = f; }
9.        public void addGridBagLayout(){
10.           JButton b;
11.           GridBagLayout gbag = new GridBagLayout(); // Specify constraints for each component
12.           GridBagConstraints constraints = new GridBagConstraints();
13.           f.setLayout(gbag); // Layout each component
14.           for (int i = 0; i < Constants.BUTTON.length; i++){
15.               b = new JButton(Constants.BUTTON[i]);
16.               switch(i) {
17.                   case 0: // Specify the (x,y) coordinate for this component
18.                       constraints.gridx = 0;
19.                       constraints.gridy = 0; // (x,y) = (0,0)
20.                       constraints.insets = new Insets(50,75,0,75);
21.                   break;
22.                   case 1:
23.                       constraints.gridx = 1;
24.                       constraints.gridy = 0;
25.                   break;
26.                   case 2:
27.                       constraints.gridx = 0;
28.                       constraints.gridy = 2;
29.                       constraints.gridwidth = 2;
30.                       constraints.fill = GridBagConstraints.HORIZONTAL;
31.                       constraints.insets = new Insets(0, 75, 50, 75);
32.                   break;
33.                   case 3:
34.                       b = new JButton(new ImageIcon(Constants.BUTTON[i]));
35.                       constraints.gridx = 0;
36.                       constraints.gridy = 1;
37.                       constraints.fill = GridBagConstraints.CENTER;
38.                       constraints.insets = new Insets(50, 50,50,50);
39.                   break;
40.               }
41.               b.addMouseListener( new MyMouseEvents( ) );
42.               gbag.setConstraints(b, constraints);
43.               f.add(b);
44.           }
45.       }
46. }
```

The result of **Listing 9.8** is shown **Figure 9.6**. Notice that the program keeps track of the mouse for everytime that there is a mouse listener activity.

Figure 9.6

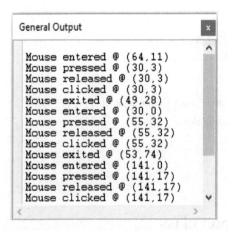

```
General Output                    ☒

  Mouse entered @ (64,11)          ⌃
  Mouse pressed @ (30,3)
  Mouse released @ (30,3)
  Mouse clicked @ (30,3)
  Mouse exited @ (49,28)
  Mouse entered @ (30,0)
  Mouse pressed @ (55,32)
  Mouse released @ (55,32)
  Mouse clicked @ (55,32)
  Mouse exited @ (53,74)
  Mouse entered @ (141,0)
  Mouse pressed @ (141,17)
  Mouse released @ (141,17)
  Mouse clicked @ (141,17)         ⌄
 ⟨                    ⟩
```

Mouse Input Listeners

The interfaces MouseListener and MouseMotionListener are incorporated into one interface called MouseInputListener, tt also has adapter class MouseInputAdapter. Not only does it incorporate these tow listeners, but it also MouseWheelListener. This interface was designed for mouse that has a third button, a scroll wheel button.

Any object that wants to listen for a mouse wheel event must use the registration method, addMouseWheelListener, or simply use the registration method addMouseInputListener.

HyperlinkListener Interface

Hyperlink is a reference to data that is located at an address, typically, outside of the current document. Typically we think of hyperlink as a web address, but it could be an icon, graphics, or text in a document. It is like the electronic version of a table of contents. The listener interface, HyperlinkListener, that response to a hyperlink events has only one method – hyperlinkUpdate. A hyperlink objects listeners for one three types of events, namely:

Hyperlink Event Types	Meaning
HyperlinkEvent.EventType.ACTIVATED	A notification that the link has been clicked.
HyperlinkEvent.EventType.ENTERED	A notification that the mouse hovers over the link.
HyperlinkEvent.EventType.EXITED	A notification that the mouse stops hovering the link.

Given that the variable **jep** is a reference to an editor pane object of type JEditorPane[1], a typical use of the HyperlinkListener interface is as follows:

```
jep.addHyperlinkListener(new HyperlinkListener() {
    public void hyperlinkUpdate(HyperlinkEvent e) {
        // Enter code here. For example

        if ( e.getEventType() ==HyperlinkEvent.EventType.ACTIVATED )
            ; // Specify what must be done
    }
}
);
```

KeyListener Interface and KeyAdapter class

The KeyListener interface processes keyboard events when a key is pressed, released, or typed. The class that is interested in processing the event either implements this interface or extends the KeyAdapter class. The relevant method in the listener object is then invoked, and the KeyEvent is passed to it. The listener object created from that class is then registered with a component using the component's addKeyListener method.

Listing 9.6 simply differentiates printable characters from the non-printable ones. That is, each time that one of the keyboard's characters is pressed, the method keyPressed is invoked, and the method getKeyChar returns the char representation, if it is an ordinary character.

// Listing 9.6

```
1.  import javax.swing.JOptionPane;
2.  import java.awt.event.KeyEvent;
3.  import java.awt.event.KeyAdapter;
4.
5.  public class MyKeyboardEvent extends KeyAdapter {
6.      public void keyPressed(KeyEvent e) // Handle the key pressed event
7.      {
8.          displayInfo(e, "KEY PRESSED: ");
9.      }
10.     private void displayInfo(KeyEvent e, String s) {
11.         String chr;
12.         char ch = e.getKeyChar();
13.
14.         if (Character.isISOControl(ch))
15.             chr = "key character = (an unprintable control character)";
16.         else
```

---

[1] JEditorPane is a class that displays text as well as graphics.

```
17.              chr = "The character is " + ch;
18.
19.          JOptionPane.showMessageDialog(null, chr, s, JOptionPane.INFORMATION_MESSAGE);
20.      }
21. }
```

Figure 9.5 shows the output from the code above.

Figure 9.5

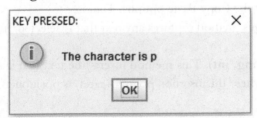

Self-Check

1. What listener interface is responsibility for window events?

2. Write the complete import statement for each of the following – WindowListener, ActionListener, KeyListener, and ItemListener.

3. Differentiate between MouseListener and MouseMotionListener interfaces?

4. Differentiate between MouseListener and MouseAdapter.

5. In what class is the method **getCaretPosition** found? Hint, start with the class JTextArea.

6. In what class is the method **getSelectedText** found? Hint, start with the class JTextArea.

7. In what class is the method **insert(String int)**, for inserting text, at a given location in a document found? Hint, start with the class JTextArea.

Chapter Summary

-   Graphical User Interface (GUI) programs allow the user to interact with the computer, using gadget such as buttons and menu items.

-   With all GUI programs, it can never be predicted what is the next segment of the code will be executed. This unpredictability is due to which gadget will be activated by some stimulus or event.

-   There are several kinds of events, and each is represented by its own interface.

- An object that is quite likely respond to an event, must be registered onto that type. The name of the method that registers an event object has the pattern **add___Listenener**, where the blank must be filled in with the appropriate type of event.

- Once an object can be identified by an event, this opens a world of possibilities for different kinds of applications.

Programming Exercises

1. Using the class DisplayText to implement the Copy-Paste options. That is,
    (a) Write a method called selectText(). This method captures any text that is selected/highlighted by the mouse.
    (b) Write a method called insertText(**String, int**). This method inserts the text that was capture by **selectText()** and places the text where the insertion pointer (caret) is positioned.

    Note: If we simply use instance variables for the copy-paste activity, then this operation can only be done from within the same frame. In order to copy from one frame and paste in another frame, you must use class variables.

    When copying, you must first highlight (select) the text. The method for retrieving the highlighted text is called getSelectedText. It is found in the hierarchy chain of JTextArea.

    In order to paste the selected text, there are two pieces of information we need – the first is the text that is to be pasted, which we have gotten already. The next is the place where to paste the text. The place where to paste the text beings where the cursor is positioned in the text area. This location is referred to as the caret position (the position marker is called caret). The method for retrieving the location of the caret is called getCaretPosition found in the class hierarchy of the class JTextArea.

    Now that we have the two pieces of information for copy and paste, is simple to place the text at the caret position. The method for inserting the text is insert, found in the class JTextrArea.

2. Using the class MyWindow that we have been using as demonstration, write appropriate Java code that will generate this popup window when the windowClosing button (X button) is clicked. Incorporate the code **System.exit(0)** to terminate and exit the program.

3. Write a class called Browser that downloads information from a website when the horizontal button marked Browser on your frame is pressed, as in Figure X Design your code so that when a document is being downloaded, the cursor changes to another style, and after the information is loaded, it changes back to its original style.

Part I
- Create a frame object
- Get the content pane of the frame

Part II
- Create a JTextField object - initialize it (optional)
  JTextField enter = new JTextField("http://");
- Register the object to the ActionListener interface - and define actionPerformed method.
  That is:
  ```
  enter.addActionListener(
          new ActionListener()
              {
                  public void actionPerformed( ActionEvent e )
                  {
                          getThePage(e.getActionCommand());
                  }
              }
      );
  ```
- Add the text field object to the NORTH of the content pane
  c.add(enter, BorderLayout.NORTH);
  Where c is the reference to the content pane of the frame.

Part III
- Create a JEditorPane object
  JEditorPane jep = new JEditorPane();
- Set editable to false
- Register object to HyperlinkListener interface - and define the hyperlinkUpdate method
  ```
  jep.addHyperlinkListener( new HyperlinkListener()
      {
              public void hyperlinkUpdate( HyperlinkEvent e )
              {
                  if ( e.getEventType() ==HyperlinkEvent.EventType.ACTIVATED )
                      getThePage(e.getURL().toString());
              }
      }
  );
  ```

- Create a JScrollPane object
- Place editorPane object in the scrollpane object
- Add the scrollpane object to the CENTER of the contentPane
- Set the size of the frame
- Set the frame visible

Part IV
- Define the method: getThePage(String)

```
void getThePage( String location )
{
        try
        {
            contents.setPage( location );
            enter.setText( location );
        }
        catch ( IOException io )
        {
            JOptionPane.showMessageDialog( this, "Error cannot access specified URL",
            "Bad URL", JOptionPane.ERROR_MESSAGE );
        }
}
```

4. Write a GUI program that features buttons to represent the digits, the arithmetic operators, the parentheses, and the equal symbol (=) on a regular arithmetic calculator.
   Operations:
   1. When a series of digits is clicked, this constitutes an operand, and is appended to a string. This string represents an arithmetic expression.
   2. When an operator or a parenthesis is clicked, this gets appended to the arithmetic expression string also.
   3. When the equal (=) sign it is clicked, the string is used in the class Arithmetic to carry out the calculations where possible, and display the answer. (Hint: Use the class Arithmetic in chapter 4).

   Hint: You may use the following to assist you:
   (a) The class Arithmetic.java in **Chapter 7**
   (b) **Listing 8.18**, in **Chapter 8**, also
   (c) The idea gathered from **Figure 8.18**, also from **Chapter 8**.

4. **Part I.** Create a window containing menus and buttons. No functionality will be attached to any of them.

- Create an application window by deriving it from the **Frame** class (See diagram below). The width and height of the window must be ½ and ¹/₃ of the parent screen size, respectively.
- Add a title bar containing the title "Chestnut Hill School Branch Library".
- Add a menu bar containing the items: Circulation, Material, and Help.
- Add pull-down menus to:
  - Circulation (New, Open, Save, Save As .., and Print. Place separators between the groups of items as indicated in the diagram)
  - Material – a pulldown menu, with items (Film and Cassette. Cassette is also a pulldown menu with items (Visual and Audio)
- Add three buttons to the right of the screen. Label them - Paint, Search and Exit. The buttons must be placed vertically to each other.
- The lettering on the buttons must be in TimesRoman, with a pitch of 16, 24 and 36 respectively.
- Choose another font for the lettering for the menu items.
- Finally, set the background color of the window to a color of your choice.

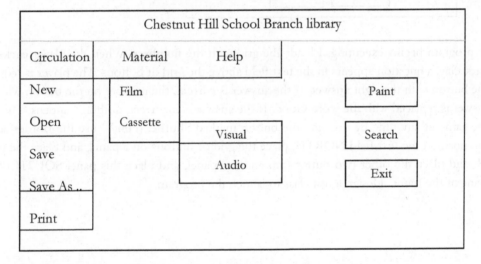

5. Write a program that will help a child learn arithmetic facts. In your solution design a class called KnowMyNumbers. This class uses the GridLayout manager to design an m by n grid with buttons similar to the sketch below.

I Know My Numbers			
What number is 10 more than 30?			
40	90	85	35
25	45	100	80
75	10	50	65
20	70	60	30
	Shuffle	Play	

When the program begins executing, I loads the grid with the numbers. When the player clicks the button mark Play, a question appears in the text field above the grid of buttons. The player is required to click the button with the right answer. If the answer is correct, the number on the button with the correct answer is replaced with the word Good. If the answer is incorrect, nothing happens. The may re-start the game at any time by pressing the button marked Shuffle. (Hint – use the BorderLayout manager to position the text field NORTH, place the grid of buttons on a panel, and place the panel CENTER, and place the other two buttons on another panel, and place this panel SOUTH of the content pane of the frame. Design a test class to launch the program.

Chapter 10 Graphics

Objectives

After reading this chapter you will know:

- How to create scenes in a frame
- The purpose of the container, JPanel, and how to use it.
- The difference between JPanel and JFrame.
- How make still life drawings.
- How to make free hand drawings.
- How to track the movement of the mouse pointer in a container, or on a component.

Introduction

All of the programs that we have written so far are text based programs. That is, in none of the programs were we ever engaged in a program whose output was pictorial. In this chapter you will learn how to create pictorial scenes, how to make still pictures, and how to make free hand drawing in containers. In order to make pictorial scenes, we need classes JLabel and JPanel. To make still images, we need the following classes - Graphics, Color, Polygon, Rectangle, and Font. In order to make free hand drawing, you must track the (x, y) coordinate of the mouse, by using MouseMotionListener interface, or the MouseListener interface, or both.

To place a single picture or image onto a frame, you first create the picture as a JLabel object, and then place the JLabel object in the content pane of the frame. To place multiple pictures, especially if they are related, you must first place them in a container other than the frame itself, and then place this container with these images in the content pane of the frame. In many instances you will have to use a layout manager, different from the default manager FlowLayout, to assist in laying out the panels of items. Once these panels have been created, it is simply a matter of positioning them in the frame, according to the layout manager of choice. The three typical layout managers that are used are GridLayout, BorderLayout, and GridBagLayout.

JLabel

If you want to display non-selectable text, or image, or both then the class JLabel is the one to use. A JLabel object can be created in one of six ways as shown by the overloaded constructors below.

Constructors	Meaning
JLabel()	Creates JLabel with no image and with no title
JLabel(Image icon)	Creates JLabel with the specified image.
JLabel(Icon image, int align)	Creates JLabel with the specified image and horizontal alignment.
JLabel(String text)	Creates JLabel with the specified title.
JLabel(String text, Icon icon, int align)	Creates JLabel with the specified title, image, and horizontal alignment.
JLabel(String text, int align)	Creates JLabel with the specified title and horizontal alignment.

The horizontal alignment in the meanings column refers to the alignment of the label's contents within the drawing area, and must be one of the following constants:

LEFT
CENTER
RIGHT
LEADING
TRAILING

By default, labels are vertically aligned center in their display area. The next section shows us how to make panoramic scenes in a frame.

Creating Picture Scenes

In order to place a single image in a frame, all that is required is an image that is embedded as a label; but first we must create that label. The class JLabel is just the right class for this purpose. Looking at **Figure 10.1**, we see a frame with a single image of a community. The placement of the picture takes a few steps:

1. Make available a file containing the image that you want to display.
2. Create a JLabel object with the image as an IconImage object as parameter. As stated earlier JLabel objects are non-clickable, therefore no event handler can be assigned to them.
3. Place the JLabel object containing the picture in the content pane of the frame, if the container is a frame.

Figure 10.1

Listing 10.1 shows a singly class that creates a generic JFrame object on which the JLabel object is placed. In this example we are using the second constructor that takes an image as parameter.

Listing 10.1

```
1.   import java.awt.Toolkit;
2.   import java.awt.Dimension;
3.   import javax.swing.ImageIcon;
4.   import java.awt.Rectangle;
5.   import java.awt.Container;
6.   import java.awt.Color;
7.   import javax.swing.JFrame;
8.   import javax.swing.JLabel;
9.
10.  public class MyWindow {
11.      public static void main(String[] arg) {
12.          JFrame f = new JFrame("Creating Picture Scene");
13.          f.setIconImage(new ImageIcon("coffee.jpg").getImage());
14.
15.          // Get properties of this frame and set frame size
16.          Toolkit toolkit = f.getToolkit();
17.          Dimension size = toolkit.getScreenSize();
18.          Rectangle r = new Rectangle(Constants.X_POS, Constants.Y_POS,
                 size.width/Constants.X_WIDTH, 2* size.height/Constants.Y_HEIGHT);
19.          f.setBounds(r);
20.          Container c =  f.getContentPane();
21.          // Create label with image and add it to the content pane of the frame
22.          JLabel label = new JLabel( new ImageIcon("nazareth3.jpg") );
```

```
23.          c.add(label);
24.
25.          c.setBackground(Color.YELLOW);
26.          f.setVisible(true);
27.      }
28. }
```

The heart of the program are **Lines 8** and **9**. Line 8 as you imports the class **JLabel**, and **Line 22** that creates the JLabel object with the picture represented by the file **nazareth3.jpg**. The default position, FlowLayout, has been assumed by the compiler; otherwise, you could have specified any of the other layout managers. To create scenes with multiple images would necessitate either using a layout manager that is different from the default, or using a panel on which to lay them out.

In this next section we will make a panoramic view of two images that will give the illusion of one continuous picture. To do this we firstly get the two JLabel objects containing the images. Secondly we position the labels using BorderLayout manager. This view will represent a sunny day of Figure 10.1, hence the picture with the sun is placed north of the picture of the community.

Listing 10.2 shows the code of two images, one that is placed north of the content pane of the frame, and the other to the south. The heart of the code, apart from the import statement of **Line 9**, are the segments **Lines 26 thru 28**, and **Lines 31 thru 32**.

```
// Listing 10. 2

1.    import java.awt.Toolkit;
2.    import java.awt.Dimension;
3.    import javax.swing.ImageIcon;
4.    import java.awt.Rectangle;
5.    import java.awt.Container;
6.    import java.awt.Color;
7.    import javax.swing.JFrame;
8.    import javax.swing.JLabel;
9.    import java.awt.BorderLayout;
10.
11.   public class MyWindow {
12.       public static void main(String[] arg) {
13.           JFrame f = new JFrame("Creating Picture Scene");
14.           f.setIconImage(new ImageIcon("coffee.jpg").getImage());
15.
16.           // Get properties of this frame and set frame size
17.           Toolkit toolkit = f.getToolkit();
18.           Dimension size = toolkit.getScreenSize();
19.           Rectangle r = new Rectangle(Constants.X_POS, Constants.Y_POS,
                  size.width/Constants.X_WIDTH, 2* size.height/Constants.Y_HEIGHT);
20.           f.setBounds(r);
21.
22.           // Laying out two images, using BorderLayout manager
23.           Container c =  f.getContentPane();
```

```
24.
25.            // First image
26.            c.setLayout(new BorderLayout());
27.            JLabel label = new JLabel(new ImageIcon("nazareth3.jpg"));
28.            c.add(label, BorderLayout.SOUTH);
29.
30.            // Second image
31.            label = new JLabel(new ImageIcon("sunshine5.jpg"));
32.            c.add(label, BorderLayout.NORTH);
33.
34.            c.setBackground(Color.YELLOW);
35.            f.setVisible(true);
36.        }
37. }
```

Figure 10.2 shows the output of the program. In the code you will see that the border layout management has been applied. If you exam the picture carefully, you will notice that the picture with the sun is placed on the content pane first, and then the community is superimposed on the picture sunshine, giving the appearance that the sun is up, and is shining.

Figure 10.2

Just as how we can place images on JPanel, the same can be done with JLabel objects. **Listing 10.3** below places five images on a JPanel object, mounted on a yellow background. See **Lines 22** thru **31**.

Listing 10.3

```
1.    import java.awt.Toolkit;
```

```
2.    import java.awt.Dimension;
3.    import javax.swing.ImageIcon;
4.    import java.awt.Rectangle;
5.    import java.awt.Container;
6.    import java.awt.Color;
7.    import javax.swing.JFrame;
8.    import javax.swing.JLabel;
9.    import java.awt.GridLayout;
10.
11.   public class MyWindow {
12.       public static void main(String[] arg){
13.           MyJFrame f = new MyJFrame(Constants.TITLE);
14.           f.setIconImage(new ImageIcon("coffee.jpg").getImage());
15.           Toolkit toolkit = f.getToolkit(); // Get properties of this frame and set frame size
16.           Dimension size = toolkit.getScreenSize();
17.           f.setBounds (new Rectangle(Constants.X_POS, Constants.Y_POS,
                  size.width/Constants.X_WIDTH, 2* size.height/Constants.Y_HEIGHT));
18.           Container c =   f.getContentPane();
19.
20.           c.setLayout(new GridLayout(2, 3, 10, 50));
21.
22.           JLabel label = new JLabel( new ImageIcon("nazareth3.jpg"));
23.           c.add(label);
24.           label = new JLabel(new ImageIcon("sunshine5.jpg"));
25.           c.add(label);
26.           label = new JLabel(new ImageIcon("nazareth3.jpg"));
27.           c.add(label);
28.           label = new JLabel(new ImageIcon("sunshine5.jpg"));
29.           c.add(label);
30.           label = new JLabel(new ImageIcon("nazareth3.jpg"));
31.           c.add(label);
32.
33.           c.setBackground(Color.YELLOW);
34.           f.setVisible(true);
35.       }
36.   }
```

The output of the program is shown in **Figure 10.3**. In the figure notice that there are spaces vertically and horizontally around components. This because the constructor was instructed to place 10 pixels of spaces horizontally between components, and 50 vertically. See **Line 20**. In addition, the GridLayout manager was used, hence two rows and three columns of spaces were reserved for components. The last position was not used, since there were only five pictures.

Figure 10.3

Self-Check

1. What is meant by the term text based programs?

2. Differentiate between a Graphical User Interface program and text based program.

3. In what package is the class JLabel found?

4. Which of the following statements are true, and which are false?
   (a) A JLabel object is a component.
   (b) A JLabel object is a container
   (c) The default layout manager for JLabel is vertical alignment.
   (d) A JLabel object is clickable.
   (e) A JLabel object cannot contain text and image at the same time.
   (f) A container object such as JFrame can accommodate multiple JLabel objects simultaneously.

5. Modify **Listing 10.2** so that the output has the following pattern. You may choose a different set of images.

6. Modify Self-Check exercise 5, so that the output has the following pattern. You may choose a different background color, also different images.

Rendering Text

One method of rendering text to a JFrame object, is by first placing the text in a JPanel object, before placing on the frame. The class JPanel contains an inherited method, called **paint**, which you must override by specifying what must be written, where it must be written, and how it must be written.

Displaying text requires knowledge of the class, Font, the class Color, and the class Graphics. We will discuss these classes, and then apply them to rendering text and images.

The class Font

A Font object is represented by a string such as "TimesRoman", "Serif", etc., which represents the name of the font; a style, such as Italic or BOLD; and an integer which represents the point size of the font. There are three styles in displaying fonts in Java. A fourth can be composed of the existing three, using the bitwise operator, as shown in the last line below.

Font Styles

Font.BOLD
Font.ITALIC
Font.PLAIN
Font.BOLD | Font.ITALIC

Two of the more frequently used constructors are shown below:

Constructors	**Description**
Font(String name, int style, int size)	Creates a font with predefined font names, a given style from the above list, and an integer value representing the font size.
Font(Font f)	Creates a font of a given font object

The class Color

When it comes to GUI programming, color images form an integral part of the look-and-feel of the user interface. With this in mind, Java provides the class called Color that allows programmers to render color of varying shades and intensities to interfaces. The class specifies colors in the default Standard-Red-Green-Blue (sRGB) color space. All the colors that are on a computer display unit are made up various mixtures (shades) of red, green, and blue light. While this works great for individual displays, the same colors are often displayed differently on different screens. To help achieve a greater color consistency between hardware devices, sRGB was established. To give you an idea of the vast variations of color – the letters RGB can each take on values in the interval [0 … 255], which makes it 256 combinations each. The spectrum of colors go from black (0, 0, 0) thru white (255, 255, 255). This means that there are 256 * 256 *256 = 2^{24} = 16,777,216 possible colors, using this scheme. In this context it would seems reasonable to define a standard to the color model, since it would be used by varying types of devices, such as display units, cameras, and printing devices.

The table below shows three of the seven constructors that are used to define a color:

Constructors	Description
Color(float r, float g, float b)	Creates an opaque sRGB color with the specified red, green, and blue values in the range (0.0 - 1.0).
Color(int rgb)	Creates an opaque sRGB color with the specified combined RGB value consisting of the red component in bits 16-23, the green component in bits 8-15, and the blue component in bits 0-7.
Color(int r, int g, int b)	Creates an opaque sRGB color with the specified red, green, and blue values in the range (0 - 255).

Apart from defining a color, the class defines some class constants, shown below. Notice that all but two of the constants are defined in both uppercase letters, and lowercase letters.

Color Constants

BLACK/black	.MAGENTA/magenta
BLUE/blue	ORANGE/orange
CYAN/cyan	PINK/pink
DARK_GRAY/darkGray	RED/red
GRAY/gray	YELLOW/yellow
GREEN/green	WHITE/white
LIGHT_GRAY/lightGray	

Although there are methods in the class we will not list them here, since much of what is being done in this book, is the setting up of a color in order to use it by subsequent codes.

The class Graphics

The class Graphics is another class which is very important in designing GUI program. The class is, an abstract class that has several class methods that are used when creating GUI programs. In a nutshell, the class lends itself to setting colors and setting fonts. It also allows for rendering of text; the drawing of the outlines of geometric shapes; the filling of geometric shapes with colors; and the drawing of images. We will list some of the more frequently used methods here.

Methods	Meaning
drawLine(int x1, int y1, int x2, int y2)	Draws a line, using the current color, between the points(x1, y1) and (x2, y2) in this graphics context's coordinate system
drawOval(int x, int y, int width, int height)	Draws the outline of an oval.
drawPolygon(int[] x, int[] y, int x.lenth)	Draws a closed polygon defined by arrays of x and y-coordinates.
drawPolygon(Polygon p)	Draws the outline of a polygon defined by the specified Polygon object.
drawRect(int x, int y, int width, int height)	Draws the outline of the specified rectangle.
drawRoundRect(int x, int y, int width, int height, int arcWidth, int arcHeight)	Draws an outlined round-cornered rectangle using this graphics context's current color.
drawString(String str, int x, int y)	Draws the text given by the specified string, using this graphics context's current font and color
fillPolygon(int[] x, int[] y, int x.length)	Fills a closed polygon defined by arrays of x and y-coordinates.
fillPolygon(Polygon p)	Fills the polygon defined by the specified Polygon object with the graphics context's current color.
fillRect(int x, int y, int width, int height)	Fills the specified rectangle.
fillRoundRect(int x, int y, int width, int height, int arcWidth, int arcHeight)	Fills the specified rounded corner rectangle with the current color.

In observation, those methods that begin with the word **draw**, except for the methods drawLine and drawString, simply give the outline of the figure in the current color. Those that begin with the word **fill**, cause the entire region of the shape to contain the current color.

Figure 10.3 shows the image of the front cover of this book. This image is not a photograph, but was generated from codes written in Java, using among other classes, the classes Color, Font, and Graphics.

Figure 10.3

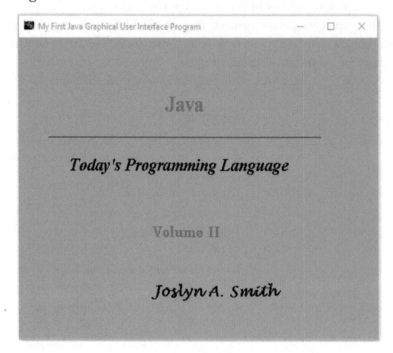

In this output there are six elements to observe:

- A green background
- Two lines of text in red color.
- Two lines of text in black, and
- A blue line.

The background was generated from the test class using the following statement:

    f.setBackground(Color.GREEN);

Where f is a reference to an object of our class MyJFrame, calling the method setBackground, with argument for setting the background color to be green. This green background will stay in place until if there is a change of background color. The first line of text Java, in red was generated by the following segment of codes:

```
g.setFont(new Font("Serif", Font.BOLD, 30));
g.setColor(Color.RED);
g.drawString("Java", 220, 100);
```

First we set the font for the upcoming text, then the color in which the text will be rendered. The order of writing these lines is not important; the third line – the actual text - must follow these lines.

The following segment of codes refers to drawing the blue line. First we set the change of color – in this case blue. The string can be drawn using either the method drawLine, or the method drawString; both methods are from the class Graphics.

```
g.setColor(Color.BLUE);              g.setColor(Color.BLUE);
                              or
g.drawLine(80, 130, 425, 130);       g.drawString("_____", 45, 130);
```

The second line of text is written with font "Times Roman", with style bold and italic. Notice the use of the bitwise operator | where the output is in both italic form and is bold.

```
Font.ITALIC | Font.BOLD
```

The complete code for this segment is as follows:

```
g.setFont(new Font("TimesRoman", Font.ITALIC|Font.BOLD, 24));
g.setColor(Color.BLACK);
g.drawString("Today's Programming Language", 75, 180);
```

The second and third lines of texts follow the pattern of the first. The difference is in the type of font that is used – "Century" and "Lucida Handwriting", respectively.

All these segments of codes are within a class that I called MyJPanel, a subclass of class JPanel. See **Listing 10.3**. The reason for making this class a subclass of JPanel is that it lest you override a method called paint of the JPanel class.

// Listing 10.3

```
1.   import java.awt.Font;
2.   import java.awt.Graphics;
3.   import java.awt.Color;
4.   import javax.swing.JPanel;
5.
6.   public class MyJPanel extends JPanel
7.   {
8.     public void paint(Graphics g)
9.     {
10.       g.setFont(new Font("Serif", Font.BOLD, 30));
11.       g.setColor(Color.RED);
```

```
12.      g.drawString("Java", 220, 100);
13.
14.      g.setColor(Color.BLUE);
15.      g.drawString("_____", 45, 130);
16.
17.      g.setFont(new Font("TimesRoman ", Font.ITALIC|Font.BOLD, 24));
18.      g.setColor(Color.BLACK);
19.      g.drawString("Today's Programming Language", 75, 180);
20.
21.      g.setFont(new Font("Century", Font.BOLD, 20));
22.      g.setColor(Color.RED);
23.      g.drawString("Volume II", 200, 270);
24.
25.      g.setFont(new Font("Lucida Handwriting", Font.BOLD, 20));
26.      g.setColor(Color.BLACK);
27.      g.drawString("Joslyn A. Smith", 200, 350);
28.    }
29.  }
```

The Method paint

As was said in **Chapter 8**, a component is an object having a graphical representation that can be displayed on the screen, and that can interact with the user. Examples of components as we said then are items such as buttons, checkboxes, and scrollbars of a typical graphical user interface. In association components is an abstract class that is called Component. Among its many methods, is this method called **paint**.

> void paint(Graphics g)

This method is called when the contents of the component needs to be painted - such as when the component is first being shown. That is when the statement setVisible (true) is encountered, or when the frame is resized, or if the method, **repaint**, from this class is called. This method never gets called directly from within your program. This method is called by what is referred to as the **Event Dispatch Thread** (EDT), which is out of the programmer's control. This EDT thread then runs in the background and, whenever your component needs to be painted, it calls the paint method.

The parameter **Graphics g** is the graphics context used to do the painting. It is this method that you will write the codes for doing the painting.

To put things into perspective, this method gets activated when this class is instantiated by some other calls, such as the test class, and the method **setVisible(true)** is called. See **Listing 10.4**, **Lines 16** and **19**.

Listing 10.4 shows the test class that launches the JPanel object. See **Lines 16** and **17**, in particular.

// Listing 10.4

```
1.   import java.awt.Color;
2.   import java.awt.Rectangle;
3.   import java.awt.Container;
4.   import javax.swing.JFrame;
5.   import javax.swing.ImageIcon;
6.
7.   class TestMyTextWindow {
8.       public static void main(String[] args) {
9.           JFrame f = new JFrame(Constants.TITLE);
10.          f.setIconImage(new ImageIcon("coffee.jpg").getImage());
11.
12.          Rectangle r = new Rectangle(Constants.X_POS, Constants.Y_POS, 600, 250);
13.          f.setBounds(r);
14.
15.          Container c = f.getContentPane();
16.          MyJPanel mjp = new MyJPanel();
17.          c.add(mjp);
18.          f.setBackground(Color.GREEN);
19.          f.setVisible(true);
20.      }
21. }
```

Geometric Shapes and Figures

Another characteristic of a GUI program is the ability to display shapes and figures, and color them to one's taste. This can be achieved by using Java predefined classes such as those we have already described, in addition to other classes such as the class Polygon. The image in **Figure 10.4** is a frame containing a star, a head, and a rectangle with tapered ends.

Figure 10.4

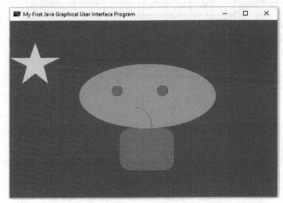

Starting with the head, its shape is an oval, created from the mutator method:

void fillOval(int x, int y, int width, int height)

x	The *x* coordinate of the upper-left corner of the arc to be filled.
y	The *y* coordinate of the upper-left corner of the arc to be filled.
width	The width of the arc to be filled.
height	The angular extent of the arc, relative to the start angle.

The eyes are circular. In Java there are no predefined methods for making a circle. To create a circle, you have to create an oval, whose width and height are the same measurement.

The nose is made from an arc – a segment of the circumference of a circle. The general format of the method is:

void fillArc(int x, int y, int width, int height, int startAngle, int arcAngle)

x	The *x* coordinate of the upper-left corner of the arc to be filled.
y	The *y* coordinate of the upper-left corner of the arc to be filled.
width	The width of the arc to be filled.
height	the height of the arc to be filled
startAngle	The beginning angle.
arcAngle	The angular extent of the arc, relative to the start angle.

Looking at the star, there is no predefined method in the class Graphics for designing figures such as a star. When designing figures over four sides, one of the best approaches is by making a scaled diagram of the figure using the Cartesian plane. See below.

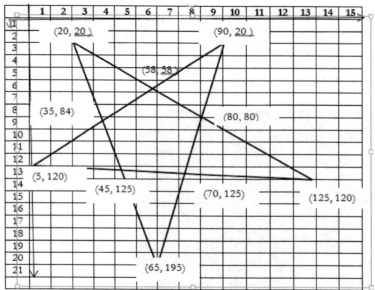

As a matter of fact the only regular figures that have methods to create them are the classes Rectangle and Oval. All others have to be constructed, either from lines, rectangles, ovals, or polygons. The graph above shows just that approximation for constructing the star. This may not be a one shot certainty that the coordinates will be correct, but after a few pulling and fixing you will get as close to your desire as possible.

In creating the program, the method fillPolygon is used to create the star. In order to create the polygon, as indicate above, the coordinate of each point must be known. According to the parametric variables of the method, two arrays of integer values must be established, one for the x-coordinates, and the other for the y-coordinates. The code necessary to create the yellow star is shown below.

```
Polygon p = new Polygon(Constants.X, Constants.Y, Constants.Y.length);
g.setColor(Color.YELLOW);
g.fillPolygon(p);
```

Finally, the body of the image was created from a rectangle that has tapered corners. The mutator method shown below creates it.

void fillRoundRect(int x, int y, int width, int height, int arcWidth, int arcHeight)

x	The x coordinate of the rectangle to be filled.
y	The y coordinate of the rectangle to be filled.
width	The width of the rectangle to be filled.
height	The height of the rectangle to be filled.
arcWidth	The horizontal diameter of the arc at the four corners.
arcHeight	The vertical diameter of the arc at the four corners.

Listing 10.5 shows the class MyJPanel which lays out the components on the panel. First it creates the yellow star whose coordinates are specified by the arrays X and Y in the interface called Constants. See **Listing 10.6.**

```
// Listing 10.5

1.   import java.awt.Graphics;
2.   import java.awt.Color;
3.   import java.awt.Polygon;
4.   import javax.swing.JPanel;
5.
6.   public class MyJPanel extends JPanel
7.   {
8.       public void paint(Graphics g)
9.       {
10.          // Define yellow star
11.          Polygon p = new Polygon(Constants.X, Constants.Y, Constants.Y.length);
12.          g.setColor(Color.YELLOW);
```

```
13.          g.fillPolygon(p);
14.
15.          // Define green oval
16.          g.setColor(Color.GREEN);
17.          g.fillOval(150, 100, 300, 150);
18.
19.          g.setColor(Color.RED);
20.
21.          // Define two eyes
22.          g.fillOval(220, 150, 25, 25);
23.          g.fillOval(320, 150, 25, 25);
24.
25.          // Define red rectangle
26.          g.fillRoundRect(240, 250, 120, 100, 50, 50);
27.
28.          // Define red nose
29.          g.drawArc(235, 200, 75, 95, 0, 90);
30.     }
31. }
```

In the listing, **Line 26** specifies the coordinates for the tapered rectangle, and **Line 29** defines the arc. **Listing 10.7** shows the modified interface, Constants. **Lines 5** and **6** shows the definition of the two arrays. Each pair of points represents an (x, y) coordinate of the star. After several trials, the array of values for the star are those shown in Figure 10.6, Lines 5 and 6.

// Listing 10.6

```
1.   public interface Constants
2.   {
3.       int X_POS = 100,
4.           Y_POS = 120,
5.           X[] = {55, 67, 109, 73, 83, 55, 27, 37, 1, 43},
6.           Y[] = {50, 86, 86, 104, 146, 122, 146, 104, 86, 86};
7.
8.       String TITLE = "My First Java Graphical User Interface Program";
9.   }
```

There are three ways that you can create a circle – using the method:
- fillOval or drawOval … as we did in Listing 10.5.
- drawRoundRect(int x, int y, a1, a1, int width, int width)
  The method fillRoundRect takes similar form.
- drawArc(int x, int y, 90, 90, 0, 360)
  The method fillArc takes similar form.

These will be left as exercises for the reader.

Self-Check

1. In what package are the following classes found? Graphics, Color, and Polygon.

2. Differentiate between the two methods drawRect(…) and drawRoundRect(…).

3. Differentiate between the two methods drawRect(…) and fillRect(…).

4. In what class is the method paint(..) defined?

5. True/False. The method called paint found in the class Graphics must be called explicitly in a program, otherwise nothung will be displayed on the screen.

6.

7. Use the methods fillRoundRec and fillArc to produce circles similar to the one shown below.

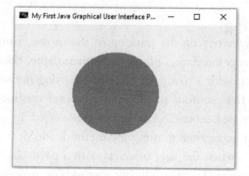

8. Use the method fillArc to produce a shape similar to the one shown below.

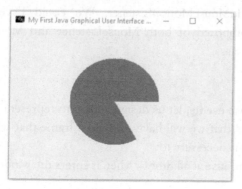

9. Write a Java application program that displays an output similar to the one shown below. The program must take into account the land on which the house and the person stands.

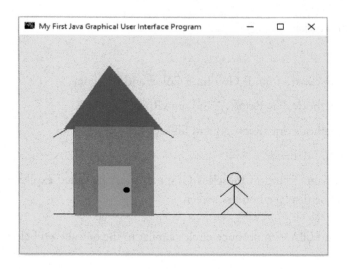

Making Free Hand Drawing

Free hand drawing almost, always rely on the tracking of the mouse, using the MouseListener interface and the MouseMotionListener interface, or their respective adapter class. As we know, mouse events occur when the user interacts with a particular component using the mouse. As a result, the reaction is captured by any of the five methods of the mouse listener methods described earlier - . mouseEntered, mouseExited, mousePressed, mouseClicked, and mouseReleased. In addition, a component that listens for a mouse event must be registered, using the method, addMouseListener. Like mouse events, mouse motion events occur when the user interacts with a particular component using the mouse. As a result, the reaction is captured by one of the two methods of mouse motion event methods - . mouseMoved, and mouseDragged. Also, a component that listens for a mouse motion event must be registered, using the method, addMouseMotionListener. We could have used the interface MouseInputAdapter, since it is composed of both MouseListener and MouseMotionListener; or simply use the MouseInputAdapter class.

Example 9.1

In an effort to understand mouse events, let us design a class to represent a canvas on which we can draw free handedly. This means that we will have to build a frame that will act like the painters canvas[1]. In designing the solution it is necessary to:

(a) Record the position of the mouse at all times - when it enters the window, and where the user presses the mouse button.

(b) Trace and display the path of the mouse when it is being dragged from one point to another.
Figure 9.5 shows a typical output. Notice that we are writing text in cursive form.

---

[1] This has nothing to do with the class Canvas

Figure 9.5

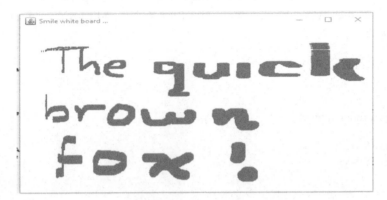

We will call this class SimpleWhiteboard – simple enough to use the mouse to draw whatever we want. As you would have noticed in **Figure 10.5**, I have written some text – The quick brown fox ! . So, in this class SimpleWhiteboard we first get the content pane of the frame and color it white. This represents the painter's canvas. When drawing in the area, the application will listen for two kinds of events continually – MouseListener event and MouseMotionListener event.

In this case MouseListener listens for when the mouse enters the container, and when the left mouse button (default) is pressed. This being the case, these actions must be defined as an entity that addresses two events:

- mouseEntered(MouseEvent), and
- mousePressed(MouseEvent)

In both cases these methods will record the (x, y) position of the mouse based on their parameter – MouseEvent. The class representing this entity is shown in **Listing 10.7**. This class will be defined as an inner class with a principal class that controls the free hand drawing.

Listing 10.7

```
private class RecordPosition extends MouseAdapter
{
    public void mouseEntered(MouseEvent e)
    {
        record( e.getX(), e.getY() );
    }
    public void mousePressed( MouseEvent e )
    {
        record( e.getX(), e.getY() );
    }
}
```

Assuming that the principal class has variables called lastX and lastY, that represent the last position of the (x, y) coordinate. It is these variables that the values for e.getX() and e.getY() are referring to. In this context the method:

record (int, int)

is defined as:

```
void record(int x, int y)
{
    lastX = x;
    lastY = y;
}
```

MouseMotionListener on the other hand listens for mouse dragged events. That is, whenever the mouse is dragged across the surface, some drawing is done. **Listing 10.8** shows a partial description of the class DrawLines. Upon recognizing a mouseDragged event, the method defines what must be drawn on the canvas.

Listing 10.8

```
private class DrawLines extends MouseMotionAdapter
{
    public void mouseDragged(MouseEvent e)
    {
        Graphics g = getGraphics();
        int y = e.getY();
        int x = e.getX();
        /**
                Write codes to make the necessary drawing with the mouse
        */
        record(x, y);
    }
}
```

Listing 10.9 shows the complete listing of the class SimpleWhiteboard.

Listing 10.9

```
1. import java.awt.Color;
2. import java.awt.Container;
3. import java.awt.event.MouseAdapter;
4. import java.awt.event.MouseEvent;
5. import java.awt.event.MouseMotionAdapter;
6. import java.awt.Graphics;
7. import javax.swing.JFrame;
```

```
8. public class SimpleWhiteboard extends JFrame {
9. protected int lastX, lastY;
10.
11.     public SimpleWhiteboard() {
12.         super("Smile white board ...");
13.
14.         Container c = getContentPane();
15.         c.setBackground(Color.white);
16.
17.         addMouseListener(new RecordPosition());
18.         addMouseMotionListener(new DrawLines());
19.
20.         setBounds(200, 150, 450, 400);
21.         setVisible(true);
22.     }
23.     protected void record(int x, int y) {
24.         lastX = x;
25.         lastY = y;
26.     }
27.     // Record position of mouse on entering window or where user pressed mouse button.
28.     private class RecordPosition extends MouseAdapter {
29.         public void mouseEntered(MouseEvent e) {
30.             record(e.getX(), e.getY());
31.         }
32.         public void mousePressed(MouseEvent e) {
33.             record(e.getX(), e.getY());
34.         }
35.     }
36.     // As user drags mouse, connect subsequent positions with short line segments.
37.     private class DrawLines extends MouseMotionAdapter {
38.         public void mouseDragged(MouseEvent e) {
39.             Graphics g = getGraphics();
40.             int y = e.getY();
41.             int x = e.getX();
42.             g.setColor(Color.red);
43.             g.fillOval(x, y, lastX/15, lastY/15) ;
44.             record(x, y);
45.         }
46.     }
47. }
```

Self-Check

1. What does the following code draw?

```
g.setColor(Color.BLACK);
g.drawLine(10, 10, 10, 50);
```

g.setColor(Color.RED);

g.drawRect(100, 100, 150, 150);

Select one:

(a) A black vertical line that is 40 pixels long and a red square with sides 150 pixels.

(b) A black vertical line that is 40 pixels and sides 100 pixels.

(c) A red vertical line that is 40 pixels long and a red square with sides 150 pixels.

(d) A red vertical line that is 50 pixels and a red square with sides 150 pixels.

(e) A black vertical line that is 50 pixels long and a red square with sides of 150 pixels.

2. Using the program segment given below, write appropriate Java code that would:

(a) Draw a polygon defined by the given arrays, and color the polygon blue.

(b) Draw the string "Hello There!" beginning at location x = 250, y = 150, on the application. Use courier font for lettering style. Bold the letters and use pitch 36 for the size of each of the letters. Color the letters magenta.

```
public void paint(Graphics g)
{
        int X[] = {10, 30, 40, 50, 70, 50, 40, 30};
        int Y[] = {40, 30, 10, 30, 40, 50, 70, 50};

        // Put part (a) here



        // Put part (b) here



}
```

3. Select from the classes below those that help in creating the graphical features of a frame.

(a) MenuItem.java

(b) JFrame.java

(c) JButton.java

(d) String.java

(e) Color.java

(f) Math.java

(g) Cursor.java

4. Given the following program segment.

```
public void paint(Graphics g)
{
        int x[] = {.........}; // array of integers
        int y[] = {......}; // array of integers
}
```

Write appropriate code that:
(a) Set the background of the container blue.
(b) Creates a yellow polygon defined by the arrays

Chapter Summary

- Graphical programming entails programs whose outputs involve images and pictures, as oppose to text based programs whose outputs are textual.

- To create a picture scene, embed the picture or image as a label, using the class JLabel, before placing it on the frame.

- The default manager for the class JLabel is FlowLayout.

- JLabel container can be used to display or image on it.

- In a picture scene images can be superimposed on one another.

- JPanle is a lightweight container, used to group components together.

- JFrame and JPanel are both containers, however there are differences between them.

- Some of the most important pre-defined class for creating graphics are Graphics, Polygon, Rectangle, Font, and Color.

Programming Exercises

1. Write a Java program that opens a frame on the screen with a title and a single red line drawn across it, similar to the figure below.

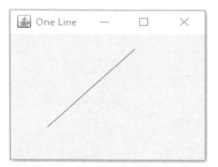

Use the class given below as the basis for this question.

```
1.    // Import the basic graphics classes.
2.    import java.awt.Color;
3.    import java.awt.Graphics;
4.    import javax.swing.JFrame;
5.
6.    public class MyBasicFrame extends JFrame
7.    {
8.        public MyBasicFrame()
9.        {
10.            super("One Line"); // Set the title
11.        }
12.        /* Redefine the paint() method in JFrame.
13.         * You don't have to call it in your program, it will get called
14.         * automatically whenever the frame needs to be redrawn
15.         */
16.        public void paint(Graphics g)
17.        {
18.            // This is where the drawing happens.
19.        }
20.    }
```

2. Using Question 1, set the background color of the frame to a color of your choice. The result should be similar to the following:

3. Using the result of Question 2, incorporate a yellow circle in the frame. Your result should be similar to the following figure. Use color of your choice.

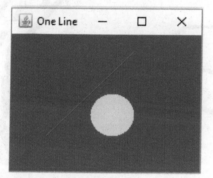

4. Using the result of Question 3, incorporate a string in the frame. Your result should be similar to the following figure. Use color of your choice.

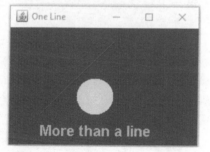

5. Using the class SimpleWhiteBoard as a basis, write a GUI program that produces an output similar to the one below. In carrying out this exercise bear the following in mind:
   - Use the class JFrame to create your drawing.
   - Create the star and the front of the house using the class Polygon
   - Create the door of the house using the method fillRect. Finish the house using freehand drawing. Use freehand drawing for the tree also.

- Use the Font class to write the label - use a font that you like- a style and size that are appealing to you.
- In your presentation, choose colors that appeal to you also.

Index

A

abstract class, 49
adapter class, 77
Adapter classes, 324
Association Diagram, 5

B

base case, 202
BufferedInputStream, 150
BufferedOutputStream, 162
BufferedReader, 169
BufferedWriter, 175
byte oriented outputs streams, 155
byte streams, 148

C

Casting, 60
Character Oriented Input Streams, 166
Character Oriented Output Streams, 172
character streams, 148
Class HashSet, 229
class Object, 67
Class TreeSet, 230
coercion polymorphism, 60
Cohesion, 7
Collection Framework, 226
concrete classes, 49
Coupling, 20

D

data structure, 225
DataInputStream, 150
DataOutputStream, 158
Dependency Diagram, 2

F

File Class, 138
FileInputStream, 149
FileOutputStream, 155

FileReader, 168
FileWriter, 174
FilterInputStream, 150
FilterOutputStream, 158
final, 69
Free Hand Drawing, 353

G

generalization diagrams, 39
Graphics, 350

H

HyperlinkListener, 333, 334, 335

I

implements, 74
Inclusion polymorphism, 59
inductive step, 202
inheritance, 39, 40, 41, 47, 49, 69, 72, 75, 80, 82
InputStream, 148
InputStreamReader, 167
interface, 73
Interface - Collection, 228
interface - List, 236
Interface - Set, 229

J

JFileChooser, 143
JLabel, 343, 345

JPanel, 343, 347

K

KeyAdapter, 333
KeyListener, 333, 334, 336

L

LineNumberReader, 170
LinkedList, 270
Listener Interfaces, 324
loosely coupled system, 21

M

MouseAdapter, 333
MouseInputAdapter, 333
MouseInputListene, 333, 334
MouseListener, 333, 334, 355
MouseMotionAdapter, 333
MouseMotionListene, 333, 334
MouseMotionListener, 355

O

Object-oriented design, 1
OOD, 1
OutputStream, 155
OutputStreamWriter, 173
Overloading polymorphism, 57
Overriding polymorphism, 59

P

polymorphism, 57
PrintStream, 162
PrintWriter, 177

Q

Queue, 264

R

Random Access File Stream, 189
Recursion, 202
Recursion vs Iteration, 215
Rendering Text, 348

S

Stack, 251
Standard Input and Output, 136
StreamTokenizer, 182
subclass, 39
super, 43
superclass, 39

T

TextListener, 333, 334
The class Reader, 166
The class Writer, 172
Tightly coupled, 21

U

UML, 2
Unified Modeling Language, 2

W

WindowAdapter, 333
WindowListener, 333, 334

CPSIA information can be obtained
at www.ICGtesting.com
Printed in the USA
LVOW05s1351260117
522281LV00005B/83/P